THE ERIC CARR STORY

D1602274

By Greg Prato

Printed and distributed by Greg Prato
Published by Greg Prato
Front cover photo by Angela Simon
Back cover photo by Richard Galbraith [myspace.com/richardgalbraith]
Book design by Linda Krieg [myspace.com/lindakriegdesign]
Book proofreading by Catherine Hensley [CLHediting.com]
Copyright © 2010, Greg Prato. All rights reserved.
First Edition, November 2010

ISBN: 978-0-578-07424-5

Contents

Introduction	*v*
Note from Eric's Parents	*vii*
Foreword from Sara-Jean	*viii*
Cast of Characters	*ix*
'50s, '60s, and '70s	*1*
Kiss: A History Lesson [1973-1976]	*5*
Kiss: A History Lesson [1977-1980]	*14*
May/June 1980	*24*
1980	*28*
1981	*42*
1982	*52*
1983	*70*
1984	*79*
1985	*99*
1986	*117*
1987	*130*
1988	*148*
1989	*161*
1990	*172*
1991 [Part One]	*196*
1991 [Part Two]	*211*
November 1991	*228*
Eric Remembered	*242*

This book is dedicated to the memory of Eric Carr,
Connie Caravello, and Bill Aucoin.

Introduction

"FLASH! PETER CRISS LEAVES KISS!" is what the headline said on the cover of the September 1980 issue of *16* magazine. I may have only been eight years old at that point (not exactly in the expected age demographic of *16* magazine's readership), but I was old enough to realize that my favorite rock band in the universe was experiencing some turbulence. Around the same time, a *People* magazine/Kiss cover story arrived, which introduced Peter Criss' replacement, a newcomer by the name of Eric Carr. His fox make-up and costume seemed cool enough, and from what I heard from friends about Kiss' appearance on *Kids are People Too* (I missed seeing it), Eric was an incredibly likable chap. Kiss' future didn't seem as doomed as I first thought. Then in the mags, it seemed like fans were in agreement with my view of what I was hoping for from the "new Kiss"—a return to some good, old-fashioned rock n' roll. Not only did they fumble the ball on their next release, *(Music From) The Elder*, but it sent me on a self-imposed exile from all things Kiss for a year or two!

When I "rediscovered" Kiss during their unmasking in '83 and pledged my allegiance once more, I went back and bought the album I missed out on a year previous, *Creatures of the Night*. WOW! The drumming propelled the album, and the band sounded absolutely reborn, thanks in large part to Mr. Carr. I was able to catch Carr in concert with Kiss several times and always wondered why Gene and Paul didn't loosen the reins a bit and give Eric a little more room to show off his songwriting and singing talents. After all, the few times they afforded him songwriting opportunities ("Escape from the Island," "All Hell's Breakin' Loose," etc.) and/or singing opportunities ("Black Diamond" in concert, "Little Caesar" on album, etc.), Eric certainly made the most of it and added a much-welcomed change of pace from the usual glut of sole Simmons and Stanley compositions.

Admittedly, by the time of Eric's tragic passing, I was in the midst of another "break from Kiss" phase (with grunge and other rock styles taking a hold over arena rock). But regardless, I still felt shocked and saddened when I found out about Eric's death on November 24, 1991 (which was an extremely sad day for yours truly, as my favorite rock singer of all time, Freddie Mercury, passed away on the same day). Later in the decade, I rediscovered Kiss' '70s work once more and ventured out to the *Creatures* album. I was once again absolutely blown away by Eric's drumming.

With Kiss' popularity returning full-on after their original line-up reunited in 1996, there have been many books written about the band's history. But very few ever thoroughly examine their '80s/non-make-up era or focus on Eric's story. After conducting interviews with those who knew Eric personally and/or were huge fans of his music and drumming, I now present to you the first-ever book that tells the true story of Eric's life (as well as quite a bit of info about '80s era Kiss that I have never read anywhere before).

Long live Eric Carr!
Greg Prato

p.s. Thanks to all my family and friends, as well as Loretta Caravello, Carrie Stevens, and Bruce Kulick for all their help. Also, special thanks to Richard Galbraith, Bev Davies, Angela Simon, Lydia Criss, Donn Young, John Walsh, Carrie Stevens, and Loretta Caravello for the great pictures.

p.p.s. Questions? Email me at gregprato@yahoo.com.

Note from Eric's Parents

To Our Dearest Eric,

Not only in our dreams, but each day that passes, we remember so many wonderful things about you.

Who can ever forget your warm smile or wonderful sense of humor, which would make us laugh?

Who can ever forget the powerful thundering sound of your drums, leaving echoes everywhere?

No one can touch our hearts the way you have.

You always let us know that, no matter what may come, you would always be there to guide the way...

In our dreams, in each day, we love and miss you so much.

Love,
Mom & Dad

[Copyright © 1998, Eric Carr's Family]

Foreword from Sara-Jean

I was only four years old when my Uncle Eric passed away. Though my time with him was short, the memories I have of him remain steadfast in my heart.

I remember how, during one of his concerts, he lifted me on top of his shoulders and walked with me through the crowd of screaming fans. Years later, my Aunt Loretta told me that my uncle had been parading me around, shouting at the top of his lungs, "This is my niece! This is my niece!" He was so proud of me.

An uncontrolled excitement filled my chest as the lights went on and the music sounded. There my uncle sat, in the center of the stage, effortlessly striking his drums, his jet-black hair rapidly swaying from side to side.

As I close my eyes now and think of my Uncle Eric, I become that little redhead sitting on top of his shoulders, surrounded by the roar of adoring fans.

I love and miss you, Uncle Eric. The pounding of your drums lives forever within the beating of my heart.

Love,
Sara-Jean *[Eric's niece]*

Cast of Characters

Mark Adelman—Kiss tour manager 1983-1988

Carmine Appice—Vanilla Fudge, Jeff Beck, Rod Stewart, Ted Nugent, Ozzy Osbourne, King Kobra drummer

Bill Aucoin—Kiss manager 1973-1982

Frankie Banali—Quiet Riot drummer

Charlie Benante—Anthrax drummer

Nina Blackwood—MTV VJ

Bobby Blotzer—Ratt drummer

Loretta Caravello—Eric's youngest sister

Gary Corbett—Kiss touring keyboardist 1987-1992

Lydia Criss—Photographer/Peter Criss' ex-wife

Scott Daggett—Eric's drum tech 1985-1987

Blas Elias—Slaughter drummer

Bob Ezrin—*Destroyer, (Music From) The Elder*, and *Revenge* producer

Bob Graw—#1 Kiss fan

Christina Harrison—Bruce Kulick's ex-wife

Michael James Jackson—*Creatures of the Night* and *Lick It Up* producer

Jaime St. James—Black N' Blue singer

Carol Kaye—Kiss publicist

Bob Kulick—Brother of Bruce Kulick, uncredited guitarist on *Alive II, Killers,* and *Creatures* [and credited guitarist on Paul Stanley's 1978 solo album and 1989 solo tour]

Bruce Kulick—Kiss guitarist 1984-1996

Larry Mazer—Kiss manager 1989-1994

Gerri Miller—Editor of *Metal Edge* magazine 1985-1998

Adam Mitchell—Songwriter

Rod Morgenstein—Winger drummer

Ron Nevison—*Crazy Nights* producer

AJ Pero—Twisted Sister drummer

Mike Portnoy—Dream Theater drummer

Marky Ramone—The Ramones drummer

Bobby Rock—Vinnie Vincent Invasion and Nelson drummer

Jack Sawyers—*Tale of the Fox* director

Wayne Sharp—Kiss tour manager [*Asylum* tour]

Mark Slaughter—Slaughter and Vinnie Vincent Invasion singer

Carrie Stevens—Eric's girlfriend 1988-1991

Ty Tabor—King's X guitarist

Eddie Trunk—Radio DJ and TV host

John Walsh—Eric's drum tech 1990

Mark Weiss—Photographer

Neil Zlozower—Photographer

'50s, '60s, and '70s

LORETTA CARAVELLO: [Paul Charles Caravello] was born July 12, 1950, in Brooklyn. I believe Lutheran Hospital. That's right off of Linden Boulevard near Kings County Hospital. My mother [Connie Caravello] and father [Albert Caravello] lived on the same block. They were just teenagers when they met. I think my father's family has like 20 brothers and sisters, and my mom had three. They met and married at about 18 or 19 years old. We have another sister. Her name is Maria. We call her "Sisie." My brother gave her that name, because he couldn't say "Maria," so he said "Sister," but he kept saying "Sisie." That's what we still call her. Eric was the oldest, Sisie's the middle, and I'm the youngest. When we were like seven or eight, [Paul and Loretta] were really inseparable. We used to play games, but as you get older—when he was thirteen or fourteen—he hung out more with his friends, and I hung out with my friends. But he was always protective of my sister and I, because he would have a lot of male friends that would come to the house. He was always there for us. He was a pretty good brother.

My grandmother bought a house about a block away, which was on Belmont Avenue in Brooklyn. She let my mother live there with my father and us, and her other son, which was Sonny, my mother's brother. It was nice, because every Sunday, we would go over to my grandmother's house, and she would make my brother's favorite—chicken with garlic and lemon. And even as he got older, that was his favorite dish, but my mother could never make it like my grandmother. But now she does. You become "the grandmother" later. We had a lot of fun. We had a very musical family, because my grandfather was a musician—he played the trombone. He used to play on Vaudeville. He played with Charlie Chaplin—that was his full-time job. He tried to teach my brother how to play the trombone, but that didn't work. And they had a piano. He tried to teach us how to play the piano.

My brother first got into drums because of the Beatles. Everybody was going nuts over that. First, he had taken up the guitar. I was going to play the drums. Then of course, we switched over. But he didn't have drums. He would have a little pad made of rubber, or he would use some cans and pots and hit them with pencils. You couldn't afford lessons too often in those days. Everybody was scrimping. But that's when he first learned the drums. He got a job with my father—my father was a stove repairman. Actually, first, my father fixed cellar doors outside, and my brother worked with him. My brother used to lay down cement. A lot of times, they used to tell us stories about going to Joe Columbo's house, and they did his backyard. He started with that job, and my father said that my brother was the best cement-layer that he ever worked with. He was really good at that kind of stuff. And then after that, my father got into the gas range business. It wasn't his business—he worked for something called Jamaica Stoves. He used to go out on jobs, and my brother would go with him. My brother learned how to fix stoves, he was really good at that, too. Even when he got into Kiss, someone told me a story that he heard noise in his kitchen, and my brother was fixing his stove! He was always good at whatever he undertook.

Early on, he got a three-piece drum set from my uncle. But then he wanted a three-piece Ludwig, because of Ringo. So my father worked out a deal with [local music instrument store] Sam Ash, because Sam Ash was moving. He said, "Look, if I help you move, can you give me these drums really cheap?" So my father and brother moved them, and they paid a little for the set. I actually have the receipts still and time-payment bills. My brother saved all that stuff. I guess it meant a lot to him.

The first band he was in was called the Allures, from Flushing. It was a three-piece band. My father always helped him. My father kind of managed him. He would drive him to jobs. We would be in the car after school, "Come on, we've got to go!" The Allures [practiced] on the fifth or sixth floor of some project, and my father always remembers how him and my brother had to carry those drums up the five or six flights of steps. That was one of the reasons why he later quit the band. Then, he started his own band, the Cellarmen. Of course, he got the name "the Cellarmen" because he used to fix cellar doors. It was four members, and he got their names from Sam Ash on the bulletin board. That was in Brooklyn, I think on Flatlands Avenue. They started to learn Beatles songs and would practice in the basement of our house every Saturday. It was constant. My brother was *so* serious about it—he never would miss it. Even during the week, he would try and do it between ... and then my mother would come down and make spaghetti and meatballs for everybody. That's what the guys loved about it. She fed them pretty good! Actually, the bass player married my sister.

They cut a couple of records. My father took them to a studio in a basement in Brooklyn, and they cut something called "I Cry at Night." Then this girl called them, her name was Crystal Collins. She wanted to record a record, so they used my brother as a back-up band. It was a really cute song that was #5 in Texas or something, called "No Matter How You Try." But that fell apart later. Her career didn't take off. The Cellarmen broke up because one of the guys went to college and another moved to Texas. Then he got into a band called Salt and Pepper. The organ player in the Cellarmen said, "Hey, why don't you come. We need a drummer." Salt and Pepper was a black and white band. They were really good—they opened for Nina Simone and Patti LaBelle at the Academy of Music, which later became the Palladium [Salt and Pepper would change their name to Creation in the early '70s].

The organ player had left Creation, and they just got this young guy in. His name was Damon, and he was only 19. [A performance at Gulliver's Restaurant/Night Club in Port Chester, New York, on June 30, 1974] was only his first or second job with them. I think the story was that somebody was angry at the people in the bowling alley, which was connected to it, and started a fire. They were in this pit area underneath—picture going down steps and being in another area. They were in a pretty bad spot. First what happened was this guy, George, said, "We smell smoke coming through, so please people, don't panic." But then all of a sudden, it came in like black smoke, all at once. It really started to fill the room and people started to panic. George died and Damon died in the fire. My brother was one of the last to get out. He was with the singer, whose name was Sarita. She kept telling him, "Paul, let's go this way." And my brother had a terrific memory. You could not top this guy's memory. A fan could come up to him twelve years later, and he'd tell them his name and exactly what he told him that night. And I heard stories like that, fans that couldn't believe that he remembered. He was very good that way with people. So he said, "No, you've got to come this way." So he pulled her through the kitchen, and they were like the last two people to get out alive.

We saw this on TV, and we were hysterical at home. He didn't call us, everybody's confused, everybody doesn't know how to reach anybody. Our only lifeline to that is you would watch the TV. For what it's worth, it was a strange night. My dog ran into his bedroom and was just crying, running around the bed. When I think about it now and things that happened, it must have been like sixth sense or something. We had no idea, and at like 12:00 the next day—we were up the whole night not knowing—my mother got a call from him, and everybody was overwhelmed. We thought he was dead. What happened was they were going into the hospitals, looking for George and Damon. Nobody could find them, so they had to go to all the area hospitals, until they realized that they had died. A lot of musicians at that time did big charity events to try and get them back their instruments. A lot of people knew about them. Once again, they were a great band.

Shortly after that, some of the members left again, and then you still had John Henderson and Sarita, and they became Mother Nature/Father Time. That band didn't last long. Then they got some kind of break where they were approached to become this cover band, Bionic Boogie. Bionic Boogie actually had a lot of songs on the radio. They thought that was going to be their big break. They played at Disneyland—they did a lot of shows there. Flasher I believe was the last one. That was a three-piece band in Long Island.

He was very, very depressed. After the thing with the fire, he never got over that. And then every time somebody said they'd do something for him, nobody did anything. He was really at a low point. At that point, he wasn't living with us. He was living in Starrett City on Linden Boulevard, and he was just back and forth—living with us, not living with us. His financial state was pretty bad. He loved his music so much, but he got jobs like driving trucks at the airport, delivering tobacco to the planes. And then he worked in the court system. He was delivering furniture with my father. My father got him a job.

Kiss: A History Lesson [1973-1976]

BOB KULICK: I answered an ad in the *Village Voice*, subsequent to my touring with several other known artists. I had just finished a stint with the English blues singer Long John Baldry. We toured with Uriah Heep and White Trash. A great tour. Looking for another gig, the *Village Voice* was the way people found gigs back in the day. I found Labelle. That's another artist that I played with, Patti Labelle and the Bluebelles, otherwise known as Labelle. I found that gig auditioning from an ad in the *Village Voice*. So Kiss ran an ad—then, they were Wicked Lester. I went to the loft, and we jammed some Zeppelin-like stuff, and they showed me the photos of the prototype make-up. We chatted for a while. The story that Ace came in, unplugged me, and plugged himself, is totally untrue. Anybody that knows me knows that that would *not* have been possible. Ace indeed did come in right after me, and he was the one who got the gig. But Paul had called me a few weeks later to say, "You were actually the best guitarist, but we want somebody who fit in better with our vision for what the band is." But we always kept in touch. That's how that started.

BILL AUCOIN: Gene was a teacher and always studious and taking notes. We didn't allow Gene to talk too much, because he always came across like a teacher and not a rock n' roller. So Paul did most of the talking. Paul tends to be a little bit shy, until you get to know him. Gene, of course, will be outspoken, almost too much. Ace probably was the ultimate rock n' roller. I'm talking about living the rock n' roll life. That was Ace. Very bright.

LYDIA CRISS: They're different now. I think they were a lot easier to talk to then. They were all funny in their own way. They were all "artists" in their own way. Not only musicians, but all of them could draw. Talking to Gene, he was a teacher [before forming Kiss]. It's like talking to a teacher—everything was facts and money, money and facts. They were all like brothers to me. I never looked at them like stars, only because when they gained their popularity, I knew them before that.

The guys were all great in their own way. Like, Ace was telling jokes and making you laugh, and Paul was the one that I think I spoke to the most, because whenever there would be a limo, Peter would share it with Paul, because they lived close to each other, like when they were going to the airport or something like that. But at the gigs, Gene always shared it with Peter, because Gene didn't want Paul's girlfriend in the middle! I would sit in the middle. I'd be in the limo before the show was over, and Peter would come in one side and Gene would come in on the other. But I knew better than to speak. [Laughs] At that time of the night, you don't talk. And Paul's girlfriend used to like to talk a lot, so Gene wanted somebody that was silent. [Laughs] But the guys were all great guys, all like brothers to me. Of course, not Peter, but they were all real sweethearts.

CARMINE APPICE: The make-up didn't matter to me. Paul or one of them told me that Gene and Paul went to see a Cactus and Alice Cooper show on Long Island, at the Commack Arena. That's when they came up with the idea to do Kiss. They said, "If we can get the power, raunchiness, and energy of Cactus and mix it up with the theatrics of Alice Cooper, we'd have a great show." I thought they had a great show. But musically, *come on.* I was playing with Jeff Beck, and before that, Cactus and Vanilla Fudge ... with *Led Zeppelin* opening up for Vanilla Fudge! But I thought it was a great show. They took the Alice Cooper thing to the extreme, and I respected them for that. But I couldn't really look at them and go, "Wow, those guys are amazing musicians." They weren't.

JAIME ST. JAMES: I was a really big fan when I was a kid. I saw Kiss live in 1974—opening up was Rush—at the Paramount Theatre in Portland, Oregon. I liked them before that. There's a little local music store in Portland called Music Millennium, and they always had records that other people really didn't have. And I saw the first Kiss record [1974's *Kiss*] with the guys with the make-up on the front. The cover was so cool that I said, "I don't even know what this is ... but I have to buy it. *I have to have this.*" I was a huge

Alice Cooper fan, so I took a chance on this Kiss thing, and of course, I loved the first Kiss record. But then I saw them in '74, and what a great band they were. Anybody that was my age—I was around thirteen—would have loved them. We all did. They were something special to me. When I saw Kiss for the first time, me and Tommy Thayer had not met yet. Tommy and I met in the late '70s, when he came and auditioned for a band that I was in. He ended up in that band—it was called Movie Star—that evolved into Black N' Blue. I was the drummer in Movie Star. I became a lead singer, and Black N' Blue formed in the fall of '81. What's funny is Tommy was at that show I was at. We just didn't know each other was there—he was off with his group, I was off with mine. Honestly, Ace Frehley was a big influence on him. He learned all those licks. Now ... *he's in the band.*

NEIL ZLOZOWER: I started back in the '70s. The first time I shot them was when they were on a show called *In Concert*, and some girl came up to me and said, "We're with Aucoin Management, and we've got this new band, Kiss. Would you like to shoot them?" I'm like, *"Kiss?"* At the time, there was a band, Bread, so that's what I thought Kiss was going to be like. I thought they were going to come out and be some folky-type thing with acoustic guitar. And then all of a sudden, they came out with the make-up and everything, and Gene with the tongue. No one did anything like that. The closest was Alice Cooper at the time, but Kiss sort of took it to a different level. I just thought it was over-the-top. I was like, "Is this a fuckin' joke or what? This band is going to be laughed out of the music industry in about two weeks!" Little did I know, 36 years later they're going as strong as ever.

TY TABOR: I saw them first on something like *The Midnight Special* and freaked out. I just thought, "What the heck is this?" I was into Alice Cooper at the moment, too, and just thought, *"Wow."* It was the only other thing I had seen that was getting way out there like that. [Laughs] And possibly, I can't remember time-wise if Peter Gabriel was doing freaky stuff with Genesis or not, but there were just a few things out early. I saw Kiss on that, but I wasn't a fan until [1975's] *Alive!* came out. I was in that age group of kids that just completely freaked on it. Of course, [I] went back and bought everything at that point. I was just one of those kids—your typical kid/Kiss fan that on Halloween would paint up and dress up. I *loved* Kiss. Through the '70s, they were one of my biggest influences. Ace Frehley was one of my biggest influences—I used to think he had such a great style and melodic sense, that you could sing his solos. That had a big impact on me.

CHARLIE BENANTE: The first time I heard [*Alive!*], I was at a party at a friend's house. The only thing I heard prior to that as far as Kiss was [1975's] *Dressed To Kill*. I was a fan, but when *Alive!* came out, it was a totally different thing. The thing that I remember most about it was just staring at the package. It opened out to a gatefold, and there was a huge booklet in it. I just remember staring at it and being like, "What the hell?" Because you would listen to the record and you would visualize in your own mind how it was. You had all these different things. And I remember early on, when I first heard Kiss, I used to think that Paul Stanley's voice was Gene Simmons' voice. It was very weird when I saw them on a TV show called *The Midnight Special*, and I was like, "Wait a minute ... he's not supposed to be singing that!"

I don't think there were any of [the songs that] were my least favorite. I loved every single one on that record. I remember playing it continuously, over and over again. I loved the way side one would kick in. It was like the introduction is the beginning of the show. Then you get to the middle portions—sides two and three—and side four was the big ending. I'll never forget listening to "Black Diamond" and being like, "What the hell is going on?" The explosions and everything. [The track-list] is a bit out of sequence. Actually, it's not even a live show. They totally rerecorded it, but who cares—it fooled me back then.

I loved [Peter Criss'] drumming on *Alive!* I think he was one of the big influences as far as having a huge drum kit. It was like, "Look at all these drums. What is he doing with all these?" Because at the time, you had like the "five-piece-kit-drummers" out there, like John Bonham and Joey Kramer. After Peter, Neil Peart had the big kit also. The end of '76 was when I saw them for the first time. [*Alive!*] prepared me. "Dude, this is fucking crazy!" I just couldn't believe it. Everything was going on, I couldn't focus on just one thing. It was just an assault on my senses. Because most of the bands at the time really didn't put on that type of a show the way they were doing. It was more or less getting up on stage and playing. It wasn't, y'know, *Kiss*. Kiss made me realize that this is what I'm going to do. And that mindset just stayed with me. It never left. Before that, I wasn't really taking it as serious as, "I'm going to make a living doing this." I absolutely still listen to [*Alive!*]. I listen to it sometimes before we play. It pumps me up. It puts me in a different state of mind.

CARMINE APPICE: As a matter of fact, when Kiss first came out, I was on their first arena headlining tour. I was playing with Leslie West, and we opened up for them.

BOB EZRIN: I met them in a stairwell at a television studio, where they had just been interviewed, and I was on my way up to be interviewed. I had heard about them by a young man in Toronto, who used to call me at home. My phone number was listed in those days, and this kid used to call me at home and say, "There's this band, Kiss. They need you to produce them! You need to find this band. They need Bob Ezrin." I had listened to their music and thought, "This is a pretty good band." And then one day, I bumped into them in a stairwell and was talking to Paul Stanley, as they were walking down the stairs. They knew who I was, which was great, because they were Alice fans. And I just said, "Listen, if you guys are ever unhappy with the way things are going with you record-wise ... call me. I'd love to work with you." And it didn't take very long—I got a phone call.

Actually [Kiss and Alice Cooper] shared a lot of the same attributes. They had a great work ethic, great sense of humor. They were not "precious" about what they were doing, but they were very serious about it. And all they wanted was to do the best they possibly could, so they could make the best stuff for their fans. That's what motivated both of them, that they were there for their fans. I think the Kiss guys are still doing that, and so is Alice. They're all great entertainers. They're all "show people," in the classic sense of it. They give the fans a great show.

I had a good time working with everybody on this particular thing [1976's *Destroyer*]. I've read the stories that Peter found it very difficult. Y'know, we worked him *really* hard. Nobody was used to working quite as hard as I had been working, just because there was so much to accomplish. We were really reaching for the sky on this record. We didn't have a lot of time to do it, so I found us having to push. We couldn't stop. We couldn't take an hour break between takes to rest our hands. So Peter in particular was working really hard, because he was having to drum like all day, every day, for the first few weeks when we were getting the rhythm tracks. He wasn't used to that. He was used to playing a two-hour show and taking the rest of the day off. That was hard for him.

For Ace, I think it was difficult because it required being somewhere on time and aiming at a particular sound or a particular part. Ace was a much more intuitive kind of visceral player/visceral personality. Not a disciplined guy by any stretch of the imagination. This was a whole new way of doing things for him. And I think, yes, there were times that he found that very difficult, and he resented me. And there were a couple of situations where we had to bring other people in to play stuff, because Ace wasn't there. And it wasn't my decision alone. This was a joint decision with Paul and Gene both. We sat there and said, "We've got to have this guitar part. We've got to have it today. Where's Ace?" So I would call Dick Wagner, who lived in the city, was a great player, and my friend to come over and fill in. That's what happened.

LYDIA CRISS: They did make me come to the studio once "Beth" was finished. They sat me down, put headphones on me, and Bob Ezrin and the band were all there. I knew the song. Peter wrote it years ago. But it was changed, because it was called "Beck" originally. And then they changed it to "Beth," and I suggested "Beth," but I'll never get that credit. [Laughs] They sat me on a stool, and they said, "What do you think?" And I just said, "It should have been called 'Lydia.'"

I didn't write it but said something to Peter, and he put it in the song. It was one of the lyrics that was added—"You say you feel so empty, That our house just ain't a home." I mean, I *had* said that to Peter. I was paying all the bills up to when we moved to Manhattan, and I was working. Once you stop working—I think I worked for twelve years—there's a void in your life. It's like, "Whoa, I don't have to get up every morning and take the train to Manhattan." I used to pay all the bills, and then all of a sudden, *the office* is paying the bills. There's a big void, so I had said that to Peter—"I don't really feel like this house is my home," meaning the apartment, actually, in Manhattan. But you get used to all of that. But that point, I had said that to him, and he had put it in a song.

It was a surprise [when "Beth" became a hit], because it was a b-side. It was definitely a surprise, especially when we heard that they won the People's Choice Awards. We were at a concert at Detroit. The show was over ... maybe the show wasn't even over. It was me, Gene, Bill, and Peter. Bill surprised us with this piece of paper. He said, "By the way, I just want to tell you that you won the People's Choice Award." We actually knew it before the show aired—that's one of the shows that they do tell you. Gene said, "Well, how are we going to accept that?" I just said, joking, "I'll accept it," and Gene looked at me, and said, "OK." And I said, *"What?"* [Laughs] So that was all a big surprise, that the song was that big.

BOB EZRIN: After they decided not to work with me after *Destroyer*, I was kind of pissed off at the band. I don't know whose decision that was. I just think it was a misguided decision, because some of the press—the initial press—really didn't like *Destroyer*, and thought that we had sold out in some way. So there were just a few reviews, not a lot, of *Destroyer*, where people said that I softened Kiss, and I "de-boned" Kiss, and I turned them into ... somebody referred to the orchestration as "Ann-Margret horns." [Laughs] Basically, they were saying it was "Las Vegas." That scared the band, but I think more than the band, it scared Bill Aucoin.

What happened was while I was on a vacation—after having finished the album and turned it in, and being pretty sure that this was a great record and we were going to do really well with it—I got a frantic message from Jack Douglas, when I got back to New York. Not one, but *many* frantic messages from Jack Douglas, that just said, "You've got to call me right away." So I did, and it turns out Bill Aucoin called him to see if he'd be interested in doing the next Kiss album. And Jack was my protégé. I trained Jack Douglas and brought Aerosmith to him. I actually gave him Aerosmith as a "graduation present," when I felt that he was ready to go out on his own. I was a little pissed off to hear that this was going on, without anybody even talking to me. Especially, as I said, we had done such a good job. So I was a little pissed ... and hurt, because I really invested a huge amount of energy and heart into doing *Destroyer* and working with the guys. And I loved them. I loved working with them. I felt like I was working with my cousins, y'know? I just felt so connected to the band that when I came back and found out I'd been effectively rejected, I was hurt.

LYDIA CRISS: When we were going to Japan, I was just going to thank them for making it possible for me to go to Japan. And I started with Gene. I said, "Gene, I just wanted to say thanks for making it possible for me to go to Japan." He said, "Don't thank me. *Thank 'Beth.'* It made it possible for all of us to go to Japan." So that's the popularity of "Beth." "Beth" was their number-one-selling record ever. It didn't hit number one, but it was their biggest selling record.

BOB GRAW: The summer of 1976, I was sleeping over my cousin's house, and she had a stack of magazines next to her bed, and John Travolta and Farrah Fawcett were on the cover of *Bananas* magazine. Do you remember *Bananas*, when we were in school, in the library? And I just happened to be flipping through it before I went to bed, and there was a picture of them and that I said, *"What is that?* That is the greatest thing I've ever seen in my life!" I asked my cousin the next morning, "Who is Kiss?" And she's like, "That's nonsense. Don't pay any attention to that. Here, listen to this." And she handed me Steve Miller *Fly Like An Eagle*, America, and Fleetwood Mac's first album with Lindsey Buckingham and Stevie Nicks. I took those home and listened to them ... and I couldn't get that picture out of my head. My grandma took me to Sears to buy some clothes, and I saw a display of Kiss' *Destroyer* and all the other albums. I told my grandma—God rest her soul— "I want that! I want that!" So she bought me the album, not knowing what it was. I took it home that day and listened to it every day after school for a couple of months. And then I made her go buy me another one, and then another one, and then another one. And then I became obsessed with them.

BLAS ELIAS: I was a Kiss fan since I saw them on a Halloween special. I can't remember the year. It was in the '70s [1976's *The Paul Lynde Halloween Special*]. I saw that, and it turned me on to the whole metal side of rock. I had been into the Beatles and the Sweet, the poppier side. That led me in the direction of some of the harder rock stuff. And at the time, I liked Peter Criss. I was leaning towards being a drummer. So yeah man, a big fan growing up.

MARK SLAUGHTER: I lived in Las Vegas, and when I grew up there, it was pretty much *Green Acres*. The Vegas we know now is a totally different Vegas. As far as Kiss coming through there, I think they came through there one time. I'm talking in the early, early '70s, when they were kicking off. When I was growing up, I thought it was really cool—the stage antics that Kiss did were cool. The thing is rock n' roll and good riffs are the key to the longevity of a track. "More Than a Feeling" by Boston for instance, is a signature. And the same thing with "Detroit Rock City" or "Rock and Roll All Nite," which is based on a blues progression. But it's the intensity of the party and the fun, and everything I learned off of Kiss and being a fan of them was these guys were more about bringing the circus into town and the show than trying to say, "Look how fast I can play" and "Look at me, look at me, look at me."

EDDIE TRUNK: Kiss was my first-ever concert. I remember very vividly walking home from junior high school with a friend of mine, and had never really been all that into real rock music at that point. As a young kid, I was into the Partridge Family and stuff like that. We walked by a record store every day on the way home from school in the seventh and eighth grade, and he said, "I'm going to go in here and buy the new album from Kiss." I said, "What's Kiss?" He said, "Well, come in here and let me show you." We went to the bin, and the new record at the time was [1976's] *Rock and Roll Over*. He said, "I don't know how this new album is, but you should buy the album that came before it, because it was really great." So he bought *Rock and Roll Over* and I bought *Destroyer*. Took it home, dropped the needle on the vinyl, looked at the cover, "Detroit Rock City" started playing, and away I went into total Kiss obsession.

Kiss: A History Lesson [1977-1980]

CAROL KAYE: I started working with Kiss in June of 1977, just as they were about to release *Love Gun*. Bill Aucoin hired me—I worked in the press department of the management company. But I had only been there a couple of months when I was moved over to a PR firm called the Press Office, that Bill was an owner of. And I was the "Aucoin Representative," so I handled Kiss, Starz, Toby Beau, and Piper. Starz were on Capitol, Toby Beau had a hit with "My Angel Baby" and was on RCA. That was pretty much where all the magic happened, as they say.

BOB KULICK: As a trusted friend and confidant of Gene and Paul's, I wrote songs with Gene, I played on Paul's solo record, played on the songs on side four of [1977's] *Alive II* that basically gave Ace Frehley his reputation as a great guitar player—"All American Man," "Larger Than Life." Those were me, not Ace Frehley. As with the Beatles, nobody volunteered the fact that Bernard Purdie played drums on some stuff, or that it was Eric Clapton on a couple of songs. There weren't advertisements in the newspaper—"Somebody else is guesting on this." It wasn't like the Beatles *and* Billy Preston. It couldn't be Kiss *and* Bob Kulick.

CAROL KAYE: Kiss were the biggest band in the world. They were voted #1 in the Gallup Poll over and over again. Their concerts were sold out. There was a frenzy around Kiss. They were on the cover of every rock n' roll magazine. We booked them on a lot of television shows. I have very funny memories of the Tom Snyder show, which I'm sure many people have seen. Back in those days, there weren't very many shows that had musical guests, and certainly there weren't as many shows as there are today. It was a treat, and it was rare to see a band on a late night talk show, or basically on any show. They had *Don Kirshner's Rock Concert* and *The Midnight Special*. You really looked forward to that night because you knew you were going to see the bands that you loved. It wasn't like it is now, where you can just access music anywhere, any time, any day.

Back in those days—again, this goes back to the fact that there weren't as many outlets as there are today—the press really worked with us in keeping the mystique. It's not like today with the paparazzi or TMZ, who are just looking to show artists in an unflattering light, or jumping out of trash cans to take photos. They really did not show photos of Kiss without the make-up. And I don't think that many of them really even knew what the guys looked like without their make-up. I do remember there was a photo that ran in one of the daily newspapers in New York on the gossip page, and they had a photo of one of the guys from the Babys, and underneath, it said, "And here's Paul Stanley taken at Studio 54!" They really thought they had it, but they didn't. It wasn't Paul. It was hard for them, because when they went out and there were cameras around, they would hide their face and put a napkin up over their face.

But again, there weren't as many newspapers and magazines, and we all really worked together. *Trouser Press* was a great magazine that I loved, who once did an "exposé" on the Kiss dolls. But all the newspapers worked together with us. We had interviews in every daily newspaper, every regional, every weekly, every rock n' roll magazine. And then we veered into the consumer magazines, and that was a big step. I remember someone called me one day and said, "Carol, you're on the front page of the *Wall Street Journal*." There was this article on the first page, and it started with, "Carol Kaye is a publicist with a problem. She cannot seem to squash the rumors that Kiss does not stand for 'Knights in Satanic Service.'" So we went through that whole thing. Working with Kiss was definitely an adventure. It was great. It was a great time, and they were the biggest band in the world. No doubt.

LYDIA CRISS: When you're involved in it ... you don't see it as much as the fans do. You don't go to the stores. You don't see the merchandise. You're really too close to it. Every now and then, you will get something that will trigger the success, like playing Madison Square Garden. And then you take a step back and say, "Wow, I can't believe I'm here!" *I* didn't play the Garden, but I stood on the stage, and it was just amazing. It was like a dream come true, especially growing up in New York. I went to school in Manhattan.

I lived in Manhattan, and Madison Square Garden is the biggest thing. That's it. Going to Japan was really exciting. The success was big. Sort of like winning the lottery. All of a sudden, everything you want, you can get. Not everything, but just about.

They told us to go out and buy a house because, "You have to spend the money, and you have to spend it wisely." We bought a car, a house, and a dog ... all in one day! And it was a Mercedes. [Laughs] It was just really exciting, especially moving out of Brooklyn was one big step, and moving into Manhattan. I had lived in Brooklyn all my life at that point, and moving to Manhattan was great. And moving to Connecticut was even greater, because the house was just something I had never, ever dreamed of. It was just amazing. The letters you get from the fans were just another thing that made you realize how big they were. There was a time that I would be home, and Peter was on the road, and I would answer some of his fan mail. Sometimes, they'd give a phone number. One day, a girl gave her phone number, and it just happened to be her birthday ... so I called her. And she started crying. [Laughs]

JAIME ST. JAMES: It was the biggest thing in rock n' roll in my life. They were the ultimate thing. I was still a kid, and I had Kiss posters all over my wall, just like everybody else probably did. In fact, I bought a Kiss t-shirt at a carnival. It was just a black shirt with the Kiss logo in little diamonds on the front, and I cherished it so much that I never wore it. I loved it so much [that] I refused to wear it.

MIKE PORTNOY: I was a Kiss fanatic in the '70s. I first saw them in '77 and then again in '79, when Peter was still in the band.

EDDIE TRUNK: My first-ever concert was December 16, 1977, at the Garden. It was *Love Gun/Alive II*. Piper opened, Billy Squier's first band. More surreal for me is my relationship with Ace Frehley, because little did I know—as a thirteen-year-old kid in this blue heaven of Madison Square Garden—that it would be about ten years later that I would be signing their lead guitar player to his first-ever solo deal. I was the vice president of

Megaforce, and one of the first things I did was go out and get Ace Frehley signed to the label. Even though Ace and I are still very close to this day, to look back on that is kind of a strange thing to think that ten short years after seeing my first show as a kid, that guy that I saw out there playing lead guitar would become a close friend, and was one of the first things that I did on the label side.

MARK WEISS: When I was 16/17, I used to sell pictures in front of Madison Square Garden in New York City. Whenever a band would play, like, Kiss played in December for three or four days, I would go to the first night, sneak my cameras in—in my boots—get real close, take pictures, stay up all night and make a couple hundred pictures, and sell them for a buck a piece the next day. So I did that for Led Zeppelin, Kiss, Frampton, all those bands that were playing multiple nights. And with Kiss, I ended up getting arrested, because they were cracking down on all the bootleggers. Here I am, I'm 17, I'm in a paddy wagon with a bunch of shirt-sellers, and here I have all my pictures. The next day, I went to *Circus* magazine, and the rest is history—I ended up working with them. I got some amazing shots from that show, still that I sell to magazines like *Classic Rock* or whoever needs them. Gene said, "You owe us your career." What was really ironic was my wife, who became my ex-wife a few weeks ago, she was Bill Aucoin's assistant when I was getting arrested. So she was back at the office, holding down the fort for Bill Aucoin, and she was like 18 years old. Sebastian Bach told me to go to the bookstore and check out a book about Lester Bangs [2000's *Let It Blurt* by Jim Derogatis], and there was a picture of Susan, my ex, with Gene, covering up [his face].

CAROL KAYE: That whole period, I was very involved in all of that. That was just such an amazing time, those four solo records [in 1978]. I remember sitting in the conference room at Aucoin Management, and we were all listening to the tracks. I was with Paul in the studio a lot at Electric Lady during the recording of his solo record, and they were each being played for us. It was just mind-boggling. And me as the publicist, my job was to get these four albums out simultaneously to the media. So we designed these little bags—it was vinyl at the time—so these four vinyl albums fit into

[them], and we had them hand-delivered to the editors of the magazines and the papers in New York. And again, there weren't 250 of them—there were maybe 30. So it was very different, but it was a time of creativity. It was a great time, those are like my happiest memories. Despite what everybody thought, they were very involved. They were all happy for one another. It wasn't like, "Oh, we're going to put out these records, and mine is going to do better than yours." It wasn't that way at all. They were very supportive of each other. But no one's ever done that again. It was amazing. And *Kiss Meets the Phantom of the Park*. [Laughs] Oh God. I can still remember sitting in the screening room, when we were watching it, and all I heard was Ace's laugh, that cackle. It was hilarious.

BRUCE KULICK: My first introduction to Kiss was really meeting Paul, because my brother befriended them after auditioning early on—the same day they checked out Ace, the legend goes. My brother Bob was an in-demand session guy in New York, and they crossed paths after a few years down the road. I think it was at a place called Bell Sound. And the next thing I know, he struck up a friendship again with Paul and Gene. Now, Gene and Paul were already famous, and suddenly, Bob had the opportunity to be social with them. So we're talking now the later '70s. Since my brother didn't have a car and I did—because I was gigging locally a lot with cover bands—I had wheels. So Bob was like, "Paul wants to go out." And for Paul, not everyone is going to be in his inner-circle, but my brother was cool, and I barely ever said a word to him, to be honest. I wasn't a Kiss fan per se, which made it much more easy for me. Appreciative of their fame and everything, but I was into the bands that influenced Kiss. I even saw similar concerts that Paul did, Led Zeppelin and stuff like that, growing up in Queens, New York. But I'd be along for the ride, where we'd all go to a club called Privates, and I remember seeing *Close Encounters of the Third Kind* with Paul and my brother. Again, I'm not going to tell you I was really his friend. I was kind of like a "tag-along guy." But it was a safe hang, and it was a lot of fun and very exciting for me, being a real lower/middle class Queens dude, to suddenly to be hanging out with Paul Stanley on the east side of Manhattan. I really got a kick out of it.

BOB KULICK: It had already reached the point where Gene and Paul were two peas in one pod, and Ace and Peter were the two peas in the other pod. It was obvious that Gene and Paul were much more businessmen, much more serious about keeping it together. Whereas shall we say Ace and Peter were party animals. Which is a fact. That was part of what was happening, and also the fact that as it was going on, who were the more important members of the band? The people that did the lion's share of the writing, the singing, and the posing—Gene and Paul. So it was the building animosity, even though Peter sang his song, and Ace was a huge idol as well. Jealousies begin, alliances form, and people leave.

CAROL KAYE: We knew that there was trouble within the band, but it was kept quiet. Bill did an amazing job with keeping it quiet. I set up all of their interviews, so I would deal with each band member individually. But I knew that Ace would do a limited amount of interviews. It was kind of difficult to schedule things with him at times. And then Peter would do some interviews, but mainly, I dealt with Paul and Gene. What greater speakers are there in rock n' roll than Gene Simmons and Paul Stanley, really? Well, Steven Tyler and Ted Nugent, yes, who I was also blessed to have worked with. But they were great. They were "quote machines."

The office wasn't very big. I think that people have the perception that there were hundreds of people employed by Aucoin Management, and it wasn't. It was very small. We were a family—we would all go out after work, have dinner together, have drinks together, even with the band. It was a great time. Companies like that do not exist today. And we were all in it together, we all had each other's backs. When we had birthday parties for Gene or Paul, we were all there. I remember when Peter and Lydia bought their house in Greenwich, Connecticut, we were all at the housewarming party. That's just the way it was.

Music was changing. It was very much about the whole new wave scene and dance in the late '70s. And Kiss were always very aware of the music that was going on, and it would seep into their music. Paul was always out at the clubs, dancing. We would go out all the time, and we were at Studio 54. I think that music kind of subconsciously seeped into some of his writing, with "I Was Made for Lovin' You." I think that that exposed them to a whole audience that would have never listened to Kiss. And they were shocked. *"This is Kiss?"* That was an interesting time. They were a little bit overexposed. It became like a runaway train, and it turned some people off.

BOB GRAW: I remember when I got [1979's] *Dynasty* the day it came out. I waited on line at Sam Goody. I went home and put it on, and I was like, "Oh my God, what the hell is this?" It was "I Was Made for Lovin' You" and "Sure Know Something." It was fluffy. I liked it ... because it was Kiss.

TY TABOR: I had kind of gone in and out of different phases with them, but in general, have remained a fan all along. How can you not love Kiss? [Laughs] But there was an era when they did "I Was Made for Lovin' You," and they started tampering around with disco, that I found myself thinking, "Hmmm, I'm not so sure about that," and feeling a little weird about the band. There were times that I lost interest and other times that I was totally into them again.

EDDIE TRUNK: The second show that I ever saw was the *Dynasty* tour at the Garden, and New England opened up [July 24 and 25, 1979]. That tour was such a big tour to introduce people to Kiss as well, but in retrospect, if you go back to the time and place, that is when the "Kiss world" was crumbling already. Even though it appeared that Kiss was still this super group—and yes, they were still bigger than most at the time—the wheels were coming off because of "I Was Made for Lovin' You" and everything else that was going on. It was the last go-around for the original band.

CHARLIE BENANTE: By the time that *Dynasty* record came out, it just seemed like they weren't hungry anymore. Now, I can look at that, and you can see how they were "breaking up" a bit at that point. I saw them on the *Dynasty* tour. The first show I saw was great. It had that excitement and that magic. Then by the second or third show I saw, I wasn't that excited anymore. And then I saw them later with Judas Priest opening, and that was awesome.

LYDIA CRISS: The thing is, it's a lot of work to be famous and to stay famous. They didn't have much time off the road. When they did, they were in the studio or they were doing photo sessions. They did put out two albums a year, so it was a lot of work. And I know Peter was the oldest in the band, and he was tired. He was tired of constantly on the go. But he was still willing to do it, as far as I knew [Lydia and Peter divorced in 1979].

BILL AUCOIN: They got tired of playing with each other. And then they wanted to take off the make-up, and they didn't like the merchandise. They thought it was too kiddy-like. So they went through a lot of changes emotionally.

CAROL KAYE: And then the '80s, it was a time of change—different music, different hairstyles. Everybody was cutting their hair short. Out went the long hair and hard rock music. It was much more short spiky hair and new wave and punk. It felt like there was an upheaval going on.

BOB GRAW: I remember buying [1980's] *Unmasked* the day it came out. It was so polished and poppy. It sounded like something you would hear on the radio. I didn't think it was bad, but *Dynasty* and *Unmasked* are not my two favorite Kiss albums, we'll just say that.

CHARLIE BENANTE: [*Unmasked*] is probably my least favorite Kiss record. I think the Ace songs on that record are good ... but that's kind of stretching it, too. I hated the sound of it. It sounded like a pop record. I hated *Dynasty*, too. It sounded like someone took all the treble and turned it up.

EDDIE TRUNK: I was loyal right through and through, with *Dynasty* and *Unmasked*. I remember hearing some rumblings around the time of *Unmasked* that Peter was in a car accident. I heard they were going to take their make-up off for *Unmasked*. The rumor was when you opened the inner sleeve, it was going to be them without make-up, which turned out not to be the case. Then I started hearing rumors that Peter didn't actually play on *Unmasked*, and then I started hearing things that he didn't play on *Dynasty*, and I said, "How is that possible? He sings on that record ... why wouldn't he play drums?" Just like we found out over the decades, things are not always what it appears to be in the Kiss world [Anton Fig played on most of *Dynasty* and all of *Unmasked*—uncredited]. I was much more naive back then and bought everything they sold hook, line, and sinker.

BILL AUCOIN: Both Ace and I were on Peter's side, and Gene, Paul, and the business manager were kind of against Peter. We kind of felt that they should have spent more time helping Peter or giving him a chance to get himself together. They were more concerned about getting rid of him. When push came to shove, I remember a meeting in a lawyer's office, where literally, Ace and I were on one side of the table, and everyone else was on the other side. And obviously, we didn't win. So Ace was a little disturbed by that. I think, also, he was getting feelers out about wanting to do his own thing, not feeling as comfortable with Gene and Paul. And Ace was always a little crazy, too, kind of the "rock n' roll guy" of the band, and he was always getting a little drunk or smashing up a car. So that didn't sit well with Gene or Paul, either. So there began to be a separation.

LYDIA CRISS: [Peter] leaving the band was a big surprise to me. I didn't know about it. I did hear things, but I didn't stay close to the band after my divorce. When you get divorced, not only do you lose your husband, you lose everything around him—the lifestyle, the family, the friends. I wasn't aware that he was actually going to leave Kiss, but they were off the road. I know his wife—at the time—didn't like Kiss.

I had heard a little about it, but I didn't know it was actually going to happen until it was in *Billboard* ... some picture announcing he was out of the band. I had heard something, because I guess throughout the year that I was separated [1978], I would hear things. I was still friends with Jeanette [Ace's then-wife] up until a certain point. As soon as they went on the road, she was told not to be friends with me. [Laughs] I guess it's hard for the band. Peter knew we were still friends. He probably didn't want to be around Jeanette, because then she'd be telling me stories. She was told not to be friends with me, but then eventually, we became friends again.

CHARLIE BENANTE: When I heard about Peter being out of the band, it was devastating. But I kind of knew it was coming.

EDDIE TRUNK: I was sad to see the original band break up. But it also brought some new interest for me because, "OK, who is this new guy? What is his persona? What is he about? What is his character? What is he going to be like?" Even at that point, it gave me a little shot in the arm of excitement. This was the first time this was happening. This was the first band of four superheroes and four characters that was about to undergo a makeover. And for me, I was very curious and very open-minded as to the whole mystique that came with a new member, his background, and his persona.

BILL AUCOIN: And then the next trauma was to find someone who could fit in the band, because it's not an easy situation. Paul and Gene are very strong personalities, and Ace was having his own problems, especially with Gene, but he wasn't exactly happy either. It's one of those odd moments. He wasn't ready to leave the band or anything, but I think what happened was everyone got very nervous. They made the decision about Peter, and then all of a sudden, they were presented with, "Oh my God ... *now what do we do?*"

May/June 1980

LORETTA CARAVELLO: To be honest, I don't think he thought too much of them. Not that he didn't like them, but he was more of a "Led Zeppelin guy" and a "heavy metal guy." He was not like a "Kiss guy." Like us, I don't think he realized how much they did. He never said anything bad about the music. He just never talked about it.

He found out that Kiss was auditioning for drummers, and one of the members [of Flasher] said, "Look, there's an article in the paper," and gave my brother the article. He wrote a resume on a typewriter—with one finger, of course—and put it inside an orange, fluorescent envelope. And basically, that's why they picked that envelope.

I got the call, that was Bill Aucoin on the other end. They wanted to talk to my brother. I remember he was in the bathroom—looking in the mirror, touching his mustache—and I just said, "Paulie, it's Bill Aucoin." He goes, "Yeah?" So he got on the phone, and after he got off, he said, "They want me to audition."

He didn't say anything [after an initial meeting with Bill Aucoin, prior to the tryout]. He came in the house and was a little excited. "I've got to go back, and I've got to cut my mustache off, though." And I remember him doing it, it was no problem. But he didn't really go, "Oh my God!" The house was very quiet and subdued. We were in our own thing. "That's just Paulie. He's going somewhere again? *Oh God.* What is it this week?"

BILL AUCOIN: He was just one of many, so he came in, he tried out, and we knew he could play well. The real question really was what kind of a human being [he was], whether he could get along with Gene and Paul, because they're strong personalities. And that was really it. We knew he played well; we knew that he could be the one. The question was when they talked to him and they spent a little time—and they always spent a little time, [but] it wasn't much time—I think it was a juxtaposition between two or three potential drummers, and he just stood out. I think he stood out because of his personality. That really separated him from everyone.

CHARLIE BENANTE: I remember going down to the auditions when I was younger, but I was too young to even get an audition! Me and my friends were there, and we actually saw Eric going in for the audition. I think we saw Carmine Appice there and some other people that I don't even know—session guys. I think we saw Anton Fig there, too.

CARMINE APPICE: I never tried out for them. I would have liked to [have] been in Kiss. I think I would have been a good addition to Kiss, but they never called me. I think they thought my image was too strong on my own.

BILL AUCOIN: There were some [potential drummers] that had been around, some that had certainly played in a lot of different bands. Some had been studio musicians. But I think a lot of them wanted to do it because they thought they could make a lot of money, as opposed to just wanting to play. That made a big difference as well.

LORETTA CARAVELLO: From what I heard, there was video recorded. But he never said there was. I'm sure there was, because how were you going to review anything if you can't look at it or listen to it? But just my assumption is they kept recording over recording. The video—if it existed—is something that probably would have surfaced on the *Kissology* DVD.

BILL AUCOIN: Eric was one of the last ones that we rehearsed with and tried out. I talked to the guys after, and they seemed to like Eric—not just his drumming, but they felt that his personality was an easy-going personality and that they could deal with that. Which is true. He really was.

LORETTA CARAVELLO: He loved it. He was fascinated. He didn't think he was really going to get anything, but he enjoyed being there. He thought he did well, but it was just one of those things. I don't think he thought he was going to do it. He was excited, but in our house, everybody was into their own thing. My mother worked in a dress shop, and so did I. My father delivered furniture. We didn't really comprehend what was going on. It was like, "What is my brother doing? I don't know." We didn't realize the extent that he was going back and forth and meeting them. We probably just thought he was going to the city that day to talk on a line with Kiss, not a personal kind of thing.

BOB KULICK: Paul told me the story of what was going on. As I recall, up at Aucoin's office, there were packages every day from drummers of all shapes and varieties, including big-name drummers, as well. I remember Paul showing me Eric's picture, with a comment about his hair. And I was just like, "Well, he can play. The hair qualifies. He looks like he could be really good. What's this guy's name? Paul Caravello? Change his first name, change the last name like you guys ... and you're set!" Paul's like, "Yeah, the guy's really great. He can really play." Eric was a real musician. He could play other styles. I was like, "Looks great, sounds great, and he can sing. He's a nice guy? *Take him."*

BILL AUCOIN: We decided to sign Eric. He was a salaried drummer—he wasn't actually part of the organization. But nevertheless, we felt more and more every day that he was a part.

LORETTA CARAVELLO: He was working with my father, and he had to go back and forth working with my father. And then he would be practicing with Kiss. But I don't think Kiss knew, because they would have stopped it, if he would have hurt his back or something. But even 'til the day of the first show at the Palladium, we were outside, and my father met the his boss' sons, and they said, "What are you doing here?" And he said, "Oh, my daughters, they love Kiss!" Little did they know that the guy that they saw every day at the furniture place was my brother.

CAROL KAYE: Eric and I became very close friends. He was just the sweetest guy in the world, and I know that they adored him. I mean, he just fit in perfectly. It was like a seamless transition—personality-wise, he fit right in. His drumming was amazing. I really think it went a lot easier and smoother than anyone thought it might.

BILL AUCOIN: They liked the fact that he was willing to do anything. But he was always the "hired hand." I think they felt a lot stronger with Eric at the beginning because it could work, but then as the years went on, they thought of him as more of a hired hand. And as Kiss was making less money, they would cut his salary down. Towards the end, he was really a hired hand.

BOB KULICK: He seemed like a really nice guy. Sweet guy, huge hair. He knew my relationship with the band, and I could see that this was his dream. This was what the guy wanted. He wanted to be in a superstar band. He lived it, and he breathed it. He was totally into the fact that this had finally happened. Your dreams come true. But as with all dreams, be careful what you dream for. Or as in the *Star Trek* episode, where Spock tells the girl that winds up with somebody else who pretended that she liked him, "Having is different than wanting." So having said that, I'm sure from other people, you know what went on after that. He was not an original member of the band, therefore, they didn't treat him as an original member of the band. And I think that was the cause of a lot of what went on that was negative. The positive side was the guy was in a huge band. Arguably, they were never better. Certainly, the original band with Ace was certainly never better than when Eric played with them. There's no question. He wiped the floor with Peter Criss. Period. And the guy was a totally nice guy and a great drummer.

LORETTA CARAVELLO: I have cards written by people that worked at the Kiss office the first year on his birthday card, and one of them wrote, "Just think if you didn't put that in an *orange* envelope!"

1980

LORETTA CARAVELLO: He was adapting well. He lived in Queens at that point, and he would be rehearsing most of the time. [Coming up with a stage name for Paul Caravello] was like a big deal, because everybody was trying to come up with a name. He had the make-up on, so you couldn't very well say "Paul Caravello," and you couldn't say "Paul" because you had Paul Stanley. He would come home and say, "Can you think of some names?" We said Tyler, Todd. Then he would ask Debbie [a.k.a. Pantera, Paul Caravello's girlfriend] and his friends. Finally, I think Debbie came up with the name "Eric." I'm not sure where the Carr part came from, but it was fitting.

BILL AUCOIN: And then they had to deal with the make-up, because Peter Criss still owned his own make-up. He hadn't signed off on that and sold it back to the guys yet. We had to come up with a new idea of make-up, a new character. That was another problem—the guys didn't know what to do. Then there was the costume. What is he going to look like? What is he going to wear?

LORETTA CARAVELLO: [An early make-up design for Eric modeled after a hawk] was one of Gene's ideas. It didn't look good. He looked like a duck! If you've seen the costume ... it looks awful. They would have laughed him right off the stage. It looked like something out of *Sesame Street*—Big Bird.

BILL AUCOIN: As we were rehearsing for the first show to announce to the press—which was being done in New York [at the Palladium on July 25, 1980] before we went to Europe—the guys really got frustrated. I remember one night in the dressing room, Gene and Paul at the end of the day said, "Look, you're the manager. *You* take care of it ... we're leaving!" And it wasn't that they were pissed off so much as they were frustrated. They weren't sure this was all going to come together. And Eric and I spent the whole night finishing the costume and deciding on the make-up, literally, the night before. The next day, when the guys walked into the dressing room, we just said, "OK, we're done. Here's what he is, here's the outfit. That's it." And they didn't really have time to think about it, because they had to perform that evening.

LORETTA CARAVELLO: I'm pretty sure he came up with "the fox." And then they came up with the make-up design they used at the Palladium, where you had no line on the nose. And what happened was when he would watch videos or look at pictures, he'd say that nobody could see the definition of his face. So he came up with putting the strip of white down the middle, and that was what it became.

BILL AUCOIN: They were all scared to death about whether the press would like Eric or hate Eric. And whether it would work, were they just kidding themselves, and should they have let Peter go. All of those emotions came into play in the Palladium show.

LORETTA CARAVELLO: He was excited [about the Palladium show]. Most of his concern was not to slip and say his real name. Because God forbid you said, "Paulie," and someone heard that. Of course, when we went, we called him Paulie, and he almost fell through the floor! So we got a little lecture when we got home—"You can't do that. Gene's going to get really mad, and I don't want to get in trouble with the band." But it was very hard. I would never call him "Eric" at home. He was always Paulie—even to my mother and father. So you just had to kind of think about it. That's why after the make-up came off, it was cool, because you didn't have to worry. You didn't have to worry about what you called him after that.

EDDIE TRUNK: I was at this first-ever show, which was at the Palladium in 1980. You have to remember that Kiss, at this point of their career in America, was a joke. I was in high school, and I was ridiculed regularly for liking Kiss. Having the balls for wearing a Kiss shirt or putting a Kiss picture in my locker. I remember that vividly. You couldn't be more uncool in your high school than to have been a Kiss fan in 1980. But I was fiercely loyal, and

I didn't care. I'm a pretty big guy in stature. If I wasn't, I probably would have physically gotten my ass kicked. But I didn't care—I was fiercely loyal to the whole thing. When I finally heard they were going to play, and I think it was the only show for the *Unmasked* album in America, it stung that the venue was the Palladium. Here's this band that went from two or three nights at Madison Square Garden, and a year later, they're playing a 2,000/3,000-seat theater. It was a tough pill to swallow, deep down inside. We knew as Kiss fans that this thing was unraveling here in America.

But I remember getting a ticket and going to that show, and I was hell-bent to go, because not only did I want to see Kiss, but I wanted to see what this new guy brought to the table, and be there for that historic night, to hear his first show playing with them. I remember there being a great buzz outside. I also remember it being—because it was such a smaller venue—a pretty tough ticket. I remember a buzz on the street of people trying to get in. I even vaguely remember there was a fire escape or emergency door on the side of that building, and people huddled up around those doors that couldn't get in, that just wanted to hear what Kiss sounded like with this new drummer. That's the one thing that I remember coming from that show being there. There was a genuine buzz amongst the Kiss fans that were still loyal, to kind of get a feel for what was happening inside—if they weren't able to get in.

And then for me, getting in and having a ticket, I remember the most immediate thing that struck me was seeing this double bass drum kit, something that you never saw in Kiss. Although Peter's kits got big at certain points, there's this *huge* kit. I think it was silver, double kick. You could feel that without even having heard Eric play yet, you just knew that this was going to be a different "machine" driving Kiss. And I say that with all due respect to Peter. I think Peter brought a tremendous amount of his style to Kiss. In the early days of Kiss, Peter was a really important weapon for them, because his background being jazz and swing, he brought that element to the sound of Kiss. And I think that's something that certainly should not be overlooked. But Eric, you just needed to look at his kit before you heard him play, and you knew this was going to be more all-out power and drive and a completely different beast than what Peter was, in his own way.

So that got me really excited, because you're also coming from a period of time in the history of Kiss where things got very poppy—*Dynasty*, "I Was Made for Lovin' You," and *Unmasked*, which is an all-out power pop record. That's one of the things that Kiss fans were getting so beat up on and disillusioned on, that Kiss was morphing into this pop band and this kiddy band. So it felt good as a fan to go in there and see this mammoth drum set with double bass, because it kind of sent the message that, "OK, maybe these guys are going to get back to some no-bullshit hard rock again." That was definitely the vibe going in, and of course, that was fully confirmed after seeing the show. Watching him play and hearing him that first show, it just drove the band to a different level. It powered the band. Whereas Peter kind of meshed with the band, had his moments, and let the band swing a little bit more, Eric drove it. Eric was a monster. He was a machine. And he put these little flourishes in, double kicks and things. These little touches in that material really gave it an extra kick.

CHARLIE BENANTE: I was at the first show that they played, at the Palladium. It was great. He was a different drummer than Peter was. Eric was more "hands and arms all over the kit." I thought he was a really good fit for those guys.

CAROL KAYE: I do remember the first show I went to that he played, and I thought it was just awesome. He just fit right in. It was great.

LORETTA CARAVELLO: Me, my sister, my brother-in-law Dave, my mother, and father [went to the Palladium show]. That's the show where he met the kids from the furniture store in Jamaica, Queens. When we were up in the audience, we did not go backstage, because my brother was too nervous. He didn't know if Gene would like it. It's like getting a new job. You don't want your mother calling. "Shhh, I'm going to get in trouble, mom. I can't get calls at work!" So he didn't know his liberties. He was very on edge, not to blow anything. But I remember we were standing up further—we didn't have close seats, we were at the top. I remember the kids were chanting, "Peter, Peter." But then after about ten minutes, you started hearing, "Eric, Eric." It was overpowering, the way the kids were screaming "Eric," from when it started out "Peter." People were wondering what these old farts were doing there—my mother and father. And we were younger, but we were creepy-looking, more like Bob Dylan-kind of kids, with long hair and a beatnik kind of look.

LYDIA CRISS: The Palladium show, that was because I wanted to see Kiss, and I hadn't seen them in a long time. And I wanted to see them with Eric. I'm not even sure who I went with, but I know I was sitting with some of the people from the office. I didn't even go backstage for that show. To me, it's a Kiss song, so it sounds like a Kiss song. Listening to Eric, it was more visuals. Being a photographer, I'm looking at the visuals as opposed to the sound. There were a lot people I knew sitting around me, so I was talking during the show. Basically, I don't really don't know the difference in the sound. I know Eric's got a double bass, and I've been told that he's a more technical drummer.

All I was looking for were the visuals. For some reason, everything seemed a lot simpler, but it was a smaller place. I'm not used to seeing Kiss from that angle. I'm usually on the stage. I didn't really take a lot of pictures of Kiss throughout the years of them performing, because Peter didn't want me in the audience. He didn't want me in the pit, which is where the photographers stay. The only place that he would let me go—and it was not every time, depending on what venue it was—was the soundboard, which was all the way in the audience, as long as I watched by some of the employees. Peter didn't want anything happening to me. I was a big girl, but he used to treat me like a little girl. And seeing that show was a little different than normal, because I'm not used to being in the audience. It was actually fun being in the audience for a change. It was a little unusual. It was sort of a "present" that I never got, that I was never able to do.

BILL AUCOIN: The performance was OK. It wasn't great, but it was good. The fact is that Gene, Paul, and Ace were very nervous. First of all, would the press accept him? This was a big press show, based on the fact that they were going back out on tour. This was the big announcement of the new drummer. I think that Gene, Paul, and Ace were as nervous as Eric was. It was really a critical time. They had a rough time talking about it. It was like, "Is this going to happen? Do you think people are going to accept him? Is our career over? Is it going to continue?" It was really that dramatic.

LORETTA CARAVELLO: Gene said how great he did. "The kids accepted you!" He felt he did great on the stage. He was overwhelmed.

LYDIA CRISS: He did a fantastic job. And I think Peter thinks so, too. Peter knows. I think Peter was friends with Eric. After the whole thing was over, I was told it was kind of a mutual thing—Kiss wanted Peter out, and Peter wanted out. You can't be angry with somebody that replaces you, because it was basically his decision. And I kind of like that Eric had a different character, that he didn't use Peter's make-up, like the current Eric. [Laughs] But Peter sold his make-up, so that was his decision, also.

BOB GRAW: I was a big subscriber to *16* magazine back then. Every month they had their standard Kiss feature and fold-out poster. I remember the cover saying, "Flash! Peter Criss Leaves Kiss!" And they had a picture of him inside with a beard, and he was like, "It's time to go on my own and record a solo album, and do this and do that." And they hadn't announced a replacement. It wasn't too long after that [that] *People* magazine came out [the August 18, 1980 issue], and it had pictures of the "new Kiss," and it had a picture of Eric Carr, before he changed his make-up. He had the original eye design. And then they had a big story in *16* magazine and a poster of him. I think it was of him standing on steps, wearing that "fox shawl." Oh God, that was awful. So I remember that.

CARMINE APPICE: Eric was a lot more powerful of a player. He had a lot more chops, more of a power drummer. More of my style of drumming than Peter. Peter was more of an old school, light kind of player. But you had him mic'd up, and it didn't matter.

CHARLIE BENANTE: Peter was more straight-ahead, kind of "keep the beat" drumming. Eric had some good hands and feet, so Eric was more on top of the kit. He was all over. Where in the early days, Peter was like that, too, and then as time went on, he kind of slowed down and just kept the beat. He didn't do much in an exciting way. And I thought Eric brought more excitement to the songs and to the playing at that point.

BILL AUCOIN: Eric I think was a lot more consistent than Peter. I think Peter had been slipping based on letting himself go a bit. From that point of view, I think the guys liked Eric a lot better in the sense that he was more consistent. Peter was very emotional, but on the other hand, he was there at the beginning and worked just as hard as the other three. And without him, it might not have happened. The split happened because of a lot of things, including Peter's problems, as well as Gene and Paul wanting it their way.

BOB GRAW: Well, I was depressed that Peter left, because him and Gene Simmons were my two favorite members. So I was pretty bent out of shape about it. But I saw Eric on *Kids Are People Too*, when they introduced him, and I watched that. I guess it was on a Saturday or Sunday morning. I instantly liked him, because he was funny and he was cool. And he looked great—he looked like he belonged in the band. I remember they had a promo clip. It was a *Dynasty* promo clip, but they inserted Eric Carr in all the spots that Peter was in in the original one. He looked cool, he looked like he fit.

CHARLIE BENANTE: He had two bass drums and a very large kit. The funny thing about Eric joining Kiss—it didn't seem odd to me. It just fit. It was just accepted. I think that's probably because of his personality and his playing. I remember at the time they did a TV show, *Kids Are People Too*, and they interviewed Eric on there. I thought Eric came across as a very likable, genuine person.

BLAS ELIAS: When Eric Carr got in the band, I was also a huge fan. I think that was one of my bigger influences, as far as my sound, my style. The really heavy, fat grooves that he laid down were a little different than the kind of shuffle-y rock n' roll rhythms that Peter Criss did. Not that it was better per se, I just liked the power that he had. It seemed like big, powerful, arena rock. As soon as I heard him in the band, I was a big fan.

BOB GRAW: Eric was a lot more technical. With no disrespect to Peter Criss, he was a lot better of a drummer. I loved Eric's interpretations on stuff like "Love Gun" and "Detroit Rock City," because he was so much better of a player, and he made those songs so much heavier. I always loved that.

CAROL KAYE: I'm trying to think of an analogy ... something you've done a hundred times, like ride a bike. You're a kid, [and] you ride your bike every day. But this one day, what made you ride that bike differently? What made you ride it a little harder and a little faster? That's kind of what it was. He added a jolt—that's probably the best word. They were revitalized, they were reenergized. There wasn't that in-fighting, it can wear you down. It's like being in a bad relationship—you're dating someone, and it's just not working out. You keep going through the motions of hoping that it will change ... it wears you down, it's exhausting. And I think that's what happened with them. And then all of a sudden, you have a new girlfriend or a new boyfriend. That's exactly what it was like. Was it different musically? I can't say one is better than the other. It was just *different.* They were more energized.

MARK WEISS: I don't think Eric could have been in Kiss when they started, and I don't think Peter could have continued where Kiss was going in the '80s.

TY TABOR: When Eric joined, all Kiss fans early on had an affinity for the original members, and it always was a strange kind of thing as different people came in and out at first. But Eric became such a long-standing part of it that it just became "Kiss Part Two."

LORETTA CARAVELLO: My brother always had naturally curly, wavy hair. When we were like 16 or 17, my brother's hair was almost down to his waist. That was a time in our lives when everybody on our block would be making fun of us and telling my mother to cut our hair, because we used to take the iron and press our hair. My brother did that, too. That's how you got it straight—years ago, you'd lay your hair on an ironing board, put on a towel, and press it. So we all had that really long hair. But then as the years went by and he got into Salt and Pepper and Bionic Boogie, he started to frizz it out. But it was always curly.

So at the time he got into Kiss, from his audition photos, his hair was more long—down to the shoulder. He had bangs, he always had natural waves. They used to do their hair in the city, so he went to the same place that Paul and Gene would go to. He came back, and he couldn't believe how he looked. His hair was beautiful. When you saw my brother or Gene or Paul, you knew that they were *somebody.* You didn't have to know who they were to know they were somebody, from the way their hair was. And that's something that the normal or regular person couldn't obtain—that type of look, unless they were in a rock band. He was a ham about it, he loved it. Took very good care of it, washed it twice a day. He was that fanatical about it.

And he was driving I believe a Dodge Colt when he got into Kiss, this old yellow car. We all had that kind of car, the ones that break down all the time. He used to drive to rehearsals in the Dodge Colt. Kiss was not going to have anybody photograph their new drummer in this car, so they surprised him with a Porsche. It was a surprise ... but I did find a lot of letters regarding, "Eric, what color car do you like? What color seats do you like?"

BILL AUCOIN: I remember when we discussed, "How is he going to jump ahead," because he had never experienced this type of thing before. So we bought him a Porsche, so he would feel more like a rock n' roller, and that he would feel like he was part of something bigger and more exciting.

NEIL ZLOZOWER: They treated him like he was one of the members. It wasn't like, "You aren't Peter, so we're going to treat you like a hired hand." They treated him like he was part of the band, and they treated him well. Gene and Paul are really nice guys. I like them.

LORETTA CARAVELLO: So here we had the hair, the car ... and then we had to get the leather pants and tight shirts! Of course, at that time, he had the make-up on, so nobody knew who he was. We lived in Woodhaven, Queens at the time, near Rockaway Boulevard. Here was Paulie basically going from this Dodge Colt to this Porsche—an entirely different look. So everybody in the neighborhood knew us. Years ago, you'd sit outside and talk to your neighbor, and everybody knew who their neighbor was. So people would say, "What's with Paulie?" They were kind of suspicious about this sudden change. But of course, nobody could say anything. And sometimes, you'd see the limousine pull up. It was a trip just to actually watch. It never really stopped getting fascinating, because we weren't the type of people to get in limousines. My father would drive—we always had old cars, and he'd drive to all the concerts. He'd never want to take a limousine, and my brother would insist, "Take a limousine!" "No, no, no, just save your money. We don't want you to waste your money." My brother would be mad, because they were old, and he didn't want them to be driving to the shows.

BILL AUCOIN: He was just a charmer. We couldn't have been any luckier to have someone as sweet as Eric. He was willing to do anything to make it happen. He was just that type of person. And the big thing about Eric that everyone used to kid about was he was so well-endowed that we said any girl that would ever go out with him would be thrilled! That was the inside joke about Eric. He was better endowed than any of us, so he was kind of "The Superman." Again, he was such a good person to work with. There was never a trauma. There was never anything he would go against. He was always willing to help as much as he could.

LORETTA CARAVELLO: He loved Gene. Paul and he got along good, but his sense of humor was more towards Gene, and Gene took him under his wing. He adored Ace.

CAROL KAYE: He and Ace were very close. I think Ace sort of took him under his wing, like his little brother, and they were really good friends. They would write a lot together, and later on, they maintained a friendship throughout all the years. But y'know, Eric was that kind of a guy. He was very friendly, very warm, very open, just really a nice guy. Very sweet. And we went out a lot when he was in Kiss, as friends. We went to a lot of the same parties together.

LORETTA CARAVELLO: I think there was a point where people in the neighborhood did know he was in Kiss. It was too hard to hide, but yet, it never got out, at least in that it made the press, that a photographer would be waiting outside our door to shoot pictures of him. That never happened. Just before he got into Kiss, he lived in our house, and he had just got through leaving Starrett City on Flatlands Avenue. And there, he lived with Debbie. Then he went back to live with Debbie after he joined Kiss. They got an apartment in the city on Bleecker Street—there were times where you would see kids sitting on the steps. He didn't mind it. But one night, somebody rang the bell at like 3:00 in the morning, and he was pissed. It was very scary. But as far as the kids, they were really respectable, and he'd come out and sit on the steps. It was really nice times, because nobody really harassed anybody. Nobody was looking to break into the house and steal. You know how things are today, if somebody knows where somebody is. We had a modest house. It was a two-family, and we had tenants up on top, and we lived on the bottom. It was something that we had gotten after we moved from Brooklyn, right off of Jamaica Avenue.

CAROL KAYE: It's funny. I don't remember the first time I met Eric, but when I did meet him, he was in the band. Wait a minute ... I remember him coming up to the office, so I guess I was still there. And I remember his girlfriend, Pantera.

LORETTA CARAVELLO: [Pantera] was with him for many years, before Kiss, even before Flasher. She was really talented. She sung just like Pat Benatar and was in a band of her own.

CAROL KAYE: Any time there was an event or a party, she was with Eric in those early days. But she was very cool. As I said, it was a small office—maybe there were 40 people. It was not the way people think it was, so we were all very close. And we all knew each other's girlfriends, boyfriends. I remember when Gene was dating Cher, and she would come up to the office with him. It was crazy. It was like we all went through everything together, it was really a very special time. I don't think that those days will ever be again ... everything was always on "ten."

BILL AUCOIN: [Kiss' 1980 tour] was mostly in Europe, and then Australia was a big tour. We had gotten a lot of fans in Australia. We didn't have any thoughts at the time [on a U.S. tour], other than getting through Europe. That was going to be the big play, also with Eric, and whether the acceptance was going to be there, and then doing a major tour in Australia, because the whole country turned out for Kiss. It was really enormous. Plus, it was very exciting to be there and to have the entire country at our beck and call—having nine limousines, a 727, and a helicopter. You can only imagine [that] it was pretty nice.

They were scared to be in another country. They thought something was going to happen to them. The hotels [in Europe] were small, the beds were small, the television went off at 11:00 at night, they couldn't get food in the middle of the night. They were just horrified—it wasn't anything like the States. It was really a trauma. And also, we didn't have sleeping buses at that point. You had a bus, but you sat up in a regular bus seat. It was a tough, tough tour. And on the other hand, they went to Australia, and the whole place opened up for them. They could have had anything, day or night. It was like the whole country wanted to see Kiss. So they went from having a so-so tour that they were unhappy and uncomfortable with in Europe, to *taking over* Australia.

CAROL KAYE: The Australia tour was crazy. It was like the Beatles coming. People were nuts, the media were all over them, the fans were ecstatic. And Eric was like a little kid in a candy shop. He really was. That's how I always think of him.

LORETTA CARAVELLO: One of the first tours was Australia. They didn't know Peter Criss there, so this was like introducing the first Beatle to Australia. He would call every night, and he was so excited. He sent postcards. He was away for a long time—that first tour—but he would constantly keep in touch with my mother and father and call us. He was having a blast. I don't know all the stories of what he was doing there. That's for somebody else to tell you.

He would go under the name "Rusty Blades," and he had all his memos—"Doctor Van"-something for Gene, "Microphone" for Paul. I have a book that he saved from Australia. It's over 2,000 news clippings from every paper, and it was presented to him and Kiss. There's two books—they're red, leather-bound books. He saved all that stuff.

Those were his favorite tours, because he was like Ringo Starr there. He told us about how the kids loved him, and he brought back souvenirs like you wouldn't believe. He had this really nice thing that was made out of metal—it was the whole country of Australia in puzzle-metal pieces. I think a mayor of one of the cities gave it to him. And he brought back this beautiful metal award from Perth, that Kiss was voted the most popular band in Perth in 1980. He was overjoyed.

BILL AUCOIN: You can imagine getting there, and Rupert Murdoch was one of the sponsors of the tour, so we took all the press everywhere. We had our own 727, nine limousines, and a helicopter. So you can imagine. They had their own masseuse on the road. They could get massages anytime they wanted to. They had big suites. Everyone had their own suite. They had the best food, the best parties. I did something that I don't think I ever did again—when there wasn't a party, I would open "Bill's Bar" at the hotel, and throw a party every night that there wasn't one. So it never really ended for the whole time we were there in Australia. It was certainly one of the best tours they had ever had up to that point.

Elton John came to one of our parties. He was touring Australia while we were there, as well. We wound up in Sydney, and he came to the Kiss party—[there's a picture] of me and him sitting together at a Japanese steakhouse. Also, he felt put-upon that night because he wasn't getting the attention. Elton was having a big party the next night and refused to invite Kiss, because he was afraid they would get too much attention. [Laughs]

They had never done anything like it. You just can't compare the two [the Australia tour to earlier tours]. A whole country turns out for you, and you have everything at your beck and call. That was an experience that most artists will never go through. You can't imagine going from someone who was picked off the street with the ability to play well, the emotion, and the personality to get along with everyone. And then being able to go to Australia and have the whole country turn out and have everything at his disposal. He certainly enjoyed it more than anyone did. But we *all* enjoyed it a lot. It was one of those "once-in-a-lifetime tours."

CAROL KAYE: I can see his face, that little smiley face. He was so proud to be in Kiss. He really was. It was a big deal for this Italian kid from Brooklyn, y'know? And that's the other reason why I think he just blended in perfectly. This is another New York guy. There's something to be said for being born and living in New York City. It's just a certain vibe, and it just worked. It was really a good fit.

LORETTA CARAVELLO: He kept that kind of stuff really private from us. You wouldn't even know he was in Kiss most of the time, because he never talked about anybody. I'm not saying that he was an angel. I don't know what he did with other people. But when it came to family, he was very, "This is my job, this is your job, and I'm not going to bring it home." I would ask questions because I was curious. It was so cool that he was in this band. But I learned to not overstep too much. He dealt with it all day long. To talk about it to me was a novelty, but to him, it was, "Oh my God ... who cares what Gene's like?" But he would once in a while offer up some things.

He was dealing with it. But when you think about it, you're sitting there going, "Hey, do you know who I am?" And he can't tell you. It was crazy because I used to go to work and say, "My brother's famous ... but I can't tell you." And they'd say, "Come on, what are you doing?" So it was very hard, but we did it because he couldn't lose his identity, because it would destroy him early on.

He didn't have such a great self-assurance before he got into Kiss. He was always thinking he wasn't that good at what he did. He was very shy growing up. I think he had his first girlfriend at 20. So the way the women were swarming over him was something he couldn't believe. He kind of started to like himself a lot, too, when they did his hair the way they did. He started to really take a lot of pride in himself. But he always had that type of personality. He never really, really believed he was as good as people thought he was.

1981

BOB GRAW: So, having this powerful new drummer infused in the band, I was really hoping that they were going to go back to the sound that they had earlier, when they were "scary," when they had albums like *Rock and Roll Over* and *Love Gun*—their heavier, darker sound. And boy, did they *not* do that.

BILL AUCOIN: *The Elder* was one that happened because they really didn't want to do an album. We had to deliver another album, plus we had a big contract, which meant every time we delivered an album, we got two million dollars. So the business managers wanted us to do it, and the guys really didn't. They were burnt out. Ace didn't want to do it, [and] Gene and Paul really didn't want to do it. That's why I hired Bob Ezrin. I knew Bob could handle them, even in a "crisis mode," because he had worked with them and had success with them. So whatever happened, I knew we would get an album out of it.

BOB EZRIN: They approached me. They came to me, and I don't even remember the circumstances, how we got back together or who called who. But as soon as I saw them again—and every time I ever did see them—I get over stuff pretty fast, so as soon as I saw them again, it was just nice to see them. I was happy that we were talking.

BILL AUCOIN: They didn't really want to write "Kiss songs," and during one meeting, we decided to do an album that was a more new and creative album. A concept album.

BOB EZRIN: We did some recording at Ace's house [in Connecticut]. That was an interesting experience. That was a bad period for me. My marriage had broken up, and I was with someone new. I was doing drugs and not in the best of shape—it was not a good experience. My recollection is I felt very claustrophobic in that area, in that house, in that little town. The walls just seemed to be closing in on me. I felt very cut off, isolated.

The Canadian [sessions] were mostly overdubbing and sort of finishing touches. We actually did that with a remote truck up at my farm, north of Toronto. And that felt far better for me, because obviously, I was on home territory. But because it was a wide-open space, with a field, I felt like we could "breathe" there. So that was a better experience. I don't think it was so good for Ace—I think Ace had a bad time there. In the same way that I had a hard time and was kind of fucked up in Connecticut, he was pretty fucked up when he came to Canada.

So I just think, all in all, the whole experience of *The Elder*, because it started off on the wrong foot, was uncomfortable, I think for everybody. And it was for Eric, too, because I think Eric was caught between Ace's grumbling and the other guys' opinions and my craziness at the time. He did a very good job of trying to rise to the occasion and give us exactly what we needed all the time. He played great drums on it. The drums are amazing on that one.

BILL AUCOIN: Eric was a good drummer. He could do anything. Don't forget, he was so devoted to the project. He never lost his enthusiasm for the project.

BOB EZRIN: Peter was from Canarsie. He was a tough, New York "street guy," with that sort of a mentality. And he had that kind of a sense of humor. Also, Peter was not really a schooled drummer. He was just a kind of natural drummer. So that's Peter's personality. Where was Eric born? [Upon being told Brooklyn] That's funny, because he didn't feel like that. Eric felt far more sort of ... did he grow up middle class? I just felt that Eric was far less a street guy and a little softer around the edges, and technically, far more schooled than Peter.

Plus, Eric came into this as "the new guy," so he was incredibly respectful and very mindful of the fact that he was being allowed this amazing opportunity. Where Peter was a founding member of the band, and in a certain way, sometimes resented me as the new guy coming in and telling him what to do. Eric, on the other hand, was the new guy and was more than willing to try anything anybody suggested. He was very, very easy to work with. And, musically, an amazing drummer.

LORETTA CARAVELLO: [Eric co-wrote] "Under the Rose" and "Escape from the Island." He was happy. I'm sure that he would have liked to do more, but to first get in the band and to do that ... I think he liked the way "Under the Rose" came out, but he wasn't too thrilled with the chorus. He thought it sounded too choir-ish.

BOB EZRIN: Allan Schwartzberg was kind of my go-to guy. Honestly, I don't remember why we did that [session musician Schwartzberg played drums on a few tracks on *The Elder*], because Eric was perfectly capable handling everything. I honestly don't remember why.

BILL AUCOIN: I think they were burning themselves out. Ace was unhappy, and Gene and Paul were tired as well.

BOB EZRIN: Ace did [voice his opinion against *The Elder*]. I think Eric was happy to be doing whatever we were doing. I don't remember Eric objecting. But Ace wasn't happy with the whole situation, from the beginning. And, as it turns out, he was right.

LORETTA CARAVELLO: I have to tell you something about my brother. He didn't say bad things about people. You had to pull something out of him. I think he confided in my parents more, but he also didn't come home and say, *"This is happening, and Ace did this."* Nothing like that at all. I mean, if something went wrong, you could see it on his face, or he didn't want to talk to anybody. Things aren't always great—when you work with people, no matter where you are, you're going to have a tiff. But he loved Ace.

BOB EZRIN: Mostly, I wasn't hanging with Eric at the time. Mostly I was pretty glued to Gene and Paul. And again, as I say, when you start something like this and you've got a limited budget and a limited amount of time, basically, we were working 20 hour days. There was no hanging out. And because it was happening not where I lived ... certainly during the recording of the rhythm tracks when Eric was around, we'd work 20 hours, I'd go to bed, and that's it. There was no time off. As soon as there was time off, I'd go home. So I didn't really get a chance to hang with him much. Though when you're with people 20 hours a day in a studio and you're working that closely together, you do form a bond. I felt very warmly towards Eric. He was just the nicest, sweetest guy and very hard-working, very inventive, and creative. I was thrilled to death to have him. I thought he was a great addition to the band.

BILL AUCOIN: I think Ace had decided that he wanted to leave. That became the beginning of Ace leaving.

CAROL KAYE: There was just so much going on in their personal lives. I believe at that point Gene was already living on the west coast. That really changed things a lot, having Gene on the west coast, Paul on the east coast, Ace upstate ... it was hard.

BOB EZRIN: [The story-line of *The Elder*] is there is a ... I don't know if you want to call it a race, [but] there are guardians every generation, that protect the world from evil. And they are set apart from the rest of humanity. They're angels, in a way, and they're there to protect the world from demons. And that class of people, they are a collective conscience that is timeless and ageless. They are collectively referred to as "The Elder." And there's this young boy, who is obviously one of them. And there's the evil genius, Mr. Blackwell, which was an interesting choice of names, because Chris Blackwell is a dear friend of mine. I don't know how we got to that, but I think it was actually Lou Reed that came up with the name "Blackwell." Because "black" and "the well," the depths of evil and so on. Anyway, so this is the boy, and the idea was to kidnap him and kill him. But he prevails because he's "the boy," and he beats the evil Mr. Blackwell back, and he's the hero that saves the world. Basically. So, kind of a fantasy of a young boy with special powers, hence that song, "Just a Boy."

BOB KULICK: What's going on with that album, when you're working with Bob Ezrin, no one says nothing negative, because Bob Ezrin was one of the big keys to their success, Alice Cooper's success, and Pink Floyd's success. The Beatles did a concept record, Pink Floyd did a concept record ... who is to think that this would not work? "A World Without Heroes," I remember Paul played me the song with his guitar solo, and I was like, "Wow, that was you?" He's like, "Yeah, I tried to play what you would play." I thought, "Wow, what a compliment from somebody who is not very open with compliments." That's about all I remember. I don't recall ever talking to Eric and him saying, "This blows. I hate playing this stuff. Why don't we go back to blah, blah, blah?" I don't recall anything like that. I wasn't privy to that.

BILL AUCOIN: It really turned out to be as much a "Bob Ezrin album" as did a "Kiss album." And, of course, it was completely different. I think *The Elder* is pretty spectacular, but it certainly wasn't a Kiss album, and we paid the penalty for that album when we handed it in.

BOB EZRIN: I thought it was great. I was so proud of it. All the sound effects, crazy production, and big songs. And the great ballad, "A World Without Heroes," and the concept, artwork, the recording of the voiceovers, and all that stuff that we had done to put this thing together. When it came together and I sat back and listened to it, I was so proud of it. And then, it came time to deliver it to the record company, and I was elected to go and play it for the record company, without the band. At the time, I thought it was an honor. I realized very soon afterwards ... *they were hiding.* I think at a certain point everybody started to cringe over the record. I think Gene and I were the most proud of it, and Paul was proud, too, because he had been doing some writing that had been so different from what he had been used to doing. So I think he was proud of it, too, to a point. But I think as soon as they started playing it for people, and people started going, *"Huh?"* then they lost faith. I remember being out there—it's like a classic scene, where everybody goes, "I'm right behind you!" And you go out into the rain, you look around, and everyone is gone. [Laughs] That was me delivering the record to the label, especially in Europe. People were trying to be polite and excited. I was all excited, and we would have big playbacks and everything. But I could really tell from the playback sessions that this was not speaking to people the way earlier stuff had.

BILL AUCOIN: It wasn't a bad move, as we got it done. We thought it would maybe bring them to another level. But the record label hated it. They wanted another straight-ahead Kiss album. So we kind of got that whole negative vibe right from the beginning. It was hard to overcome that when the record label and everyone is saying, "We don't like it. You can do another one. Please let's not put out this one." It was very negative. But there was no way they were going to go back in the studio.

BOB EZRIN: I think *The Elder* was a victim of my "Pink Floyd era" [Ezrin produced Pink Floyd's 1979 album, *The Wall*] and Gene's restlessness and everybody's sort of aspirations to be taken seriously. I feel like that motivated us, unfortunately, almost more than good sense. Once you begin with that premise, you start off by saying, "You have to do something that is more important," then right off the bat, you lose the essence of Kiss. And that was a mistake. I take as much responsibility for that as much as anybody, if not more. Because I kind of convinced them at the time that we could do something that would be really amazing and trippy and kind of based on a story that we would make a film out of.

We were really thinking *The Elder* as a full multimedia project. Making a cartoon, a film, a book, you name it. And that, of course, appealed to Gene, who comes out of that whole "comic book ethos." He was a comic fanatic, and also, was starting to do movies and get really excited about working in other media—and expanding his profile and his career. So the idea of doing something like that really appealed to him. And then we brought in other people to help us out with it. They were all very excited.

But I think what we ended up making instead of a great Kiss record was a very precious ... the very thing that typified them in the beginning, the fact that they were not precious, is the thing that we injected into this project, and it's the thing that made it not work. We got precious. Now, that being said, there are moments on that record that are pretty amazing. Maybe if you put them in a different context, they'd be better received. And there are some people who are just rabid fans of that album, because I think there are some things that appeal to ... there are some people that like fantasy and science fiction, and they're Kiss fans too, so this is a perfect marriage of those things for them. But I think for the average Kiss fan, who's really into just the "cock and balls of Kiss," I think this album let them down.

CHARLIE BENANTE: I thought it was kind of modeled after *The Wall*. But there were some pretty cool tunes on there, the song "The Oath." They changed the image a bit there and were trying to be kind of artsy. They were trying to do their version of *The Wall*, and I don't think it came across.

BOB GRAW: I remember seeing the pictures. The pictures came out before the album came out. It was like, "Kiss' New Look." They all cut their hair and were wearing completely different outfits from their *Dynasty* or *Unmasked* outfits. I was like, "Wow, that's cool. This looks pretty tough." Except for Paul Stanley's purple headband. But I remember waiting on line at Modell's to buy it. I got it home, put it on, and the first track on the original printing of *The Elder* was "The Oath," which was a great, kick-ass, hard rock song. I was like, "Alright, they're back!" And boy, where did it go wrong? Song after song, I was like, "What is this? Why are Kiss trying to reproduce *Tommy* by the Who?" I didn't get it. Not a lot of people did. After 25 years, the album eventually grew on me, and I love it. But, yeah, I didn't get it.

EDDIE TRUNK: Having seen the show [at the Palladium] and seen what Eric was about, I was excited that this new blood was going to drive Kiss back into more of a hard rock band. And I, like a lot of fans, was shocked to see what the by-product of him joining the band became, with *The Elder*. I remember hearing "The Oath" from *The Elder* and liking it. I was excited about that, because that was kind of a big Zeppelin groove. That was a hard rock song. But then getting more into the record and hearing the different styles to it ... *The Elder* is one of those "love/hate" things. The band hates it, some of the fans hate it, [and] some of the fans love it and think it's this masterpiece. I'm somewhere in the middle. I don't hate it, [but] I don't love it. It is what it is.

But I was very curious in listening to it, because it was the first recorded music with Eric on drums in the band, and I really wanted to hear what he was going to do and what they were going to sound like on record. And the same thing—there's some double kick, and there's more of a different groove and pocket going on than what Peter was doing. It's funny, because over the years knowing Eric, he had told me many stories about how against the record he was. And what a curveball it was for him, to join this high energy/ hard rock band and couldn't wait to get in the studio and start bashing it out, and the next thing you know, you're working with orchestras and conductors, and writing this concept piece. He was kind of lost. He was like, "Wait a minute ... *this is Kiss?* This is what I joined?" But, of course, being a new guy at the time and happy to have the gig, he didn't really have a lot of leg to stand on, to open his mouth. He kind of did the best he could.

MIKE PORTNOY: It's strange. I love *The Elder* album! I know that's such a controversial album for so many people. It's a love/hate album, but I fall in the category of "love." I thought that was an awesome album and still completely underrated and under-appreciated. At the time, it was a hard pill for Kiss fans to swallow. They had cut their hair, which was a weird enough adjustment to make visually, but also, them doing a concept album was really controversial. And I've seen many interviews with Gene in recent years where he poo-poos it because it wasn't a successful album. But to me, a good album isn't determined by whether or not it was successful. In fact, I think some of the best albums of all time were ones that were under-appreciated at the time and considered a flop at the time. So I don't buy into that. The success doesn't equal good or bad to me. Now, listening back to that album, there's some great stuff on there. Just about a month ago, I was listening to my iPod on shuffle, and there's an instrumental on that album, "Escape from the Island." I hadn't heard that in so many years. I was like, "What the fuck is this? That's pretty cool!" And sure enough, it was from *The Elder*. I just think it's an incredibly under-appreciated album. I think it holds up even better. I think it was cool that they were willing to take a chance to do a concept album and do something out of the norm. It's a shame that Kiss doesn't look fondly on it, because it would be awesome for them to pull out some of those tunes and still play them to this day.

TY TABOR: When *The Elder* came out, I didn't know anyone else that was listening to that record, and it was, for me, one of my favorite things they had done in a very long time. I freaked on that record. I loved it. What I liked about it was it just had this foreboding and serious feel to it. And a whole lot of it, I had no idea what they were singing about or what this was from. Like, is there some movie I don't know about or some story I don't know about? It just intrigued me as so not like anything they had ever written before lyrically, and musically, really. It had a medieval kind of freaky vibe to it, and they're singing about subject matter other than girls. For me, it was just like, "Wow, they've done it again!"

BOB GRAW: The band sounded good on it. It was produced by Bob Ezrin, and he always brought that great sound. It was a great-sounding album. But it just was not Kiss—I don't know why they went for that. And I remember reading quotes back then, and Ace hated it. Ace wanted really nothing to do with it. It was pretty much why he ended up quitting the band. And Eric was like ... I remember hearing quotes that he said, "Why did we do this? Why didn't we go back to the way you sounded?" He was disappointed that it was his first album and it was a "rock opera." Very disappointing.

CAROL KAYE: They weren't working as a unit any longer. It was very fragmented, and I think it showed. Although years later, I've heard people say that that was such a great record, and that when it came out, they hated it, because it didn't sound like Kiss, and it was much more of a conceptual album. I have also heard fans say years later, "It was a really good record. We just didn't give [it] its proper due when it came out," because they didn't want to like it.

LORETTA CARAVELLO: Eric didn't like the direction at that point. He didn't like it, because when he joined the band, it was more a heavy metal type of thing. He wasn't really vocal to everybody. I only knew it from a few things I might have overheard him say to Debbie or something. But I found out later that he wasn't really thrilled about the look. When they cut his hair, he was like a basket case. He loved his long hair—I think that bothered him more than the record! But as the years went by, he started to like *The Elder* because I think with that the kids started to appreciate that it was just part of the history. At that point, really, who would want to listen to it? But if you really do listen to it, it's a good album. But for Kiss fans, it was so unusual, with Peter not being there. They didn't want to accept it. As far as *The Elder*, people respect that now, and there are a lot of people I know that are collectors from *The Elder* era, because you cannot get anything. He saved what's called "The Black Smurf Award," I think it was from Germany. There are a lot of pictures of him with the band holding that. It says on it, "The Shrieker of the Year," whatever that means.

BILL AUCOIN: There was [talk of a tour in support of *The Elder*], but it never came to fruition.

LORETTA CARAVELLO: [A stage design for a proposed *The Elder* tour] was like a play more or less. There were different concepts, where Ace would fly to the ceiling with a backpack on him and smoke coming out. They had tanks drawn there. It was like a fantasy. They would take somebody from the audience and pull them up and go through this thing with them. And there would be a wishing well. It's like 15 different stage designs.

BILL AUCOIN: They potentially thought this would be turned into a feature film, which never happened. It didn't come close at all.

BOB EZRIN: When you're making something like this, your head is in it, and you're in the moment. You might have casual conversations about futures and other things, but you have no time to dwell on it. There's so much to do. So we talked about wanting to get a film and a comic book and all sorts of stuff made. But when it was clear that people were hating it, I think everybody's aspirations changed. Then I think it became more a question of the band trying to figure out how to undo the damage or how to make up for it as quickly as possible. So once again, they moved on from me.

1982

BILL AUCOIN: 1982 [was when Bill and Kiss parted ways]. I was going in a different direction. I didn't like the fact that the band was splitting up. They wanted to take off the make-up, and they didn't want to do the merchandising. It was completely opposite of what I wanted to do—so we had a meeting, and we decided to split. It was really that simple. Ace was still in the band, but at that point, Gene and Paul really took over the band. Ace didn't show up for very many things. Eric was a hired hand—he would not be at those [meetings].

CAROL KAYE: Behind the scenes, things were very different. Something was missing. I don't want to say "fun," because that's the wrong word. You knew things were changed. Bill was gone. Peter was gone. It was different. It was a new time for them.

LYDIA CRISS: I didn't really pay much attention to Kiss [during the early '80s]. I felt that they were fairly dying out. See, I worked in a photo agency, and I had my original photos of Kiss from the Daisy and all that in the file, and they were never used. People just didn't ask for photos of Kiss.

BOB GRAW: Well, it was hard to tell people I was a Kiss fan all my life! Kiss, in our school, *was hated*. You wore a Kiss shirt, and you got punched. People ragged on me no matter what. In '79/'80/'81/'82, people were like, "I can't believe you still like them ... they're still around?" Because they had no popularity whatsoever in this country. The only way to see them was the occasional TV appearance, which was *Solid Gold* and *Fridays*. You wouldn't even know they were around, because they didn't tour. All of 1980 was spent overseas, and in 1981, they didn't tour.

LORETTA CARAVELLO: [During this time] Eric wrote something with Bryan Adams. If you listen to the song "Don't Leave Me Lonely," which is from *Cuts Like a Knife* [released in 1983], that turned out to be one of the best songs on that album. He knew him from the songwriter Jim Vallance, and Bryan Adams would write music for them, too. They knew each other that way. I didn't really know too much about Bryan Adams until later on.

MICHAEL JAMES JACKSON: [Kiss and Michael's initial meeting] came about through my attorney, who was close with their business manager. My attorney represented Diana Ross. Diana Ross was also business-managed by Howard Marks, who was Kiss' business manager. Kiss was at a seminal point in their career, where they needed to make a change. They needed to start making some records that returned them to being song-oriented records. This was right after they had done *The Elder*. *The Elder* signaled a decline in some ways, maybe for them as an artist, in terms of how they were perceived. They were really a tremendous performance band, and they had a character that belonged totally to them. But those records, right around the period of time of *The Elder*, started to take them away from that character, and I think the audience got a little confused.

So I was introduced to Gene and Paul initially and had a meeting with them. I didn't have any particular background whatsoever in doing metal or heavy rock n' roll. So I was an unusual choice. I had some kind of reputation of being a very song-oriented producer. When I met with them, it was not as if it was a job I was vying for, because they were outside of their frame of reference, and I was probably outside of theirs. But there was a certain amount of "good sense" that we came to in our conversations, and for whatever reason, they seemed to be interested in what I was talking about. Doing a Kiss record was bound to be a very unusual experience for me. So we developed a relationship and proceeded. Just before I started working with them, I was finishing a record with Jesse Colin Young, from the Youngbloods. So I went from being in a studio up in the woods in Point Reyes to being in Manhattan with Gene, Paul, and Eric.

ADAM MITCHELL: I had met a guy back in the late 1960s, Michael James Jackson, who eventually went on to produce Kiss. I met him up in Toronto. I was producing a group at the time called Fludd. They were on A&M, they had a couple of hits, and he happened to be up in Toronto—he lived in L.A.—I can't remember why he was up there. But I happened to meet him in Fludd's manager's office, and he and I just became good friends. So when I moved to L.A. in 1976—I had a deal with Warner Brothers Records—just by coincidence, when I was recording my record at Sunset Sound, he happened to be in the next studio, recording I think Pablo Cruise. And so he and I reconnected, and he came in and listened to my songs. I had a lot of good songs, and a lot were getting cut by other artists. That was 1978, probably. So a few years later, when Kiss was coming off the disaster of *The Elder*, they felt they needed songwriting help. Michael was by this time signed on as producer, and he called me. Even though I was not what you would call a conventional Kiss writer ... I mean, I always loved rock n' roll—AC/DC, Led Zeppelin, and so on, and I played in the Paupers, which was a rock band in the '60s—he called me for whatever reason. We just hit it off.

MICHAEL JAMES JACKSON: *Killers* was a compilation record [released in 1982 overseas and only available in the U.S. as an import], and we were going to do four additional tracks. There was a lot of pressure on it, because there was a contractual obligation to deliver that record quickly. I recorded them at the Record Plant in Los Angeles, on Third Street. My process of recording was probably different than what they had been doing before, so it was kind of a "getting to know each other" period. Very quickly, when we were finishing that, we had to start *Creatures of the Night*. So the strongest memory I have of that particular period is it was very "pressurized."

ADAM MITCHELL: Paul usually would come up with a title that he would write about. At that point, I had a pretty nice house in the Hollywood Hills, and I had a nice little studio in one of my bedrooms. And my friend, Roger Linn—who was a guitar player in my band—had only a year or two before invented the drum machine. And once the drum machine was invented—in fact, Herbie Hancock had the first one, and I had the second one—you could have a home studio. Because prior to that, unless you were Paul McCartney or a star of that magnitude, you had to have a full set of drums, mics, [and] isolation booths. You had to have a full studio. But once you had a drum machine, you could do effective home demos. So that's what Paul and I would do. We'd write at my house, and then we'd demo. Gene and Paul's arrangement was for a song to go on a record, they both had to like the song. And I think that's the only two songs he and I actually wrote ["I'm a Legend Tonight" and "Partners in Crime"], and they both ended up going on the record. But the thing that I remembered the most about that record is the cover is rather unfortunate. It's kind of arty, kind of a weird color scheme. It didn't seem like a Kiss cover at all.

MICHAEL JAMES JACKSON: My impression of Gene was Gene was a very smart guy. He was interesting and very clearly focused on they had to reinvigorate their career at that point. Paul was very studious and warm. Paul and I got on great. Eric was a really heartfelt guy. He really, really gave a shit. Not that the others didn't; they did. But Eric was *really* focused on his love of the music. He was focused on his love of playing and his particular determination to be considered a solid musician and solid drummer, and most particularly in the field of metal, which is very competitive. Particularly with guitar and drums, guitarists are very competitive with each other, and the drummers are very competitive. Eric was very dedicated to being a good player and wanting to be perceived as a good player.

ADAM MITCHELL: Eric could put away alcohol like nobody's business. When I first met him, I remember we went to a sushi bar on Ventura Boulevard, called Domo. And my house, technically, I lived on the valley side of Mulholland up near the top, and my street, Berry Drive, ran all the way down to Ventura Boulevard. It exited Ventura Boulevard very close to this restaurant, Domo. So I said, "Let's just meet down there." So we met, and as I remember, Eric had like ten sakes or something, and was just as sober as a judge! And me, who is not a drinker, trying to keep up with him. By the time I had three—I think in the end I had four—I was cross-eyed. To see straight, I had to put one hand over an eye and sit in the parking lot for like an hour or something before I was sober enough even to make the 50 yards back to my street. But Eric was one of those people that could drink, and it never showed a bit.

We met at that sushi restaurant, and he was totally down-to-earth, as everybody will tell you. Funny, funny, funny. And he loved Monty Python, as I did. He knew every word of everything they'd ever done. He just had a great sense of humor. I heard him play by that time, and I just thought he was the perfect drummer for Kiss. Technically, he was very good. Much, much better than Peter Criss. And the fans liked Eric. If you can imagine, stepping into Peter Criss' shoes ... stepping into the shoes of an original member of Kiss must not have been easy. And it really would have gone to a lot of people's heads, but not Eric. He was down-to-earth. He was just hilariously funny. So we became very good friends right away. We used to hang out a lot.

The thing I remember about all of them—but particularly true of Eric— Eric was funny as hell. Eric was one of the funniest guys I ever knew. When he finally moved to L.A., he had this apartment, right down the hill from the Whiskey A Go Go. And I dropped him off there one night, pulled over to the curb, and he stepped out. He was talking to me and wasn't looking where he was going ... and stepped right into the biggest pile of dog shit you've ever seen! Eric was fussy about his clothes and appearance. That was hilarious.

I remember lots of funny stories, things that happened. One time, he and I ... Eric's hair was so big. Eric's hair was so big that it would drive Gene and Paul crazy. Even in the era of big hair, Eric had the biggest hair anyone ever saw. Gene and Paul were constantly trying to get him to cut it down, and he wouldn't. One day, there's a restaurant on Sunset Boulevard, right across the street from where the old Tower Records used to be, called the Old World Cafe. He and I were having lunch there one day. We're sitting out in the front patio, and two blondes go by in a Camaro. They look out the window, and they see us sitting in the patio. They immediately do a u-turn in L.A. traffic, and they pull up. And Eric gives me that look, like, "They recognize me." And they're two good-looking blondes. So they pulled over to the curb, get out of the car, and one of them walks up, looks at him, and goes, "Guy ... *big hair!*" She had no idea who he was! She got back in the car, and they took off.

BOB KULICK: Anybody that knows anything about guitar knows that that was not Ace Frehley—that was me [on the four new songs on *Killers*]. Paul's solo record obviously showcased that. I "ghosted" for the band when they asked me to as a friend, i.e., *Alive II* and the *Killers* stuff. I played as a member of Paul Stanley's band when he did his tour [in 1989], and I played on his record and got him other musicians to use. Basically [I] was Paul's best friend for several years. He even gave me his apartment to live in! I had a really great relationship, and still do.

MICHAEL JAMES JACKSON: Working with Bob was great. Bob is a really fine player and a tremendous amount of energy, a great determination to do the right thing. Bob was wonderful. He really cared how things came out.

BOB KULICK: What I had to deal with was Paul and Gene, and that was pretty much it. By that time, they were looking for "Eddie Van Halen." They were looking for somebody that could plunk the magic twanger and do it for them in that way. Hence, my frustration, because Paul's record, the *Alive II* stuff, everything I played was like, "Wow, that's great." Whereas by the time these sessions rolled around, it was like, "Eh ... I don't know about that." "What? What don't you know about it?" "Try something else." "What? I've tried everything. I tried melodies, I tried just winging it, I tried some wang-bar stuff. Do you have an idea? I'm listening." So all that Eric got to see was how they tortured somebody else, because they basically tortured the shit out of me. Me, who [earlier] anything I played was like, "Great!" Then it turned into, "What else you got?" That's when it was time to get somebody. You need somebody in the band now. Stop doing this, because you're barking up the wrong tree now.

BOB GRAW: I thought the four new songs on *Killers* were a step in the right direction. I thought they were starting to come back. They were kind of *Unmasked*-y type of songs. I don't think that they were the best songs, but at least it was a step back in the right direction. Wasn't one of the songs written by Bryan Adams? ["Down on Your Knees" was co-written by Bryan] At least they were back to playing rock songs, y'know? And I think "Down on Your

Knees" is a great song. I love that. And "I'm a Legend Tonight" is a good song. They're not the worst Kiss could have done, so at least it was a step in the right direction.

EDDIE TRUNK: I think it's important to note what came between *The Elder* and *Creatures*, because it very much was "the bridge," and that was the import *Killers* album. It had those four new songs on it, and even though at the time it was only available on import here, I remember getting that record and being very excited that what I heard was the steps back to Kiss being Kiss again. So when I heard "Partners in Crime," "Nowhere to Run," and those songs, I said, "OK, I'm starting to hear the Kiss I love again." It's not fully there, but it's getting there. So I think that's a very important bridge from *The Elder* to *Creatures*.

MICHAEL JAMES JACKSON: At the time, Ace was not around. It was really Gene, Paul, and Eric. So the tracks were cut with Eric, Gene, and Paul, and my tendency was to focus on drum tracks—cut the drum tracks with a scratch guitar, and build everything on top of the drums once I'd done that.

BOB KULICK: What I was privy to was the tail-end of *Killers* into *Creatures of the Night*. That's when they were trying to find a guitar player. I was playing, and other people were playing. Robben Ford played, the guy from Mr. Mister [Steve Farris], Vinnie Cusano was around. And I was hanging out with Eric, because I was the "de facto guitar player," and Gene and Paul were *Gene and Paul*. Sometimes, he'd pick me up from the hotel, take me to the studio. I believe we were at Record Plant. After, we'd go have a drink or dinner. That was the period of time where I was probably his best friend as far as the closest I ever got to him. The role of guitar—that's what I was at the time. Ace had not officially left, but he was no longer playing. So with me, the big joke was, "Yeah, we'll get Bob a wig." They had already replaced Peter, they were about to replace Ace.

It was always a joke [the possibility of Bob joining Kiss], because by that time, the joke became, "Did he take it seriously?" It was like, "Look, I already have a record deal, I'm already managed by Leber-Krebs. I don't need you." Not that I wouldn't have said that to them—if they asked, I would have joined in a minute, of course. But the point was I had graduated past that point already. I was their friend and confidant who had his own deal, had his own manager, was an artist in his own right. I had passed the point of, "What do you think? Can he help us out?" I'd help whenever I could, as far as playing, or in Gene's case, write a couple of songs with him. The same with Paul's solo record. "Do you know a bass player?" "Yeah, Steve Buslowe. The guy I worked with in Meat Loaf." He got hired because I recommended him. That's what it turned into. They had more respect for me, actually, because it wasn't just somebody to hire anymore. It was somebody like, "Oh, the guy's got his own record deal." And they were fans. That's the other thing. They were *my* fans.

ADAM MITCHELL: I met Vinnie through Sue Saad and the Next. I don't remember who introduced us, who introduced me to Sue Saad. I don't remember quite how I met him ... he might have been playing guitar with Sue Saad and the Next. They really were one of the God-almighty-dreadful '80s bands. Sue Saad and the Next unfortunately were part of that really terribly named new wave, which never went anywhere. Oh God, everything was just eighth notes. It was *so* lame. Anyway, I met Vinnie through Sue Saad and the Next. And I was immediately taken by what a phenomenal musical talent Vinnie really was, and probably still is. He is really a beautiful player ... but personality will defeat talent, every time. And I introduced him to Gene. Gene and I were writing one day, and Vinnie stopped by my house.

MICHAEL JAMES JACKSON: Vinnie was not a heavy metal player. He was *a rock n' roll player.* He was a melodic player, and that didn't necessarily fit in with what Kiss was. In those days, that kind of metal music was about raw and pure aggression. And one of the problems with a lot of the guitarists who worked in that genre was they were all about their left hand, meaning they were all about a lot of notes, how fast can you do them, and "How fancy is this?" Most of those guys that got known for their dexterity with their left hand were not very good at creating a feel. Because to create a feel, you've got to have a great right hand. Vinnie Cusano was a good rhythm player, and he had a good feel for doing that kind of strong rock n' roll. But once again, he was very melodic. His melodic sense had not much place with Kiss, because it didn't fit the genre. But these records, like all records, were a constant moving target. When you're in the process of doing it, you're defining it and redefining it, almost as if it's never going to get done. So what happened organically, what happened by direction, and what happened by pure accident are all part of the process. Was he easy? Was he difficult? Was he talented? He was very talented. But it was not always an easy fit. Pure stylistic differences. Vinnie, like I said, was very melodic. Kiss records are about raw, tough feel. If you do something that's too melodic, it sounds wussy. That's not going to fit. So there would be discussions about that. And some of that produced conflicts that had to be worked out.

LORETTA CARAVELLO: He was sad, because Ace was a really big part of the band. Ace was very close to him, and they were good friends. You can see it in the videos. My brother had a tendency to go towards Ace and Gene. My brother you could see was a person that would be attached to somebody. He looked up to somebody. They were scared—all of them were—because you can't replace Ace. And then they got Vinnie, and Vinnie was actually a really great guitarist. From all accounts that I saw, my brother took more pictures of him than he did any other member! So, apparently, he must have liked him.

MICHAEL JAMES JACKSON: I did [see Ace at the sessions]. We cut the tracks in Los Angeles for *Killers* and *Creatures*. And then we flew back to New York and recorded Ace on some of it. But Ace was not around during the tracking. Ace *did* play. To be honest, it's a long time ago, I don't remember [which tracks Ace played on]. Ace played some parts on those records. It was kind of fragmented, because those guys had gone through a lot together. Gene and Paul were very focused on reorganizing what they were going to do as a business and what they were going to do as a band. And Ace was certainly a part of it, but he was also simultaneously disconnected from it, because Gene and Paul were the ones in control. So Ace made a contribution, and he did play on both those records. But the performances were somewhat minimal.

ADAM MITCHELL: We did absolutely terrific demos at my studio on "Creatures of the Night" and "Danger." In fact, "Danger" especially, our demo was way better [than the album version], and I'm sure Paul would tell you the same thing. The drum part that I had programmed in the drum machine for "Danger"—just because of the tempo—was particularly difficult to play. And Eric did a tremendous job on it. "Creatures," that lick that comes halfway through and at the end, I came up with that lick and actually played it on the demo. When they went in to record it, I kept on saying, "You've got to get somebody else in to play this." They brought in Robben Ford and tremendous guitar players—much, much better guitar players than me. But nobody could play quite like me, so I ended up playing it on the record. So what you hear on the record is actually me, playing my blue Charvel.

MICHAEL JAMES JACKSON: We ran two studios at the same time, in the same building, and we'd go back and forth between the two of them. We put Eric in a separate room by himself. There was a big focus on trying to get as close as possible ... not to the exact sound of John Bonham, but we tried to get some of the character of Bonham's sound. You can't ever duplicate what anybody else has done, because it's not just the echo, it's not just the environment, it's not the ambience—it's also the sound of the drums, the way they're hit. There's so many factors involved, [like] the humidity in the room. All those factors are involved in what the overall ambience is and sound is. But there was a real determination to try and create a sound that really had a character to it, that was along those same lines. So Eric was put in a separate room—not even a booth [but] a separate room—and was close-mic'd and distant-mic'd. We had spent a lot of time—we might have spent a couple days—trying to really work and find the sound, specifically around the drums. Because on that record, the drums have a character to them. That is what gives that record an identity.

Eric was way into it, because it was his "glory moment." It was when all the focus was on Eric. He was willing to do whatever it took to achieve that particular thing, and also, was very focused on his playing. I always appreciated that he really cared about exactly what he did and how he was going to sound. And then later, that record was mixed by Bob Clearmountain. It was made very clear to Bob that the particular overall character of the drum sound was a key element in the record. So when he mixed it, he added some of the echo that the Power Station became very famous for. There was an elevator shaft there, that he had put a microphone down. He could send the signal into the elevator shaft, which would resonate, and the mic would bring that back. So some of that is also mixed into the drum sound on *Creatures*. Clearmountain did a great job, because one of the hallmarks of Clearmountain in those days was he had the unique ability to get more low end onto a record that would translate over the radio. A lot of engineers can put it on a record, but you never hear it on the radio. Bob had a methodology where he could really sculpt that in, in a way that if the record got played on the radio, you could hear that low-end character very clearly.

LORETTA CARAVELLO: That was his favorite album. I think he said "Saint and Sinner" was his favorite song to play. From what I heard, the drums were recorded in an elevator shaft. And they never were able to duplicate that sound again. They tried and tried, and he tried and tried, but no one has been able to duplicate that sound. It just hit it right. It's like the weather, when you see the ice on the trees, it has to be perfect and the same, and it never is again. He was very proud of the album.

MICHAEL JAMES JACKSON: The feel of the album and the character of the sound was built around Eric's drums. So I'd have to say his drums certainly played a significant role. But the other thing that I'd say about Eric in relationship to that was since he was the "new kid on the block"—even though he'd been with the band for a while—he still was not [a member of] the original band. But Eric had a deep love of Kiss and a deep love of Kiss' persona and what the concept of Kiss was. So Eric at times was very vocal about wanting to be ensured that Kiss was going to be Kiss. And that was all about the sound and trying to translate some of that "alive-ness" on disc.

BRUCE KULICK: There was a time when, for some reason, I was able to stop by the studio when they were doing *Creatures*, and that was the first time I saw Eric. I love that they were working on "I Love It Loud." They were checking the mix. You know, the mix at the end when the song fades out and then comes back in. I thought *Creatures of the Night* was a brilliant Kiss album, because it has such a huge Zeppelin-ish/metal sound to it. I was really impressed with that. And I'm sure that was their reaction to *The Elder*. And there was Eric on the couch. His hair was huge. I only knew of him—that he was the new drummer—but I didn't know him. So I felt like from his own personal insecurities, he put up a bit of a wall with me. Of which, getting to know him in the latter years, I totally understood. So at the time, I thought that he was kind of "guarded," and I didn't get a chance to really say, "I really got to experience Eric." It was more like, "What are you doing here, tall guitar player dude? Invading our space here?" But I kept it kind of neutral in my mind, what I thought of him. But I will say I was like, "Hmm, is he playing the rock star, or is he just uncomfortable meeting people socially?" And Gene was always all Gene. I don't even remember how I wound up there, but that was obviously exciting for me. And "I Love It Loud" sounded amazing!

MICHAEL JAMES JACKSON: "I Love It Loud" is really Gene's persona. It was very "Kiss-like" in the sense that it was very much the persona that Gene puts forward. "I Still Love You" was a big favorite of Paul's. A lot of time was put into trying to really make that be something. Even "Creatures." A lot of effort went into trying to make these records be a step above the norm.

BOB KULICK: And when Vinnie got the gig [replacing Ace], Vinnie could really play, but that was not the problem for Vinnie. His problem was another issue.

ADAM MITCHELL: I knew Vinnie musically was perfect for Kiss. And I told Gene right away, "This guy's a great player. Personally, you may have problems with him." Vinnie was a great player. That's the thing. In life, it's almost difficult to separate the talent, because sometimes the most talented people bring along personality issues with them. But make no mistake, Vinnie musically is really, really talented. I've heard Vinnie play, on acoustic guitar, versions of "White Christmas" which would break your heart. He's a great guitar player.

BOB GRAW: The writing was on the wall, because Ace was in bad shape at that time. I remember reading in the newspaper that he had wrecked his car. He was like driving a hundred miles an hour on a bridge, going in the city somewhere. He was almost killed. So I knew it. And when they said they were going to tour without him because he was hurt, you could pretty much see it, that he wasn't coming back.

MICHAEL JAMES JACKSON: We were all confident that we had done something that was the right thing and something that was real. And that represented the band now in a way that was really appropriate. Whatever albums had preceded *Creatures* immediately, I think everybody felt that *Creatures* was the real thing.

BOB GRAW: Eric's defining moment in his entire career, his "coming out party," was *Creatures of the Night*. The sound of his drums on that album, especially on the original vinyl pressing, is just sonically *booming*. Every song on that album, he sounds great. It's like ear-shattering, every song.

LORETTA CARAVELLO: That's what basically brought the fans back. When they heard this guy, they said, "Wow, can this guy play! This is heavy stuff." And that was what Kiss was basically supposed to be. Peter had a different style. He wasn't as heavy. But my brother had more of a tendency to be more like John Bonham, who became his favorite drummer, other than Ringo, when he was a kid. For real heavy drumming and style, it was John Bonham.

EDDIE TRUNK: Getting *Creatures*, it was eye-opening. It was just *monstrous*. One of the heaviest albums Kiss has ever done, and one of the reasons for it, not only the material, but obviously, the drums. The drums are monstrous-sounding. I never heard drums booming like that on a Kiss record before or played like that on a Kiss record. It all came together—the material, Eric finally being Eric and getting to be what he signed on to be coming to that band. And Kiss being a heavier band than they'd ever been. The irony of all of this, of course, is that you had Ace Frehley out the door.

CHARLIE BENANTE: I think Eric was a big Led Zeppelin fan, and he was always into the whole "John Bonham thing." He played Ludwig, as well. I just think he captured what he wanted to on that record. The drums sound so big and large. If you listen to the fourth side of *Alive II*, the drum sounds on that record were great. They had some big tones on that record. And I think on *Creatures of the Night*, they captured that sound as well. It just fit the songs. So I thought that was a great Kiss record.

MIKE PORTNOY: *Creatures of the Night* is an amazing album. It's got some great drumming on there. He was a double bass player for starters, which Peter was not. And in the early '80s, there were very few double bass players. At that point in the '80s, I had only been really listening to ... maybe Mötley Crüe was just coming around, but there were very few double bass guys I was listening to, and Eric was one of them. And that's one of the things that made his drumming stand out different form Peter's. And the *Creatures* album has some great double bass drumming and some real aggressive type of stuff that made the drumming stand out.

AJ PERO: Twisted Sister just did a show in France, and I did an interview with the French affiliate for *Modern Drummer*. I was one of his mentors, and we went through different phases, and Eric Carr's name was brought up. I said he was a great drummer. Like me, we were really able to show what we were all about. I said one of my favorite albums to this day is *Creatures of the Night*. The way the drums sound and the way he played, you can just *feel* that power coming off it.

JAIME ST. JAMES: I liked the heaviness of it. Kiss has been a lot of different versions through the years, but I like the heaviness of *Creatures of the Night*. That's great.

BLAS ELIAS: *Creatures of the Night*—yeah! The fatness of the grooves. The '70s-style drums were groovy, but it wasn't as heavy. He was the first drummer to me that I ever heard really laying down a solid two-and-four, heavy backbeat groove, without a whole lot of embellishment. Just laying it down, heavy metal style. That was a turning point for me, because I had been studying jazz in high school, played in the jazz band, and came from that kind of a background. And that got me interested in playing heavy rock. I loved the sound he had. It was bigger and thicker. The bass drum and snare drum were huge. It was just different. I'm not sure how much he had to do with the sound, but I just dug the power.

BILL AUCOIN: [*Creatures of the Night*] was a very good album, and I do think Eric was great on it. At that point, he really had learned so much and had experienced so much, that he was coming into his own. He was really becoming a great drummer. I think that's the reason. He really was a spectacular drummer, and he just got better and better.

AJ PERO: He had a great sound and played great on the album. Unfortunately, *Creatures of the Night* and *The Elder* were the least popular albums of Kiss. Just like with us, *Come Out and Play*, which I thought that I did some really intricate, not over-the-top, but things that a lot of musicians and drummers complimented me on. You take a thing like "We're Not Gonna Take It"—the most simple beat. But the way that I approached it, people say, "Wow, that's really cool. How did you come up with that?" And I'm like, "Well, I was told to come up with some kind of beginning like a 'Stargazer' or a 'We're an American Band'-type beginning," where the minute you hear it, you don't even have to hear the first chord. You know that's "We're Not Gonna Take It." It's something that sticks out in people's minds. I was thrilled to do that.

CHARLIE BENANTE: "I Love It Loud" was on that record, which became a classic. "Creatures of the Night," "War Machine," which I loved. I always thought that Stone Temple Pilots ripped the riff off on "Sex Type Thing." "Saint and Sinner," "I Still Love You" became one of their "live songs," where he would do his "I Want You"-type thing. That record had some good tunes on it. The drums were so up front and loud. It kind of captured you. If you were a drummer, you had to love that record, especially the sound of it.

BOB GRAW: I loved the "I Love It Loud" video, because it was Kiss the way Kiss was supposed to look, [the way] they were supposed to sound, with the fire. I remember Eric Carr's drum set was just *enormous*. And it was set up on top of the tank. It was cool. It was a great video.

NEIL ZLOZOWER: The first time I shot them was at A&M Studios, and they had a listening party. They didn't play or anything, but they had four stools on stage, and they basically had press people there, and they were allowed to ask the band various questions they had on their mind. I think Ace was still in the band at that point, before he got kicked out and before Vinnie Vincent was in the band. So it was the three originals and Eric. I do remember that was the first time I ever shot the band with Eric. At the end, they all got together and put their hands together, and I think fireworks went off. I do have photos, too.

BOB GRAW: You could also tell by listening to *Creatures of the Night*, there is nothing that sounds like Ace Frehley on that album. Ace Frehley has a very distinctive guitar sound. It was nowhere on that album. So his face is on the album cover, but it credits him nowhere on the album—no songs and no definitive Ace Frehley leads. Vinnie Vincent had very much his own sound. And probably, Vinnie Vincent and Eric Carr made that band a much, much better *sounding* band. And then they gave Vinnie Vincent his own make-up and his own costume.

TY TABOR: For me, it was unfortunately one of those times when I'd lost interest for a minute. That particular one just wasn't my favorite thing they'd ever done before. I had missed Ace, and I'm partial to his guitar playing—big-time. That one, it just was a moment like I said, I went in and out. That was an "out" moment.

WAYNE SHARP: I was working for a concert promoter based in New Orleans, which is where I'm from. The manager at the time, Howard Marks, was working with Diana Ross, and we had promoted some Diana Ross shows. Chris Lendt was on the road with Diana Ross, and we just got to talking with Chris. I was a huge Kiss fan, and they were getting ready to go back on the road for the *Creatures of the Night* tour, which intrigued me, but I was young. I was in college. So the first time I met Eric, my boss and I took a day trip over to Dallas, where they were rehearsing. I knew Eric was in the band, but I didn't know Vinnie Vincent was in the band, because they had Ace on the publicity shots for the record. We went over there and got to watch them rehearse. I don't remember actually talking to Eric, but got to watch them rehearse and was impressed.

And then we did promote some shows on that tour, including a big show in New Orleans the night before Mardi Gras in the Superdome. I guess that was the first time I had a chance to actually meet Eric and get to talk to him. We did a press conference before we put the tickets on sale, which the band came in for. So that was my first time meeting Eric. What I saw of the show—and I did get to see a good bit of the show in New Orleans—I thought was great. Eric was such a better drummer than Peter Criss, I thought, just in terms of power. That was a tour where his drum kit was on top of a tank. And Vinnie Vincent was amazing live. Gene and Paul, that was I guess the last tour with the make-up. They still had it. I thought it was a great tour. And that record, they had some really strong songs on that record that worked live in concert. I thought it was a great show that I saw.

EDDIE TRUNK: As great and highly regarded as *Creatures* is now, going back to that time and place, Kiss was never lower in their life in America. The album still to this day is one of the poorest-selling albums in their catalog, and the tour in support of it was one of the most poorly attended, to the point of 2,000 in a 20,000 [seat arena]. It was a joke. You had this group that creatively had made this great record, and whose newest member was really starting to contribute and came up with this monster performance. But at least in the U.S., you had this band that was just on the balls of their ass.

LORETTA CARAVELLO: He was very sad. He was upset [that the *Creatures* album and tour did not do well]. If the band did not do well, where was he going to be? He felt it was a reflection on him.

BOB GRAW: Well, it's a shame that they didn't put that out in 1979 or 1980, because it would have been, without a shadow of a doubt, one of their biggest albums. Because people had pretty much forgotten about them when this album came out. I remember it was kind of hard to find when it first came out. And there wasn't really that much about them in the magazines anymore. Maybe the occasional page in *Hit Parader* or *Circus*. But other than that, you really wouldn't know Kiss was around. And that's what was so disappointing. The only way you would really know that they were still around is if you saw the "I Love It Loud" video late at night on MTV. They would only play it once in a while. And that's why it's such a disappointment, because it's probably one of the top five Kiss albums of all time. There's not a bad song on it. A lot of the songs have become staples of their concerts. "Creatures of the Night" has been in the set, "I Love It Loud," "I Still Love You," and my favorite song on the album, "War Machine." Every song was great on that.

MICHAEL JAMES JACKSON: There may have been some disappointment about it, but there was too much pride in it to worry about that too much. The one thing that we all knew was Kiss had been returned to a place where it was going to get perceived the right way. That's what *Creatures* did. It returned whatever credibility may have been slipping. It was really an authentic Kiss record.

1983

NEIL ZLOZOWER: I did those two shows [when Mötley Crüe opened for Kiss in California on March 26 and 27]. As a matter of fact, that was the first time I shot Mötley live. They opened up at the Universal Amphitheater, the next night was something called Irvine Meadows—which is now called Verizon Amphitheater [Note: There is a possibility that the Irvine show was the night before the Universal show]. I was there, and I was backstage hanging out with Mötley, because there wasn't really much to do hanging out with Kiss. It was the very last show, and Nikki being a wise-ass, goes, "Hey Zloz, we're going to go on, and when we thank Kiss, we're going to go, 'And we'd like to thank our mother and father's favorite band, Kiss, for letting us open!'" I'm like, "Nikki, I don't think that's too wise of an idea to do. You don't want to burn bridges with Kiss." Because Mötley Crüe, at that point, *Shout at the Devil* was not even out. Me and Nikki were getting tight back then. It was still before our infamous trip to Club Med, which I guess Nikki talks about in *The Dirt*.

JAIME ST. JAMES: I thought it might be kind of weird—a new guy with new make-up, a different look. But I saw the *Creatures of the Night* tour, and I thought, "God, that guy's great!" I saw them at Universal Amphitheater with Mötley Crüe opening for them. The stage set-up was really great, and it was centered around the giant drum kit that he had. I was totally blown away by the show. I saw Mötley Crüe at the Troubadour and the Country Club before their record [*Too Fast For Love*] came out, so I saw Mötley Crüe many times. Mötley Crüe looked different when they were first playing the clubs around L.A. They stemmed more from what Nikki was doing, a more New York Dolls-ish kind of a thing. But then they went more towards the "Kiss look." It was a perfect match [Mötley Crüe opening for Kiss]. I'm a big Mötley Crüe fan.

NEIL ZLOZOWER: Mötley Crüe was pretty potent back then, and they were young and hungry. They did a pretty "blitzkrieg" set, I remember. I wouldn't say [Mötley Crüe blew away Kiss], because Kiss fans are so fanatical that if you're at a Kiss show, chances are 95% of those people are there to see Kiss. I wouldn't say they blew them away, but that was the beginning of Mötley Crüe. That was the first time I ever saw them. They looked mean, nasty. They were hungry, they were young, and they put on some good shows.

LORETTA CARAVELLO: That was the most people they ever played for [when Kiss played three mammoth Brazil shows on June 18, 23, and 25]. Once again, he thought it was phenomenal. He saved t-shirts from there. He has a lot of memos and stuff.

MARK WEISS: My first studio in New York was a block from the Garden, and they were one of the first bands that came into my studio. They came in without any make-up on. I did one of their first photo shoots without make-up—they were kidding around with hiding their faces a little bit. Before that, in *Circus* magazine, I know Gene and Paul went in and did an interview with Gerald Rothberg, and they didn't have make-up on, and covered up their faces a little bit. They were just ready to unmask, so they were teasing him a little bit. But I also shot them when they were rehearsing at SIR. I remember one picture I have, where Eric is holding a birthday card. Some fan gave it to him. There's a big bunny rabbit on the card. It said something about hugging or something cute. I've got a lot of those kind of shots—hanging around, rehearsing, posing at video shoots. I think I'm the only photographer who shot every incarnation of the band.

MICHAEL JAMES JACKSON: Vinnie had become more "Kiss-torized." He had become more adapted to becoming a member of Kiss and the idea of being able to alter their style musically, which is maybe what he thought he was going to bring to the table at that point, was pretty much out the window. He had adapted himself to the fact that, "This was a Kiss record" and "This was a Kiss career," and he was going to have to modify himself to fit that mold. Which he did.

It was the same procedure [recording *Lick It Up*], cutting the drum tracks with scratch guitar and building on top of those tracks. *Creatures* was a unique experience, and the drum sound that *Creatures* is so known for was a unique experience. To try and duplicate that, you'd have to go back into the same room, use the same microphones. I tended to record the drums in ways that they hadn't done before. I used Telefunken 251s, and I put them all over the drums. It's a very rare microphone—there are probably only 700 left in the world. But it captured a broad spectrum of the low end. I did the same with *Lick It Up*. It was just the way that I did things. But to make *Lick It Up* sound like *Creatures*, we would have had to record in the same studio, under the same circumstances. And even then, it wouldn't have been the same. But it would have been closer. *Lick It Up* was recorded at Right Track Studios in New York—spent a lot of time on the drum tracks. It was a fun record to make.

LORETTA CARAVELLO: He was happy about it. Came home, he just said, "They're going to use some of my music!" And Gene loved the song ["All Hell's Breakin' Loose," the album's second single and video, was co-written by Eric and the other three members]. It came out just the way he wanted it to, basically.

MICHAEL JAMES JACKSON: As I remember, I was running two studios once again. We were recording at Atlantic and also recording at another studio, because we were always up against a schedule. There was a contractual schedule that had to be met, and it was hard. We always worked 12 to 15-hour days, six days a week. We'd start at noon and finish at 3:00 or 4:00 in the morning. It was always like that. The third studio was a little studio downtown. I don't remember the name of it. It was a funky little studio. We were doing overdubbing at the time.

LORETTA CARAVELLO: The *Creatures* tour didn't do good, so they had to try a different direction. They had to do something different. They figured just to put that era behind them. They needed something to perk them up, so he told us at that point in 1983 that they were thinking of doing that [taking the make-up off].

CAROL KAYE: The '80s were a time of change. New wave music, which Kiss were not. It was MTV, and they were not played on MTV ... until, of course, when they went on and unveiled their faces.

MICHAEL JAMES JACKSON: Those conversations were probably occurring during the sessions, and then certainly afterwards. It was a huge, huge decision for them. Kiss has always been about shocking people, so if you look at that strategically, that they were going to play that one ace, that was a card that they always withheld, and [it] was bound to happen sooner or later—whether it happened then or five years later. Sooner or later, they would have done that and tried it. It just so happened that at that point in their career, they thought, "It's time. Why don't we do this? We'll see what happens." You can see what happened. It had its moment. But perhaps, they then just became "a band."

CHARLIE BENANTE: I think after that, they conformed into a different type of band, and they just followed it. I think if they would have remained with the make-up on for a little bit longer, everything would have come back. I don't know. I just think the guys were looking for the next thing that was going to bring them back into the public eye.

CAROL KAYE: I thought it was great. I thought it was time for them to do that. And look at all the success they had then, with all those records without the make-up, and the tours were still selling out. It was time.

TY TABOR: I remember thinking they were in need of a little boost, and I thought, "Good move." It seemed like it was time for something like that to happen.

BOBBY BLOTZER: I thought it was a good time to do it. Ultimately, it's like Heinz Ketchup taking the label off the ketchup bottle and putting on Springfield's Ketchup. People don't want Springfield's Ketchup. *They want Heinz.* Kiss and the Kiss make-up is synonymous, and that's what people want.

MARK WEISS: To me, Kiss should have make-up on. When they took it off, I was a little disappointed. I thought Eric looked better without make-up. He looked more like a rock star. I always thought he looked a little silly with the fox make-up on. I thought Peter Criss looked cool with the cat make-up on, but I don't know ... it was something about "the fox." It hit too close to home. Maybe he shouldn't have been an animal.

EDDIE TRUNK: I think taking off the make-up was somewhat of a non-event. I mean, they needed something. They needed a kick in their career, without question. It was useful in the sense that it was a little bit of that "press kick" that they needed. But it's really important to put yourself in the time and place that this stuff happened. Kiss was a joke, and very few people cared. I remember one of the magazines at the time even having a caption with the photo of them without the make-up, saying, "If anyone still cares, here's Kiss without the make-up." It was that sort of sentiment. But it got them on MTV for that moment, and it let people know that they were still there. And let's face it, what really everyone cared about was seeing Gene and Paul, because you had Eric who was only in the band for a couple of years and didn't really have any level of mystique. And you also had Vinnie Vincent, who no one knew—with or without make-up at that time. So Eric and Vinnie, it didn't really mean all that much. But for the long-time Kiss fans, seeing Gene and Paul was a big deal.

BOB GRAW: I remember reading somewhere that it was going to be on MTV, and that they were going to show them without make-up. I remember waiting all day to see it, and then they showed them. JJ Jackson had them all sitting at a table, and they showed a flash of them with make-up and then without make-up. I was like, "Wow ... they are really *not* good-looking guys!" I mean, Eric had a baby face. He was probably the only one who could get away with it.

JAIME ST. JAMES: I remember seeing that. They kind of looked like pretty much what I thought they were going to look like, because at that point, I hadn't met them.

NINA BLACKWOOD: Kiss is the most brilliantly executed marketing and promotional product in the history of rock. I think of them more as an entity unto themselves rather than just a rock band. Everything about them was a calculated move, down to their "unmasking." For some reason, that was my personal favorite era. I liked seeing the "men behind the curtain."

MARK WEISS: I thought when they took the make-up off, they were more musical. They had something to prove, so they tried harder, maybe. Their songs were more produced. They started hiring writers. I just think they had more to prove. They wanted it to work, because now, they were moving on. They were trying to get ahead of the game ... in a different game.

BOB GRAW: They were actually playing that video ["Lick It Up"] a lot on TV. I remember it was on *Friday Night Videos* and that Casey Kasem show, *America's Top 10*. It was on everything. I saw that video a million times before that album came out. I remember *16* magazine went back and did a story about Kiss without make-up. That was a big, big, big deal, when they took that make-up off. It probably was what resurrected their career.

NEIL ZLOZOWER: What I do remember is they went to this radio station in Los Angeles, and this was their first appearance where they were going to be unmasked. They went to this radio station, and I was hired to shoot it. I actually got some of the very first shots of them unmasked. One thing that stuck out—it was on the second or third floor, and Gene was sort of hanging out the window, and I was maybe 50 yards away. And there was a big crowd of people at this radio station, because Kiss fans are the most fanatical fans of any band I've ever worked with. And Gene was in this window sort of hanging, and I saw him throw something. A half second later, something landed one foot away from me on a hood of a car. It was this big, obnoxious bracelet, and in the middle of it, was this clear thing that had this black widow spider. And I thought it was the coolest fuckin' thing in the world. So I stuck out my hand and snatched it in the blink of an eye. There were other people around me, but my reflexes were faster than everybody. I kept it for years and years. And one day, I was like, "You know what ... this isn't even mine. *It's Gene's.* " So one day when I was with him, I was like, "Hey Gene, I got something of yours, and I think maybe you want it back." And I gave it back to him. Little did I know, somebody told me he had like 50 or 100 of those things, and he used to give them out all the time. It was really cool, though. It was a black widow spider encased in this plastic bubble or something.

BOB GRAW: I thought *Lick It Up* was fantastic. Like I said, I think with *Creatures of the Night*, they put everything they had into making that album, but it didn't get the recognition it deserved. But I think *Lick It Up* is up there. There's not a weak song on it. I wasn't crazy about Paul Stanley "rapping" on "All Hell's Breakin' Loose." I wasn't thrilled with that when it first came out, but I love the song now. It's one of my favorite Kiss songs. The heavy chorus—it's an unbelievable song. But like I said, there's not a bad song on that album. A lot of the songs on *Lick It Up* are faster and heavier than *Creatures of the Night*, like "Exciter" and "Young and Wasted." It's dirtier, and it's filled with sex. It's a great, great album.

EDDIE TRUNK: The *Lick It Up* album, I don't think the album is nearly as good as *Creatures of the Night*, but I think that because they took off the make-up, and because *Lick It Up* was a very catchy song, and because MTV really had started to shape and take hold and get into more homes at that point, it all came together to get them back on the map. I remember there was an ad in *Billboard* magazine, that *Lick It Up* went gold. That it was a celebration when that record finally went gold. I was working in a record store at the time, and that was a big deal. You can imagine, though, just a few years earlier, Kiss—who had shipped platinum—are celebrating a gold record? But that's how far they had fallen at that point. Reaching gold status was an accomplishment. So it all came together—the power of MTV, which had really emerged at that time, the little pop from taking off the make-up, the fact that *Lick It Up* was a good record, and the song itself was real catchy. So I think it all came together.

MARK ADELMAN: I was managing some bands in New York City, and a friend of mine called me. Kiss was looking for a road manager. I met with the accountant or the business managers, and then I met with Gene and Paul, and everything went well. The next thing I knew, I was in Portugal with them two weeks later. That was the first tour without make-up. [Mark's first show with Kiss—which was also Kiss' first-ever without make-up—on October 11] was exciting. It was the first time I'd ever worked with the band. I remember being in Lisbon and just the excitement of pulling into the city with them, and there were posters all over the roads, from the airport to the hotel, of Kiss without make-up on. It was kind of crazy.

I remember Eric fast becoming one of my good friends. We would hang out. I think the first day, we had lunch together. It was not much of a separation between the elite—being Gene and Paul, and Eric and Vinnie. Everybody melded well together. Eric had a pretty good sense of humor and personality. We used to make jokes about him, and everybody had nicknames for each other. We used to call him "Bud Carr Rooney"—he was the illegitimate son of Mickey Rooney and Buddy Hackett. We always did stupid things. At airports, we would go on computer terminals when the flight attendants weren't there, and we would type in crazy things, so when they'd sign on, it would be hysterical.

I remember just thinking how huge this thing [the tank stage] is. He had this massive drum set. I think early on in the tour, the guys would mess with him. He'd be doing a drum solo, and they wouldn't come out on time, and he'd be looking over, like, "Where are these guys?" Gene and Paul are very self-confident guys, and Eric was there to work, and he was a great drummer. I think everybody was excited at the spectacle of the whole thing, including the band.

BRUCE KULICK: There was an occasion later on when I actually jammed with those guys. I was on the list of guitarists. Not a lot of people know that. At one time, I did audition when they did the big cattle call. I wonder, chronologically, that might have been when they weren't sure about Vinnie [Note: This could have occurred between the European and U.S. legs of the *Lick It Up* tour, which resulted in Vinnie supposedly being fired and then re-hired by the band, ot later in 1984]. I can't remember. But it was just "Come in, play, bang out two songs really loud, and leave." I had no interaction with anybody, except hearing a compliment from Gene, like, "Great vibrato." I definitely didn't project the right vibe to be accepted in the band then. And it wasn't something that I used to talk about a lot.

I just remember the "goulash story" [when asked if he discussed Vinnie with the band]. When you serve goulash in one of the European countries, he was dipping the bread in it, biting the bread, and then dipping it in again. I think all the guys were chiming in on some bad table manners from Vinnie. But again, it's heresy from me, because the story was pretty old. I think in some ways, because Eric had such a big heart, Vinnie at times was trying to latch on. First of all, he knew Eric was in the band, and Vinnie wasn't officially in the band. "Hey, let's go eat here!" I would hear things like that, how he wound up with like, "Hey, you got that covered, right Eric?" I would hear various stories like that, that just made me realize that Vinnie may have taken advantage of Eric's good heart. He was very much a generous person.

MARK ADELMAN: The American tour, I don't remember the numbers at how big we played. I think we played at Radio City Music Hall-type venues—5,000 seaters and stuff like that. Some less, some more. I remember being in L.A. with them for one of my first times, and Eric and I went shopping. We bought blazers, and he would wear my sport coat, and I'd say, "Come on, I need it back," and he would say, "But it looks better on me!" It was always banter back and forth. We'd always rent cars and drive around L.A. He had a couple of little girlfriends, I think. It was just guys in their late 20s/early 30s having a good time, y'know?

BILL AUCOIN: No, I didn't [ever see a "non-make-up era" Kiss concert]. I didn't really believe in that. I was one of these people that thought they should have kept it on. However, Eric and I kept in touch on the phone, mostly phone calls.

1984

BOBBY BLOTZER: I saw them once in '84. It was in L.A. I thought it was a trip to see Kiss without their make-up on. I thought they played great. He was a great drummer, had a great sound, and he picked up the pieces well from the old days. I thought he was very solid and held his own with everybody else.

MIKE PORTNOY: I guess the first time I would have seen Eric was the *Creatures of the Night* tour, and then I saw the *Lick It Up* tour and the *Animalize* tour. I saw them on all those tours and still followed them. As much as Peter was my hero in the early days—just because he was such a big influence on me—there was no question that Eric was obviously the better drummer. Technically a better drummer. I was very impressed with his drumming.

MARK SLAUGHTER: I met the guys when they were walking around the Aladdin Hotel on the *Lick It Up* tour. My local band opened for Stryper and a lot of the bands that made it through there at that time. I actually gave Eric Carr the demo tape of my band. And lo and behold [years later], he called me up and said, "Dude, you're not going to believe this. I found the demo tape!" He was a full rat packer, and he held onto everything. He says, "I have it. It's right here in front of me." My perception was that it was an incredible show. Any time I've ever seen Kiss, these guys understand how to work an audience.

EDDIE TRUNK: The closest that Kiss came on the *Creatures* tour to New York was Worcester, Massachusetts, which was not very close. The Centrum in Worcester, they played a gig. I was supposed to go, and I couldn't because I had an appendix attack, and was in the hospital the day before I was supposed to leave. The next year for the *Lick It Up* tour, they also played Worcester, Massachusetts [on February 24]. I went up with a few friends, because I didn't know if they would wind up playing in New York. I took the road trip, and we got to the hotel that we were staying at. We brought our cooler, some beer, and our boom-box. We were there at maybe 3:00 or 4:00, and the hotel was right across from the venue. We said, "Let's have a little party and get ready to go to Kiss." We had the door open to the hotel room that we were all hanging out in, playing music, and seeing if any fans were walking by. And I will never forget it—who walks by and stops, but Eric Carr! We were all kind of like, "Holy shit ... you've got to be kidding me!" He was like—in typical Eric fashion—a lovable, great guy. "Hey, what's all that racket? I'm trying to get some sleep!" Like we'd known him forever. We couldn't believe it. He walked into the room, and we were drinking Michelob out of the cooler, and he had a beer with us. We talked, took pictures, and there he was a few hours before he played with the band, hanging out in our hotel, because he was staying in the hotel as well. Came, sat, had a beer with us before the show, and talked. That alone speaks to the type of person Eric was. That was the first time I met him. We didn't become friends because of that, but it was my first connection with him.

BOB GRAW: The first time I saw Kiss was on the *Lick It Up* tour at Radio City Music Hall in New York City, and Accept opened the show, on the *Balls to the Wall* tour [Kiss played two nights, on March 9 and 10]. I was disappointed that I wasn't going to see Kiss in make-up, because that was my life-long dream. And every time I tried to see them, something happened. I was still excited. I remember my step-mom took me, and we sat in the first row of the first balcony, so there was nobody standing in front of me. But I remember watching all those old videos, and I remember how big the stage was and the staircases and the big huge Kiss logo. And this was nothing more than a stripped-down stage. They were re-using the tank. But other than that, because it was Radio City, it wasn't a very big stage. I loved the show. It's one of my fondest memories, because it was my first. You always remember your first. Eric was great—I think he definitely brought a heavier sound to their older material, as well. Like, when they played "Cold Gin," they sped everything up. It was faster and heavier, and that's definitely what he brought to that line-up of the band.

LORETTA CARAVELLO: We went to the Radio City show. First off, when we got there, the people were really nice, and they took us to the back of Radio City, and they showed us all the hidden doorways. You wouldn't believe what's back there. It looks like *The Phantom of the Opera*. The guys there took us through the doors, and they had secret steps that went down. So that was nice. We have a very big family—my father has like 18 brothers and sisters, and they had kids, so they took not only us but the family, fans, and groupies in a gigantic room. The band came in, and they started to mingle. They had a really big food table in the center. And it was kind of comical. There were some girls there ... they looked like they were there for "a good time." What happened was they were lined up in front of the food table, and the minute the band saw them, they told [the workers at Radio City] to take all the food off and throw it out. Nobody wanted to go near the table. [Laughs] You had to see my brother's face—"Oh man, they're sitting on the table, and the food's there." The band was cracking up. There was also somebody in there that we always thought was my brother—the drummer from Quiet Riot, Frankie Banali. From the back, we always mistook him, no matter where we went. We would tap him on the shoulder and think he was my brother.

FRANKIE BANALI: I arrived at Radio City late and missed the show, so I never did see—or have ever seen—Kiss live. Yes, people were coming up to me asking for my autograph, thinking I was Eric. When I told them that it was me, thankfully they still wanted the autograph! I do vaguely remember someone being very nice and hugging me, thinking I was Eric. If they were Eric's family, they were really sweet.

I am sorry to say that I only had one opportunity to meet Eric. Between Eric's schedule with Kiss and mine with Quiet Riot, our paths only crossed once. This was at a record release party for Judas Priest. It was held at the Queen Mary liner that is permanently docked at the harbor in Long Beach, California. Eric and I were talking about drums. A fan walked up to us and asked me for my autograph. I was getting ready to sign it and add "Quiet Riot," when he says, "I love your drumming with Kiss!" I looked over at Eric, and he starts to laugh. I said to the fan, "Well, you better have the real

Kiss drummer sign this then," and winked at Eric. Afterwards, Eric said to me, "Earlier tonight, I signed two autographs for Quiet Riot fans before they realized I wasn't you." We both cracked up, talked a little longer, hugged, and went our separate ways. It's a shame that I never had the opportunity to spend time with Eric. But I have one memorable meeting to reflect back on, and he was a genuinely nice person.

LORETTA CARAVELLO: It was a lot of fun. It was a blast. I remember when we went to see the show, Radio City had given everybody 30 or 40 posters, and we left all our private property back there. When we came back, of course, everything was missing. Not handbags, but somebody helped themselves to the posters. I'm not talking about just my family, [but] everybody that left their stuff. I thought that was pretty tacky, but you live and learn. There really isn't that many posters of Radio City around at all. I think they were just in the venue or in the window. [Gene and Paul were] very respectful. Paul was always like a gentleman. He would come up to my mother and father—"Hello Mr. and Mrs. Caravello. How are you?" He was very quiet and soft-spoken. And Gene was Gene—"Hello," shook your hand, and talked for a few minutes. In the earlier days, they were more out and socializing, but as the years went by, they came out for a few minutes, and then went away.

CHARLIE BENANTE: The next time I saw them after that was *Lick It Up* at Radio City with Accept opening up ... and I left. It wasn't Kiss. I just wasn't into it.

BOB GRAW: I was really surprised [when it was announced that Vinnie had left Kiss for good], because like I said, he had really injected life back into that band and gave them a totally new sound and an exciting sound. I was really sorry to see him go. I didn't understand it at the time. I think I might have heard it on *Fingers Metal Shop* [a New York area radio show] on WBAB. I heard, "Vinnie Vincent has left Kiss," or "Vinnie Vincent was fired from Kiss." I was like, "Well, maybe they'll get lucky, and Ace Frehley will come back." But that didn't happen.

ADAM MITCHELL: I know they had a great deal of trouble having Vinnie sign any kind of contract with them. I know that lasted like ... it seemed at the time like a year. He wouldn't sign a contract, but I didn't know the details of it. It wasn't a marriage made in heaven, let's put it that way.

BOB KULICK: If you had a business, like any business, and you set up the business and carry the business to success, and then you hire somebody to fill one of the slots, they have to earn their way to participate in the way that you're participating. I think that he too soon asked for too much. And for guys who by that time were more businessmen—or at least as much businessmen as they were rock stars—that was not acceptable. No matter what he wrote, it was not yet acceptable. So he had to go. That's when Gene called me and was like, "Do you know any guitar players?" I knew what *that* meant. [Laughs]

ADAM MITCHELL: Just guitar-wise, Vinnie was a perfect fit. He really was. Vinnie had played with this guy ... when I was doing my own solo record, my drummer, Art Wood, had played with Dan Hartman. He had a big hit with James Brown, "Living in America." Vinnie had played in his band, and he would tell me ... we had dinner at Art Wood's house one night, and we got to talking about Vinnie one night. And he said, "We'd be doing some show in Italy, and I'd be like half-way through the second verse, and in the middle of the verse, Vinnie is upstaging me! He's up there, shredding some solo ... in the middle of the second verse!" Vinnie's problem ... he just wasn't a good fit with Kiss. I had heard stories about Vinnie before I had started writing with him. I will not take away Vinnie's undeniable musical talent. Musically, he is very, very talented. He really is. But personally ... it's something I can't get into, because I haven't seen him since then. I only wrote two or three songs with Vinnie. Musically, he was a phenomenally talented guy. Paul Stanley would tell you the same thing. And they had huge difficulties with him as a person. But musically, Vinnie is a major, major talent.

LORETTA CARAVELLO: He liked Vinnie. I can tell just from the pictures he took of them. He thought he was a great guitar player. But whatever opinion he had, he had to basically keep to himself, because that's not his decision. But you've got to do what's best for the band, and if Gene and Paul didn't want him, then that's how it had to be. He just mentioned that Vinnie was leaving. He didn't say much, I'm telling you—he tried to keep a lot of the stuff out of the house.

BOB GRAW: It's been twenty-something years since I've listened to that album [Wendy O. Williams' *WOW*, which was produced by Gene, and on which Eric, Gene, Paul, and even Ace, played on]. I remember seeing the video for "It's My Life" on *Night Flight* on the USA Network, and I didn't even know that any of Kiss' members were on that album, until I went to the record store, and there was a sticker on the cover that said "With special guest Ace Frehley and special appearances by Paul Stanley, Eric Carr, Reginald Van Helsing [Gene's alias]." I thought the album was not that great, but I loved that song, "It's My Life."

LORETTA CARAVELLO: "Ain't None of Your Business" I'm not too crazy about, but "Legends Never Die," I could listen to that ten times in a row. I think it's a great song. I think it's kind of sad, but it's nicely played. The other one, eh, I can take it or leave it. He liked Wendy. I have a tour book she signed for him that says "'F' n' roll Eric, Let's rock! Wendy O." Typical Wendy O. I just think it's sad what she did to herself—I don't understand that [Wendy committed suicide in 1998]. She would have been good today. I think today would have been her time. People would have loved them. Everything old is new now.

BOB GRAW: I think I was reading either *Hit Parader* or *Circus*, and they had a quote from somebody, saying Vinnie Vincent had left Kiss, and Mark St. John was joining the band. Actually, they said, "Mark Norton" was the new guitar player in Kiss. I'd never heard of him. I didn't know who he was, so I was like, "I guess we'll wait and see."

MICHAEL JAMES JACKSON: By that time [of *Animalize*], we had established a pretty solid sense of teamwork. This was the fourth album that we did, and they were pretty used to my methods in terms of tracking. I had a very organized way of doing it. So we got through all the tracking as we normally had. But once again, everything was built around the drums—everything was built around Eric. The overriding thing that I would say always about Eric is Eric just really cared. He had a tremendous amount of heart for Kiss. He was one of those people that if he could have chosen a dream to have in his life, it would have been doing exactly what he was doing with Kiss. You can't really say that about a lot of people. I respected his dedication. I respected his fierce protection of how he perceived Kiss, and I think he was a really good-hearted guy.

BRUCE KULICK: I popped up there [during the recording of *Animalize*], and it was just me and Paul. The only thing I heard was, "I'm not happy with what Mark was doing on this. Do you have a guitar with a Floyd Rose [tremolo bar]?" Which at the time was very new. And I said, "Yeah." Instead of them calling my brother, it was me, which was great. But I didn't have any interaction with anybody but Paul. *Animalize* was kind of like [2009's] *Sonic Boom*—that was Paul's baby. The session went well, and I was thrilled to finally do something like my brother did. Before I left, Paul told me, "Don't cut your hair." I had *no idea* why he said that, as it was kind of shoulder-length. But, obviously, Paul was thinking ahead.

MICHAEL JAMES JACKSON: I might have had some experience with Mark St. John, but I don't remember much of it. I remember he was a nice guy.

BRUCE KULICK: "Lonely is the Hunter," and there's a tiny bit on another song ["Murder in High Heels"], but it's just a couple of riffs that he needed.

MICHAEL JAMES JACKSON: I cut the tracks [for *Animalize*], because by then, they were used to the way I cut tracks. I had a specific way of doing it. I did a lot of editing and splicing between tracks. So I made sure all the tracks were done, and everything was very solid. And then I didn't finish the record. At the time, we had some disagreements that needed to get worked out, and it was uncertain whether they would. Somebody offered me another project, and I took the other project. But the disagreements at the time were significant enough that it was the appropriate thing for me to do. And then Paul and Gene finished the record. We'll just say [it was] some contractual things. I remained very close friends with Paul and certainly friends with Gene. We had a great run, and it was a great experience. If the question ever came up [of working with Kiss again], it would be perfectly fine. [Eric] would call me occasionally, and we would talk. We remained friendly.

BOB GRAW: I love *Animalize* because it was fast and heavy. Mark St. John was almost like a Vinnie Vincent clone. He played very fast and technical. But that album had some of the best songs of 1980's Kiss—"Heaven's on Fire," "Under the Gun," "Thrills in the Night."

"Under the Gun" [a song Eric co-wrote with Paul and Desmond Child] is heavy, and it's fast. It's a kick-ass rock song, and Eric plays his heart out on it. It's just a great heavy metal song. Eric's drumming on his first three Kiss albums—you can forget about *The Elder*, don't even include that—which were *Creatures*, *Lick It Up*, and *Animalize*, his drum sound is just great. I don't know who was behind mic-ing his drums, but his drums are out front and in-your-face on all three of those albums. Those are my three favorite albums of the Eric Carr era.

The "Heaven's on Fire" video ... with Paul jumping through the ring? It was them lip-synching the song, and it was all cutaways from a hotel party they were having with a bunch of amazing-looking women. And I remember Eric is under a table in that video, making out with a girl. He looks up at the camera and mouths the words. At one point, he comes out from behind the drums, jumps on Paul's back, and he sings part of the verse. It's a good video, for that time. And Eric's wearing a leopard-skin jumpsuit in the video!

BRUCE KULICK: Paul was certainly excited that the new record had a hit with "Heaven's on Fire." I think *Lick It Up* was a good starting point for them coming back. It just seemed like the timing was good for them to start climbing back up. But then again, there was that whole attraction towards them now being a "hair band" and what was going on with MTV. They were doing some great videos. The opportunity was there for people to get into

Kiss without make-up, even though it's hard for some new Kiss fans to think about that now, again, if they'd only been exposed to them in the past ten or fourteen years. If you're one of those new fans, you might not know how important Kiss without make-up was. It was ripe for it to grow, and in general, yeah, there was that period of Gene having his flirtations with Hollywood, of which Paul always made sure, "I have my eye on the ball, and everything's going to be great here. I'll man the ship." And he did. Paul definitely had a strong vision for the band. Both of them worked incredibly hard, so it was just like, "OK, who's going to run with the ball?" Although they didn't always agree, of course, but they know how to work hard. I learned a lot from them.

NEIL ZLOZOWER: I actually got hired to do their big photo shoot with Mark St. John. And then after that, they did a video shoot somewhere with Mark St. John. And the funny thing I remember is even at the video shoot, a little bit of [Mark's] illness was already taking effect. Because I remember, he could only stand up and do whatever for very short periods of time. And I remember going up to Paul, saying, "Paul, no offense, but are you going to take this guy on the road with you? How is that going to work? He can barely do a video shoot, let alone go on tour." So I was sort of doubting their judgment there.

LORETTA CARAVELLO: All I remember him talking about was how [Mark's] hand was swollen, and they had to get rid of him. Who knows what it is with that one, that poor soul. Actually, on the CD that I'm putting out, there is music that Mark had given me that my brother had wrote and gave each member of Kiss a copy, but they never used it. So we took that, and I'm putting music together from that. He was supposed to play on that song, but he passed away [on April 5, 2007, of a cerebral hemorrhage]. He was a nice guy.

BOB KULICK: Paul called me in London while I was working with Meat Loaf. He's like, "Do you have Bruce's number?" "Of course. What's going on?" "Uh ... Mark St. John has a problem." So my brother called me back, and he's like, "Paul just called me. You know what's going on, right?" About six weeks later, I'm still in London with Meat Loaf, and they are coming over to play! I got to see the first shows that my brother played with the band, vis a vis that first tour that they did, which was England.

MARK ADELMAN: It was really awkward. I think we had Bruce as a stand-by, and Mark would be watching the show with Bruce playing. It was the most bizarre thing I'd ever seen.

BRUCE KULICK: It was easy to get the gig in '84 when they were like, "Hey, can you fill in?" By then, I had a little more seasoning. I was more confident, and they needed me. [Laughs] So, really, outside of those two quick encounters—jamming two songs and just seeing him on the couch—I didn't know Eric very well at all. And then it took me suddenly going from playing "ghost guitar" on *Animalize* and Paul saying, "Don't cut your hair," and me going, "What does that mean?" to three months later getting called to say, "We need you to come to Europe for at least two weeks, maybe more." They told me what the deal was, and I was obviously on cloud nine, because even if I thought I had Kiss on my resume for two weeks, I still thought it was the biggest thing in the world. I didn't know two weeks would turn into *twelve years*, but there it was.

I remember missing some of the time of rehearsals because I injured my arm. By the time I was ready to rehearse, it was getting kind of close to leaving, maybe ten days. I was very familiar with the songs, anyway. I don't remember much what it was like to rehearse or hang with Eric at that point. When we got to touring, I certainly did—that's when I got to know him. That's when you're sitting in the limousine, that's when you're traveling together and hanging. And for the most part, here I am, whisked away off to England, first class, with Kiss. And my first gig, my knees were shaking, I was so nervous. But I got through it, and I played well. I thought everything was a little fast, but that was a little bit indicative of that time period, don't know why. But I clearly understood the pecking order, which was Gene and Paul—and their competitive nature—with Eric. He might have had tenure over me, but he was still one of the "hired guys." And then there was me, who was like a "temporary hired guy" [laughs], but who's living the dream.

That tour, it was always Gene and Paul who rode together in the limo after the show. So there I was with Eric, and lots of times, I heard him complaining. And I was really kind of disappointed. He probably had some valid points about how the band was being handled or what he might have been bitching about at the time. But, come on, *we were in Kiss.* We just played a sold-out show, we're in limousines, and we're going to the finest hotel in town. And we didn't play half bad, either. So, chill. It was like somebody raining on my parade. Now, years later, as I got to experience the same kind of things that happened when you're familiar and you see how things are going down and you don't feel included, you don't really know what you can and can't say ... again, every situation about being in Kiss was about, "How are you going to handle it? How does your personality determine?" Clearly, you're working for somebody. And, in some ways, that's actually healthy for the band, because if everybody thought they were equal, sometimes, that's how you have a lot of problems. When there's the natural pecking order, things get done. You're either going to do the job, or you're not.

So it was a little hard for me to get close to Eric, because I just saw him as a negative. And again, I do know—and I understood years later—what bugged him so much. But it always came down to life—and I'm as guilty as anyone—where you just can't help but bitch and look at the glass half empty instead of half full. And that was his choice. And you could see me walking into this situation, even temporarily, going like, "I wish he'd stop. This is ridiculous." And, at some point, I know during that tour, in the backseat of a lovely limousine in England, I said something like, "Do you know how many guys would give their left arm to be in the band? Stop it!" I don't even remember if I got much of a reply or him understanding it. I can't remember [exactly what Eric was upset with]. It was the usual kind of drama that happens when you're not really feeling like your say matters. And I got a taste of it, when I was given an old wireless system, for example, and it would start to falter on stage, and it would be very frustrating. And then the opening act is Bon Jovi, and they're nobody at this point, by the way. They're destined to be huge, but they're nobody, and they've got all brand new equipment. And I go backstage and complain about it to Gene, and Gene didn't appreciate it. He definitely heard, "Why does the opening act have better gear than us? *We're Kiss.*" But he still didn't appreciate it. So, put that in the column that, "OK, I get it." Even though Gene had his point and I had my point, the way I think Gene handled that was that kind of a thing where I could see how Eric—maybe what he needed to be in his comfort zone—they weren't giving him.

MARK ADELMAN: We had Bon Jovi as the opening act. I remember they were really just a small, little band, and it was obvious that this band was going to be huge. I remember being in Norway and walking by a McDonald's, and they were pounding on the window because they didn't have any money to pay for their burgers and french fries. So I walked in and bought them all burgers and french fries. I should call them now and see if they want to buy *me* some burgers and french fries. But it was fun to be with Bon Jovi. Eric was friends with everybody. I'm sure he and Tico [Torres] were close, because they were both drummers. It was very warm and fuzzy back then. There were no egos. Gene and Paul, however they were big rock superstars, they were pretty approachable.

BRUCE KULICK: Although I still think, in general, because I was the guy plucked from obscurity, basically, even though I had played with Meat Loaf, Michael Bolton, and Billy Squier before, but here I am, as the lead guitarist of Kiss ... I didn't want him raining on my parade. And what was kind of funny was I think he liked to play the role of "I'm going to be the bratty kid." And Gene and Paul will definitely be your "parents" in a band situation, because Kiss is *them.* Everything that comes off great in Kiss, in one way or another, is a reflection of them. And when it doesn't look good, it's a reflection of them, not other people. So they are very "parental" and in control in that way. By that point, even though they had more business to learn—they went through a lot of crazy stuff during the '80s, with another management company ... well actually, at some point, they got rid of the one they had when I joined a few years later. But it really came down to his kind of needs, and I don't think he was always feeling unhappy. Just I was a good ear to bitch to! Now, no one was better than Eric with the fans, and I'm not saying that he didn't play his heart out. But that was just one thing about that whole tour that kind of freaked me out about him. And then in time, he saw that I was not trying to side with Gene and Paul, although in latter years, he actually accused me of that, where I just decided to "side" with not wanting to be upset about something that I couldn't change.

And that's real important that everybody understands that. His points could be valid for him, but they're not realistic. The real choice would be for him to say, "I'm not happy. I don't want to be in the band anymore." And sometimes, when you actually say that to someone who's your boss, maybe they actually make it better for you. Or they don't. But until you're ready to say that, you're either in that situation or you're not. And I don't think I need to defend Eric not being happy. I mean, was Peter ever very happy? Was Ace ever very happy? I have to admit that, for the most part, I was happy, although I had my battles and my frustrations. But I don't think I was ever as unhappy as the three members I just mentioned. But then again, I think my personality was a little more understanding of like, "This is the way it is. And look at how successful the band has been the way that this is. So who am I to re-invent it? I didn't start it."

But there was one pivotal thing that happened during that tour that was really kind of crazy. And I know there's some documentation of it somewhere. But like I was saying about him wanting to be "the brat," y'know, Gene and Paul are always very guarded about the journalists and stuff. Although now in this day and age, you've got Gene on Twitter, so how guarded are we? Or the reality show [*Gene Simmons Family Jewels*], which is of course entertainment, but he's showing sides of himself that no one ever knew. But for sure, back then, journalists were not their friends, in general. There was this really cute girl who worked for *Melody Maker*, who somehow weaseled her way to be in Eric's room and do an interview. And then got him in the bathtub and posing in bubble bath with a glass of champagne or something. Basically, because *Melody Maker* was not the *Kerrang!* of England, made fun of him. And there was a picture of him half-naked in the bathtub. And the girl didn't sleep with him. I think he got in the bathtub to be funny and to be outrageous and to be cute ... and to maybe get lucky. I mean, Eric would definitely go the extra mile to get some attention, especially in a situation with a pretty girl. Why not? It's freakin' rock n' roll. What's the big deal? Here you are, touring in England, and it's fun.

When it came out in the paper, they were *really* pissed at him, Gene and Paul. Again, for me, I was the observer. It's one thing to do that in front of the girl, but to then actually pose for a picture, you're asking for it. And that gave you an indication of "I'm going to be the misbehaved kid." Was it as bad as some of the other shenanigans that other members put Gene and Paul through? No. But still, it probably, once again, put them in that situation where they could make him feel bad, and then he could be unhappy again. "Oh, now they're pissed at me." So you see how he kind of created that. Even though I thought it was classic, it was unbelievable. I loved it. Let's face it. Drama always surrounds a band, period. You don't even have to look for it. I have that picture somewhere—it was in *Kisstory*.

BOB KULICK: The tension—or the *frustration* is probably a better word— somebody who wanted to contribute more than he was allowed. It was a constant frustration for him, as it would have been to anybody. As it was to my brother to a lesser degree, because for whatever reason, my brother had thicker skin. Like, Eric might show up with something—"Here's an idea for a song." But guys in bands—and it's not just Gene and Paul, it's everybody— the pressure of that and the sense of humor to keep yourself stable and able at the table, somebody jokingly saying, "That sucks," hurts people's feelings. So I think Eric unfortunately took too many of the "joke comments" to heart, rather than just like, "These fucking guys, can't you be nice? If you don't like it, just say you don't like it. You don't have to insult me." But that's the way it is. You dish it out, [so] you've got to be able to take it. He could dish it out, too, believe me. He would make fun of me sometimes. It would be like, "Give me a fucking break, you and your hair." It was part and parcel.

MARK ADELMAN: It was a good time. People had seen them [without make-up], the mystique of them coming in and out of buildings in make-up was gone. They could just walk out of a hotel room, and there would be fans there. It was just different, and it was accepted that, "This can actually work now." I mean, fast forward 20 years, and they went back to the make-up again.

JACK SAWYERS: How it all started for me was I grew up on South Jersey, which our venue for concerts was mostly the Spectrum in Philadelphia. So every once in a while, Kiss would come to town. Sometimes it would be a Thursday night or Friday night. But I remember on the nights they were coming, a few of us would skip school and take the bus up to Philly in the morning and just hang out all day, because most of it was general seating. I think the first Kiss concert I saw of them with Eric was the *Animalize* tour [on November 25]. That's when they had that crazy thing, where Mark St. John was sitting on the side of the stage and Bruce was on stage. That was kind of weird. I think that was the first time I ever saw Bruce Kulick, too.

But the cool thing about that was before the concert—we were there way early—I noticed that the buses had all rolled up. On the tour buses, they had on the plate on top, "Women Wanted." Which I guess was the theme of time. Instead of saying "Toledo, Ohio," or wherever they were headed, it said "Women Wanted." But I met Eric by the buses back there for the first time. He was always so gracious. I remember it being a little bit chilly that day. So we talked to Eric a couple of times, and he would go back and forth, between the venue and the bus. We'd walk back there, he'd see us and go, "Oh ... you guys again!" Because there weren't many people there yet. So he would stop and talk to us again and sign stuff for other people that were waiting. So the day goes on. I guess he saw our faces enough at the beginning of the show that when the show was over, we immediately ran back to where they were letting people backstage. So we're standing there, and Eric was walking by. Eric was the only one that would come back out and sign stuff randomly for people. He saw me standing there with my friends and goes, "Hey ... you again! You're still here?" And he waved us back, past security. So we went back, where all the after-party stuff was. It was kind of cool, 'cause we were hanging out there, got to talk to him a little bit. And then it was time to leave, and everybody went home.

BOB GRAW: I remember going to Nassau Coliseum [on November 21], and it said, "Tonight's show has been cancelled. Call Ticketron for refunds and exchanges." And I remember we went to A&S the next day at the Walt Whitman Mall, and they said, "No, it's been rescheduled [for November 26].

Paul Stanley has laryngitis." And I said, "Why didn't we hear about this on the radio or anything?" But they never talked about Kiss on the radio. They never played Kiss on the radio. You didn't get Kiss news. It's not like today, where you can just get on the Internet and go right to their website. But, yeah, I remember we drove all the way to Nassau Coliseum. My dad and my step-mom took me to that show. Queensrÿche opened up that show. Once again, finally, I was seeing them on a big stage. And they had the explosions. They had the big Kiss logo over the stage. It was really good. But very scaled down. They didn't have a lot of gadgets and gizmos on the stage. But it was still cool to see them on a big stage. I remember they were all dressed in like animal skins. Mark St. John didn't play at that show. Mark St. John had problems with his hands, and Bruce Kulick joined.

BRUCE KULICK: My two weeks turned into six weeks, of which I really started to get in a groove with the guys. I remember the only time I got very, very nervous was playing Wembley, which was a big deal for me. I know Gene and Paul were happy with me, and I felt great about that. The fans in England knew who I was, because *Kerrang!* came out rather quickly, where the U.S. magazines were two or three months behind. And then all of a sudden we're back in the States, and we're rehearsing in Allentown, Pennsylvania, with the big *Animalize* show. The record's gold already. Everything is coming our way. Now ... how will they handle Mark St. John? I am still only a "fill-in player." Well, they're giving him photos in the tour book, and I couldn't tell you if it was contractual or what. Mark's hand healed, and they wanted to have him watch the show. But I had the home court advantage by touring with them. I remember overhearing Gene in the limo listening to a board mix—how the band was sounding—and him being really pleased and complimenting me. And I was really stoked. I mean, they didn't go out of their way to do things like that, but that gave me some justification for feeling like, "Let's see what's going to happen." But I had a very healthy attitude when Mark was even traveling with us, because I knew that this is something out of my control. I'm not going to be like the ice skating people, like break their knees. [Laughs] Nancy Kerrigan, what happened to her, and Tonya Harding. But, potentially, it could have been this terrible, competitive thing. I used to even jam with Mark, as that would be healthy behavior. So, it didn't take too long for them to realize that it was time to send Mark home.

I was in my hotel room, and Paul called me from another room and told me I was the new guitarist. I kind of saw the writing on the wall. I didn't need any psychic ability. I knew they weren't pleased on the biggest opportunity they gave him, I think he tried to up-stage them a little bit. I thought Mark was a really talented guitarist, but I always thought he was wrong for the band, and I feel that they hired him for the wrong reasons. Eric never really had much of an opinion. He used to talk about Vinnie a lot, to be honest with you. Because Vinnie would follow him around and mooch meals off of him and just befriend him. Well, they were the Italians in the band. I heard a lot of stories from Eric about Vinnie that were pretty funny, just them touring and funny things he would do. But Eric didn't have much relationship with Mark at all. It was kind of odd. Mark was definitely the odd man out, and that was a very unusual situation. But I don't know if it was for contractual reasons or, "Hey, we hired this guy, raved about him ... and now we don't even give him a chance?" Not that there was ever any big announcement, just like when Tommy [Thayer] joined Kiss there wasn't a big announcement. Be careful when you make the big announcement. If that guy falls, then the next guy doesn't get *any* announcement. [Laughs]

LORETTA CARAVELLO: Other than Gene, Bruce was his great friend.

MARK ADELMAN: Bruce was great to be with, too. It was a good pack of guys—me, Bruce, Eric, Gene, Paul, [and] we had a tour accountant, Chris Lendt. [Lendt] did the numbers, and I did the road managing.

BRUCE KULICK: I didn't have a real contract with the band until they asked me to really join. Before that, it was just a work-for-hire/working agreement. And Eric always had a contract. That was always something that they never wanted me to know what was in Eric's or Eric to know what was in mine, which, of course, is wise for them.

BOB GRAW: To be honest with you, the first couple of times I saw Bruce, I wasn't crazy about Bruce's playing. Vinnie Vincent live, he played Ace's stuff completely different. I think Bruce tried to play Ace's stuff exactly the way Ace played it almost, but he wasn't as "dirty" of a player. Bruce's sound is very polished—Bruce is a very polished musician. Everything he does is very technical, whereas with Ace, it's just a sloppy mess. That's why he sounds so good. But Bruce brought a much more technical sound, where he wasn't playing a million notes like Vinnie Vincent or Mark St. John played. He was a very technical, sound player. And during the next three Kiss albums, it fit perfectly with the direction they were going in, because they were going for a much more polished, almost like '80s rock sound. Whereas the first few albums with Eric were just metal, and then they went the way of a lot of bands of the '80s, a very polished, very MTV-friendly, not scary sound.

NINA BLACKWOOD: I particularly enjoyed guitarist Bruce Kulick's deft and inspired musicianship, which could be better appreciated without the outrageous staging and theatrics.

BRUCE KULICK: I remember hearing stories about Eric knowing Diana Ross, from the years when she was part of the Kiss family, because she was dating Gene. And he would tell me that she would invite him to her house for a party, and he'd be kind of like, "I don't know if I want to go." And I'm listening to that, going, *"Are you kidding me?* You're even thinking twice about going to Diana Ross' house in Beverly Hills?" And that's the stuff that would blow my mind about Eric. Now again, when you know Eric, you totally get it. But when you're just hearing it for the first time, you're going, "Huh?" And I'm not going to remember all of his little run-ins with Diana Ross, but he had some really funny ones. I can't remember the incident, but something where he was trying to be polite, where instead of it, he ends up spilling the drink on her. That wasn't it. I just remember that it was something that he did that I remember him telling the story.
   I was just thrilled at the taping of [the December 12 show at Cobo Hall, released in 1985 as the *Animalize Live Uncensored* home video], because I'd never met her before. I only heard about her fame, etc. Years before that even, my brother worked with her, because of Gene, actually. But there she

was, backstage at the Detroit show. There she is helping me get my whacky "boot wrap" around my leg. I'm like, "Oh my God ... Diana Ross is helping me. This is crazy!" But she was cool. She was a pro and a great performer, and she knew what we were doing. It wasn't that long into my tenure in the band that Gene moved right on to Shannon [Tweed]. So I had a full twelve years of Shannon, which has been great, [and] because of the *Gene Simmons Family Jewels* show, I'm re-living a lot of the old footage, y'know? I couldn't tell [if Diana Ross was a fan of Kiss' music], but she couldn't have been more supportive and wonderful backstage. I was blown away by it, because my brother had his good and bad stories with her, but he was working for her. This is a little different. She's there as Gene's date. And she was wonderful.

BOB KULICK: I don't recall anything other than how infatuated they were with the "new thing," and that's why the fact that my brother was able to play some of that while still being a core rock-blues player, to be able to play what Ace played was the ticket. Where Mark St. John was more of "Eddie Van Halen" and less "Ace Frehley," and then also, he had his problem as well.

[Bruce brought] a stability that they hadn't had before, because unfortunately, Ace had reached that point where once the "thrill is gone," shall we say, what to us seems like, "How can the thrill be gone? Isn't it great to get up there and do that every night?" Sometimes, the answer is no. So my brother brought an enthusiasm and a positive vibe, whereby those guys— Gene and Paul—could feel comfortable, and Eric could have a friend. As I said to you about the two peas in the pod, that never changed. Whoever the other peas were—whether it was Eric Singer and my brother, Eric Carr and my brother—they were the two peas in one pod, and Gene and Paul were the two peas in the other pod.

Fortunately for Eric, Bruce came along, and I think it really helped, because they really bonded and became really good friends. I think that helped Eric to cope with the difference between "having" and "wanting." When you want something, you think the best of it. But when you have it, it comes with the pimples. You've heard people say it—"Be careful what you wish for." You know the *Twilight Zone* episode, where the guy wishes for that girl's love, and now, she won't leave him alone. And now, the guy wants to kill himself. [Laughs]

MARK ADELMAN: I remember it being a lot more calm than I thought touring with them would be. Like, instead of going back to the hotel at night and getting drunk, we'd be wondering what kind of soup they were serving and if room service was still open. It was more like a traveling group of shoe-salesmen than rock stars.

When I was there, it wasn't [as wild on tour with Kiss than is usually portrayed]. There was always girls, but whether or not you'd actually want to be with them is another story. I mean, there was always one member of the band—I won't mention his name, [because] I'm sure everybody knows who—he was always the one that was most interested in the big, fat, ugly ones. But it was pretty laid back and mellow. We all had girlfriends back home. It was a business.

I remember off tour, Eric would always be at my house, and we'd go out and hang out together in the Village. We would just drink a little too much. It was just fun, because at that point, Kiss was kind of being revitalized, and he was enjoying some "rock star adulation." It was kind of a revitalization.

BOB KULICK: The difference between a band wearing make-up and putting on a show compared to a band where the make-up was gone and they tried to be more musical is really like comparing apples and oranges. To say, "Well, my brother's a better guitar player than Ace," well, fair enough. But it never was a contest of better or worse. It was a contest of who was more entertaining. Each band had their own thing. Obviously, the original band with the make-up and the fire and the brimstone, what can you say? As a spectacle, few could rival that. As a band—whether it was Eric Carr and my brother or Eric Singer—was a superior *playing* band, a superior *musical* band. It was a band that could compete better with what was going on at that time. Just like when someone says, "Who's better, you or your brother?" There isn't a "better." It's a "different." I never viewed it as a better or worse. You may do that with a baseball player—"Well, his stats are better." It's hard to judge with a guitar player. "Did what you play affect that person?" "Yes, they were emotionally touched." "Well, no different than when he did it." "Right. Well, so what's the difference?"

1985

AJ PERO: I knew Eric for years. The first time we met, we looked at each other, and we almost resembled each other. We hit it off, and people would come up to us, look at Eric, and look at me, and sometimes, we would goof around and say, "No, *he's* Eric Carr!" And I would say, "No, *I'm* Eric Carr!" We would fuck around like that, and people would believe us. It had to be in the early '80s. I was a Ludwig endorser, and he was a Ludwig endorser. We met at a couple of the functions and really became friends about '85. I was doing a demonstration for Ludwig at the NAMM show, and Eric came down. One thing about Eric, I don't know if he was shy, but he wasn't aggressive. Like, I was very aggressive—I was the loudmouth. We hung out, we had a lot of dinners together, [and] we went out to clubs together. We've always been tight.

Sometimes, you come across people in big bands, and they're a little bit above what they feel than anybody else. Me? Yeah, I'm in Twisted, I've always been respected, but [I] never became big-headed. And that's the way Eric was. He was in Kiss, but he never would say, *"You know who I am?"* Where you get a lot of these groups that they go into a place, and it's like, "Hey, do you know who I am? I can do anything I want!" Where me and him always tried to be laid-back, didn't try to make a big scene. We just wanted to have a good time and hang out, and if people approached us, we were very approachable. We always kept in touch with each other, and we would always talk shop. He would always ask me about certain things that I did, like, "How the fuck do you do that?" And I would say to him, "It's just like this thing."

I always asked him, "When you play with the guys, do they let you shine, or do they try and hold you back a little bit?" And he didn't really want to get into it, but I could tell that maybe he was. Just like with Twisted—I was hired to do a certain job. I was brought up with jazz and big band, I played prog metal. At 14/15 years old, I was playing Rush, Emerson Lake & Palmer, Yes. But then when I joined Twisted, I had to do the "AC/DC thing." Which was not bad, but the thing is, a lot of times, drummers don't see the talent that other drummers have, because they're not able to show it. At the clinics, I was able to show it, and Eric saw me perform. He came up to me and said, "Dude ... *wow!* I know you have to play a certain way on the albums, but shit, you're a monster!" That was that mutual respect that we always had. And as a person, great guy. He'd give you the shirt off his back. He would call me, and we would just talk about stupid things. It was a cool thing, to have a friend like Eric Carr.

We were doing a table-type thing [at NAMM]. He complimented me on my sneakers—I was wearing Converse. I'm talking, not paying attention, and he puts matches in the eyelets of the sneakers, lights them up, and all of a sudden, I go, *"WOOOOOW!"* I thought he was going go to pee himself. But I got him back later that night. He had this leather jacket, a very thin leather jacket. At that time, I was a lot bigger. I was working out, very muscular. I put his jacket on and said, "Wow, this is a nice jacket, Eric." He goes, "It fit you?" And I go, "Not really." I did a flex, and I split the whole back of his jacket! He says, "That's a $500 jacket!" I said, "Well ... *bill me.*"

We were at the NAMM show, so Ludwig puts us up in this hotel and tells us that, on the top floor, in the restaurant, they're having this big to-do. Eric meets me in the lobby, and we're both "rocked out." My hair is down to my ass, as is his. I've got my cut-off Twisted Sister jacket on. We get into an elevator, and there's a couple of like "surfer boys" in the elevator, snickering and laughing. I said to one guy, "Is there a problem?" The guy goes, "You look familiar," and Eric says, "Yeah, I'm AJ Pero from Twisted Sister." "Oh shit ... Twisted Sister!" And I go, "I'm Eric Carr from Kiss." They got out, we got to the top floor, we got out of the elevator, we looked at each other, and we bust out laughing.

NEIL ZLOZOWER: I think I did the *Creatures of the Night* reissue. That was at my studio. Bruce was in the band at that point.

BRUCE KULICK: The record company wanted to cash in on the fact that, suddenly, the band was selling a ton of records. And it made sense to get the make-up thing off of there and show the "new band." I had no say in the matter, and I understood that some fans would see it as sacrilege, but it was just a marketing thing. It was just like when somebody has a hit song, and it wasn't on their last record—because they did a soundtrack or something—and suddenly, that thing goes through the roof. You throw it on the last record, so people will buy that.

NEIL ZLOZOWER: I remember they came to my studio [for the *Creatures* reissue album cover photo], and if I remember correctly, drummers always come first to the session. Drummers are usually the low man on the totem pole. On stage, they always sit in the back—you don't see much of them. Being a photographer in the photo pit, the angle that you shoot at, the drummer is so high that, sometimes, you don't even see their head. Because you're at such an angle, you may see their bass drums and cymbals, but especially Kiss, the drummer is so high you can barely even see them.

I think I remember Eric showed up first, and drummers are always like ... you don't need as many shots of drummers as the singer or the guitarist. Especially with Kiss, you've got Gene and Paul, and then their guitarist is next. Bruce was a little bit lower man on the totem pole, even though I love Bruce, and he's a good, close friend of mine. So the drummers always show up early, and you don't really need that many [shots] of the drummer. But when you're done shooting, they're like, "Hey Neil, can we do this? Can we do that?" And I think Eric was the same way. He was sort of like hoping that I shot more photos of him than I really needed. And I tried to oblige. Gene and Paul are really nice people. I really like bagging on them—they're really easy to bag on, 'cause sometimes they're just so arrogant. Those are the people I really like bagging on more than anybody. So I did a good job of bagging on them, I'm sure.

BRUCE KULICK: All I can think of, it was so thrilling [the recording of *Asylum*]. I recorded a few years earlier a record for Michael Bolton at Electric Lady. That's just such a magical place, although Jimi Hendrix barely got a chance to use it. But the point is, he built it. It was like just kind of special to be there. We worked our asses off. It was great being there on Eighth Street at that time. Good vibe there. I remember, back then, it was still kind of "rock n' roll." I don't think it is anymore. There were a lot of cool clothing shops, and it was just the Village, which is so iconic. It was great. Eric hung around, even though you usually do the drums first. I have some cool pictures from that era. For me, it was kind of funny, because Gene and Paul didn't always have to be there at the same times, so they'd pass me off. So, sometimes, I'd be working three weeks in a row. But it's like, why would I be complaining? I'm in Kiss, doing what I love—playing guitar.

LORETTA CARAVELLO: "King of the Mountain" was one of his favorite songs. On "King of the Mountain," he excelled. The sound he was getting on that, he thought it was similar to *Creatures*.

MARK SLAUGHTER: When Bruce Kulick was in the band, I love the drums on [those albums]. I'd say more *Asylum* was probably the one that I was really into, because they had more [of] a harder edge to it. Eric had a thing where he would play a backbeat also. He'd play straight four/four time. The best way I can describe it is kind of like how Charlie Watts and how he would skip that one/two. On two and four, he would actually lift up on the hi-hat, and that's part of his drumming style. What Eric would do is he would go one/two, and on the two and the four, he would actually double it with his floor tom. And that was a really cool thing, because there's a really good, huge bottom. He was really one of the only drummers I saw who consciously did that throughout the set, to give it a bigger sound.

BOB GRAW: Very over-produced. I know Paul Stanley and Gene Simmons produced that album, and I think Gene's head was not really there. He was doing a movie at the time. Whatever the case was, the sound on that album I still think to this day is awful. It got cleaned up a little bit better when it was remastered. But it was very polished and poppy. The whole highlight of that album is the opening track, which is Eric Carr's drum solo opening up that album and going into "King of the Mountain." That was really the highlight of the album. Everybody will say, "'Tears Are Falling' is the highlight of that album," because they just beat that song to death on MTV. Great song, but very polished and poppy-sounding. It's an OK Kiss album, [but] it's by far not their best album.

BRUCE KULICK: Certainly, by the time we got the artwork all done, which I thought was kind of like pop art, which probably didn't go over that well with everybody. But I liked the record. I thought there were some really good songs. But, for some reason, it just didn't have a hit that "Heavens on Fire" or "Lick It Up" was able to do for the band.

CHRISTINA HARRISON: We're still kind of on the fence whether Bruce and I met in '84 or '85. I was modeling then, and a model asked me to go to a party at Peppy Castro's house. He was a jingle writer. I met Bruce at the party ... but I wasn't into guys with long hair at all—that's another story. But we started dating rather quickly. Then I know that Bruce took me to SIR Studios, and they were rehearsing for a tour. I think it might have been *Asylum*. So he took me to SIR, and he was introducing me to everyone. And this I clearly remember like it was yesterday. He said, "This is Eric." And Eric was standing up, he whirled around, and he was literally—as we're meeting and shaking hands—spraying Aqua Net in his hair. And he's spraying it continuously in a big circle around his head. I just thought he was the cutest happy-go-lucky guy I'd ever met in my life. Little did I know that he had the darker side, too. But he really was a happy-go-lucky guy, and he was nicest out of all the guys. He was super-friendly to me. You just wanted to hug him.

WAYNE SHARP: I was still working my way through college, and I got to know the band from those shows [on the *Creatures* tour] and got to work with Howard's office. Didn't really have a whole lot to do with Howard. But Roseanne Shelnutt, who was his marketing person, I got to know her. And then they started to tell me about this other pop band that they were managing that was based out of L.A. called Candy. I really fell in love with that band, too, and we made a deal with Howard to bring Candy to New Orleans for a month, to get them out of L.A., before they released their record, so they could get some more live experience outside of L.A. And then what happened was when I graduated from college ... during that time, I got to spend more time with Howard, especially with the Candy stuff. He always said to me, "When you're done with school, if you ever want a job, give me a call." So when I graduated from college, I called him. I saw a full-page ad in *Billboard* for the tour that the band was getting ready to do. So

I called Howard and said, "I see that you've got a tour going out with Kiss. I'm finished with school. I'd love to know if you were serious about that job." And he said, "Absolutely. I'm going to put you on the road with Kiss." This was for the *Asylum* tour. "And then, when you're done with that, by that time, Candy's record will be out, and you can be the day-to-day manager for Candy." So that was pretty much it. That tour started in Little Rock, but it went to New York for like a week before. They were still doing some photo shoots and some other stuff. We met up with the band at LaGuardia and flew to Little Rock, and they did some dress rehearsals for the tour.

BRUCE KULICK: Usually, bands of that era, the band thinks about what they want to do [fashion wise], but we had help with a clothing designer and somebody who could actually get someone to make certain things. So when you see some outrageous thing that Paul's wearing, he didn't buy it at the local shop!

WAYNE SHARP: [The costumes] was pretty ridiculous. But I was 21, and it was my first time being in management and being on the road. And plus, I was a huge Kiss fan, so anything they did would have been fine for me. But the costumes ... I remember in Little Rock, one of the things I had to do was arrange for this cape [to arrive] that Gene was going to wear for the bass solo on the tour, that they had made by a costume maker in Los Angeles. And the thing came in this gigantic box. It was *huge*. It was this gigantic silver cape that had lights sewn into it, these crazy lights that would flicker on and off and do patterns. It needed so much power that you couldn't run it off batteries. It had to be plugged in! And it had to weigh at least 50 pounds. I'll never forget, he put that thing on, the stage lights are off, and the cape lights are going on and off. And then when the lights went on, Gene's standing there with his arms crossed—you know that look he does—he's looking around, and then he just starts cracking up, laughing. He was laughing his ass off. And then he threw the cape off, did his solo, and that was it. That was the one and only time he wore that thing in concert.

But those costumes were so bad, and I wasn't quite sure at the time whether they knew they were bad or not. I mean, Paul's wasn't that bad, for the time. Gene's was horrible, and I'm sure he would be the first to admit it. We had a lot of fun in the dressing room before the show, especially with Eric. They would say Gene looked like Lainie Kazan, and he would put on his "Lainie Kazan costume." And Eric had these crazy, neon-colored unitards that were painted and stuff. That's pretty much all he wore. That and I think he wore like boxer shoes to play in ... and his gigantic hair. But some of the best times on that tour for me, besides the shows, was when they were getting ready, because they would sit in the dressing rooms, and it was hilarious the jokes that they would tell amongst each other. Those guys have great senses of humor. And Eric was ... Gene used to call him his "little buddy." And his other nickname was "Bud Carr Rooney." That was like his alter-ego.

On that tour, when we went into cities where the attendance numbers were pretty low, Gene and Paul would start teasing Eric. One city we were at, we were staying at like a Fairmont, and at the showroom at the Fairmont Hotel was the Platters, but it was "Buck Ram's Platters." I don't even know if Buck Ram was an original member of the Platters or not, but he was like the only guy, and everybody else was sidemen that he hired, and he would do Platters songs. So the joke became in cities where attendance was bad, they'd be like, "Eric, a couple of years from now, it's going to be 'Appearing at the Holiday Inn ... *Eric Carr's* Kiss!'"

MARK ADELMAN: There was definitely a drop in record sales, [and] there was a drop in ticket sales. The business at that point was changing, and music of that ilk was just not as popular as it was. We had a big attraction that Kiss is unmasked [on the previous two tours], so a lot of people came to see that. But it was a little more difficult on the next run, as one would expect for a band that's been around for 20 years at that point.

BRUCE KULICK: The attendance dropped, and that was very disappointing for the guys. And when they're disappointed, everybody's going to suffer. So, suddenly, you don't have as big a crew, or we're trying to look at ways to keep the cost down of the tour. We had a bus instead of flying everywhere. I still knew that, as much as it might not have been the news that we all wanted, we were still playing arenas, rocking out, and the fans are digging us. And my attitude was I didn't know how long I'd be in Kiss for. I thought, "Maybe the band will be around for five years." Not necessarily I'd be there for twelve, and then they'd go on for another gazillion years. It's crazy. Remarkable.

SCOTT DAGGETT: I was living in Chicago at the time, and I got a call from a company called DV Sound, which is a concert-touring sound company. And a friend of mine was out with Kiss and had worked for them for a while, and they lost or fired their drum tech. At the time, I think I was 19 or 20. They gave me a call, and it was the first national act I had gotten a chance to do, so, of course, I jumped at the opportunity. At the time, I didn't know much about Kiss, and I didn't know anything about Eric. I got to look at the drum set, and to this day—I just finished up with Limp Bizkit—I've never seen a drum kit that big. *Ever.* In hindsight, it was a great way for me to get initiated into "the club," but man, that kit was huge. At first, I was very nervous. But Eric calmed me down. We became fast friends. The initial impression was I was intimidated by the size of the band, by the arenas and things like that. But real quick, I got adjusted. The crew guys were something else. It was an incredible bunch of guys.

I got to know Bruce and Eric the best. Eric had unbelievable wit, and [he was] just a funny motherfucker. Besides the size of the drum kit, every drum was triggered. So I would spend a good portion of the day just getting that kit up, and then literally, right up until showtime, I was tweaking the electronics on it. So our relationship, probably after the first two months or so of *Asylum*, we started becoming friends. We spent an awful lot of time discussing his solo and how we were going to change it for [future tours]. We went to the Ludwig factory. He'd pay me to go with him to the factory, and we'd talk about different kits. Eric's drum set, for every one bass drum, they used two normal bass drums, so you can imagine, with three kick drums, there were six bass drums used. He was a big client of theirs. It was an awfully big custom kit.

JAIME ST. JAMES: I forget what booking agency we were with at the time, but they said, "You're up for this Kiss tour. We're going to try and get this for you." The year before, we were touring with Aerosmith, and that was great. I thought, "If I'm going to get the Kiss tour on back of this thing, I'm a happy guy." I'm very fortunate we got half the tour. I think W.A.S.P. did the last half, and we did the first half. For me, it was a brilliant thing in my life—"I just opened for Aerosmith ... and now Kiss? This is crazy for me!" It was a lot of fun, particularly for me, because I would sit out in the arena, watching Kiss do their soundcheck during the afternoon. Paul would always get on the mic and say, "OK Jaime, what do you want to hear?" And I could name *any* Kiss song I'd want. I'd say, "I want to hear 'Got to Choose.'" And they'd play it, as far as they could go with it. I always remember Eric would go, "I don't know that one!" And the last night of the tour that we were on it, Paul goes, "Hey Jaime, I got one for you," and they started playing a song by Black N' Blue, called "Rockin' on Heaven's Door."

SCOTT DAGGETT: A couple of times we had verbal fights, usually problems with the drums. One night, when I first got to the band, Eric had these ... on stage left and stage right, above the drum kit, we had special cymbal stands made to hold these ... they were called Simmons pads at the time. They're electronic drums, and in the middle of his drum solo, he had these power chords inside of them, and he would play a song and play the kit behind that song. Anyway, they were very top-heavy. If you've seen any pictures of the old kit, they were a pain in the ass, and I was always worried about them.

Back in the days before they had these metal drum risers that you could actually weld the drum kit down to, I used to nail his kit to the riser. I was that paranoid about stuff moving and falling down. Knowing that, a couple of the guys on the crew sabotaged me one night. I forget what arena—it was a big show—and Eric gets up ... it was real dramatic. He had this little box [that] they custom-made it to fit next to the right kick drum foot pedal. It was probably close to a foot in height. And, after the solo, Eric would jump on the two bass drums, stand up, and hold his sticks up. But he used that box as sort of a springboard.

That night, we get to the drum solo, and there's three stands to hold six pads. And he starts out on the right side—boom! And, sure enough, at the swivel point where those pads were, they fell down. So I'm freaking out. And then the next pads, as soon as he hits them, they fall down. The third set of pads, they fall down. I'm sure the [tour's] carpenter—I knew later, [that] he's the guy who did it—must have been peeing in his pants, laughing so hard. But it sure wasn't funny up there, and it was really not funny to Eric. He was very pissed about that. He knew it was someone in our crew, just by the way it happened. It wasn't an accident. So the next night, and for about five or six shows after that, he would call in the head of security for the tour, which was one of the band's employees, and have two guards posted on the drum riser before the show, to let everyone know that he was pissed about it.

JAIME ST. JAMES: It was a great time of my life. Our *Without Love* album was a killer record. It's one that a lot of the fans really like a lot. This is going to bring me to an Eric Carr story. I don't even remember what city we were in, but it was during the day, backstage in one of the big arenas. I was hanging out, talking with Eric, and I was actually showing him how to spin his sticks, because he didn't know how to! He goes, "I don't know how to do that. I've never tried." So I go, "Well, let me now show you how to do it." So I was teaching him how to spin his sticks, and this little kid and his mom come walking up. They say, "Can you take a picture with us?" And Eric goes, "Let me see your camera." He grabs the kid's camera and throws it on the ground—smashed it! I'm going, "Where are we going with this? What just happened here?" Eric goes, "That camera sucks," and Eric pulls out of his bag his camera, and gave it to the kid. He says, *"That's a camera!"* He literally gave this kid a camera that was probably ten times as much as the one the kid had. That's the kind of guy he was, such a nice guy.

CHRISTINA HARRISON: I wasn't a rock n' roll fan. I was more into Sting. But it was exciting for me, a kid from Michigan. I remember the first time I went to Madison Square Garden [to see Kiss on December 16], I was sitting with all the parents and girlfriends. It was usually stage right. And [I] was sitting there by myself, and one of the security guards came to get me and said, "Bruce wants to see you." We were just dating then. So they took me backstage, and it was super-exciting. I'm thinking, "Oh my God ... what happened that Bruce would need to see me before a show?" And all that Bruce wanted was for me to help him with his hair. [Laughs] I helped him tease the back, and Eric was probably spraying his hair with Aqua Net ... or in the bathroom, one of the two, because he had a little nervous stomach before the show. But he was hyped up and happy all the time. I just thought, "Oh my God, I'm backstage, and they're getting ready for this big show." You can't get bigger than Madison Square Garden. It was so cool. Gene and Paul were always in the "Zen moment." They were more serious, and Eric was just so bubbly and friendly all the time.

BOB GRAW: December 1985—Kiss at Madison Square Garden, with Black N' Blue opening up. I was happy in the way that it was the biggest Kiss show I had seen, as far as a lot of pyro and the Kiss sign they used was the size of a small town. The logo would change colors every song. It was just enormous. But I remember their costumes were atrocious. They looked like they should be a lounge act in Vegas. It was all sparkly. And I remember Gene wore a wig on that tour. It was just awful. I've heard him say that he "looked like Phyllis Diller's sister" a couple of times in interviews. And I remember Paul Stanley with the sequins ... *oh God.* It was not their finest moment. Like I said, I'm happy that they stayed relevant and stayed current, and "Uh! All Night" was a hit for them also off of that album. They did what they had to do. Those albums probably could have been Paul Stanley solo albums, because he did most of the "heavy lifting."

JAIME ST. JAMES: [The Madison Square Garden show] was *huge.* I actually met Gene and Paul's moms at that show. I always remember Gene's mom looked at me and said, "Which one of you is 'Black,' and which one of you is 'Blue?'" Gene goes, "It doesn't work that way, mom." But to play Madison Square Garden was pretty killer, especially because there was some New York paper that came out the next day it seemed, or maybe it was that weekend, and I was on the cover of it. It was a great shot of me. I don't have a copy of it—I wish I did, it's really cool. But yeah, Madison Square Garden ... come on, that was huge, opening for Kiss. I remember Gene said, "Hey, nobody threw chairs at you. You guys did alright!"

JACK SAWYERS: The second time [Jack talked to Eric] was the *Asylum* tour. When the buses got there, we were early, so we were hanging around, standing around, and Eric and Bruce and all these guys come off the bus. So Eric sees me and totally recognizes me. He recognized a lot of people from a lot of different places. He would know faces and names. So, at that point, he was like, "Come on in," so we went in before the show, and he was showing us them setting up the stuff. He got us those little patches to wear on our legs, and we were walking around for about an hour. It was pretty cool. And then he had to go, and we went back around front. Then the show went on, and then after the show, we could get backstage with those after-show passes. We went back, hung out, and talked to everybody, got to meet the band. I think that was the first time I ever met Bruce, was at that show.

CARMINE APPICE: I met Eric on tour, when King Kobra opened for Kiss. But I think I met him before the tour. I was involved with Aucoin Management. This guy, Alan Miller, who was the president of Aucoin Management on the west coast, he was my manager for many years. So he was well-tied-in with Aucoin and Kiss. That's how we got to go on tour with Kiss in '86. Living in L.A. and Kiss being in L.A., I ran into Kiss members. I'm sure I ran into Eric somewhere, maybe even at a Ludwig event. But I remember hanging out with him on tour on the King Kobra/Kiss tour. He was playing Ludwig at the time, and I was playing Pearl. I had been a Ludwig guy for a long time. He was a really cool guy, a nice guy. A good drummer. I really liked the way he played. Kiss seemed to be doing fine with Eric.

SCOTT DAGGETT: Eric was the first heavy metal drummer to incorporate electronic drums into his live solo. And that was just his own creativity. He started thinking about it with I think the album before it [*Animalize*]. At any rate, he got hip to that—the technology—by one of his acquaintances at Electric Lady in New York. At the time we were doing it, it was so new that there were all kinds of problems and things that we had to get over, like triggering on those pads. Which is nothing today, but we had some trigger problems, and we had shows where he'd hit it, and nothing would happen. But, yeah, he was absolutely [the first]. And if you notice, so many drummers came in after that, and to this day, they're still using that idea of playing some toms and some chords and then playing a kit behind it. It's used a lot, and that absolutely came from Eric Carr. He was a very creative guy.

BRUCE KULICK: He was definitely one of the first [heavy metal drummers to use electronic drums in his drum solo]. He embraced it and incorporated it into his big solo moment, with lasers and everything. And it was exciting. I thought it was very musical. He wanted to get into, "What if we sample this? What if we trigger this?" I loved that he was trying to be creative and take it to another level. I mean, was Kiss going to spend the money like Mötley Crüe did for Tommy Lee with a hydraulic system? No, and that was done already. But I thought that was great.

ADAM MITCHELL: As you can imagine, I saw countless Kiss shows. To me, Eric's drum solo was always absolutely the highlight of the show. In many respects, Eric Carr was the quintessential Kiss drummer.

MARK ADELMAN: He had a great drum solo. I remember watching him, going, "How does he do that?" I wasn't really even sure about the electronics, because there was always sounds happening when he wasn't hitting. It was kind of at the beginning of electronic additions to drum kits. He was a master. He was just a great player.

CARMINE APPICE: I remember it was a good solo, and he had a lot of drums. I'm not sure about the synth pad thing [regarding if Eric was the first metal drummer to use synth pads in his solo], because I was using something called Synsonic since 1978. Those were like synthesized drums.

MIKE PORTNOY: His drum solo was very different to Peter's, because he was a better player. Whereas Peter's was a lot of flash and single bass drumming, Eric's was way more technically advanced and didn't rely on flash. It relied on the drumming itself. He had these huge, long-kick drums, and he was playing double bass patterns that I hadn't seen many drummers play at that point. He was a "drummer's drummer" in terms of Kiss. Peter was more of a character—and I say that with all due respect, because I grew up on that era—but it was Eric that was more of a drummer than a character.

MARK SLAUGHTER: Eric Carr's drum solo was one of the best drum solos, because he integrated melody with drums. And he did it by the samples of the Simmons pads in the early years and changed it around over time. It was really cool, because he would play as if he would play those hits or power chords along with the drum solo. It was cool, because I saw Eric Carr as "that drummer" in the very beginning.

BOBBY BLOTZER: I met him on several occasions. He was a hell of a nice guy. He respected me; I respected him. The first time I met him was at the Limelight in New York City. It was funny, because he made a comment to me that I thought was really weird. He goes, "I can't believe I'm standing here partying with the drummer of Ratt." I go, "Dude, I was just thinking the same thing. I couldn't believe I was standing there partying with the drummer of Kiss!"

GERRI MILLER: The first time [Gerri met Eric] must have been one of the shows. I saw so many, though, I really couldn't pin-point. It probably was in the New York area. He was always really nice, really fun, in a good mood most of the time. I don't think I ever saw him in a snit or anything like that. He always had a smile on his face and friendly. And nice words for everybody. It was pretty much the backstage type of thing or at a show afterwards, that kind of situation. And the studio occasionally, while they were recording or rehearsing. We didn't go out to dinner ourselves or anything, but we did sometimes speak on the phone, just us.

   Kiss was on the cover [of *Metal Edge* magazine] more than anybody during that period. Every time there was a new album or a tour was starting, there was something. And then we often did special issues focusing on the drummers or the guitarists or whatever, so he was always in the drummer one. I think I did six of them [special Kiss/*Metal Edge* issues], but not only all in the '80s. We always did one for the tour. They were very cooperative with us, as far as access. Went to video shoots, went backstage, got phone interviews for updates, [and] they would give us stuff for giveaways. It was a pretty good relationship. They had a good relationship with our publisher— it was very beneficial to both sides.

WAYNE SHARP: I guess the other reason Gene would sometimes call him his "little buddy" was because, remember those My Buddy dolls? Eric went out and actually bought one, and he would take it around with him on tour, just for fun and laughs. And I guess that was part of Gene calling him his buddy, because he had a My Buddy doll. It was this creepy little doll, this little boy with a baseball cap. I remember another time, Eric got these crazy slippers in one of the airports we were in, that were like giant dinosaur feet, and they made sound, too. He'd be walking around in the dressing room with them on.

JAIME ST. JAMES: They're not a party band. That doesn't happen. Paul might have a little whiskey in his coffee afterwards or something, but that's about the extent of it. We were the "party guys." We had a good time. We had fun. Basically, Kiss was like Elvis. After the show, they're gone. Boom, *done.* Jump in something, they're out, and you never see them.

WAYNE SHARP: We used to go bowling a lot on that tour on nights off. I just remembered how much he liked to laugh and how much he liked to make Gene laugh.

NEIL ZLOZOWER: As far as being wild, I would say the other bands in their "off-stage antics" were a billion times wilder than Kiss. I mean, Kiss, they don't do drugs. Gene has never had a sip of alcohol in his life; he's got *his* vices. Once the band was off stage, it wasn't like, "Hey Zloz, let's get a drink! Let's go get some drugs! Hey Zloz, there's five hot girls. Go get them, and let's all go fuck them!" It wasn't like that at all with Kiss. But [it] was like that with Van Halen, Mötley Crüe, Poison, Ratt, and Guns N' Roses. It was just a different type. The audience scene was obviously pretty wild for Kiss shows, but there wasn't really after-show parties, debauchery, or human degradation. It was just a whole different type of vibe.

Back in those days, when you were on tour with Kiss, it was sort of like in a way being on tour with Michael Jackson. You had to know what to do, what not to do, what to say, what not to say. Now, they know me, so they see me bringing five girls to my hotel room, or they see me drunk after a show, they know what to expect from the Zloz. I've got a 35-year relationship with those guys. I don't tippy-toe around them anymore, and they know what I say to them. I had to thrash one or two of them a couple of times here and there, but I actually really like the guys a lot. Gene's one of my idols in life. Sometimes, I hate him, and other times, I just love him, like people like Carroll Shelby or Howard Hughes or Stirling Moss, people that mean a lot to me. Sometimes, I'll see him with Shannon, and he'll be like, "Neil, are you married again?" and then I like to gas him up, "Oh yeah, I got married a couple of weeks ago." "Neil, 50%, *don't do it!*" And then I look at Shannon, and I'm like, "Shannon, what's wrong with this guy?" He's funny. I love Gene, and I love Paul.

SCOTT DAGGETT: They were partiers. The odd thing about this band is Gene and Paul didn't do any drugs at all. But they were very much into pussy. One night, we were in I believe it was Pittsburgh. But during the soundcheck, the band—literally—blew out the electricity in about a quarter of the downtown area. One of the transformers at the arena blew. It resulted in a cancelled show, so everyone's feeling pretty good about not having to work that night. By that time, my usual routine was to load up the drums and head to the hotel that Eric was at, because the crew had stayed at a different hotel. So I go over, I call him, and he says come up to this room. I get up in the room, and Chris Lendt's assistant was there, Bruce was there, Eric was there, I think the tour manager at the time was up there, and a couple of others hangers-on, and this one girl.

This girl from *Hustler* magazine—she was the "Hustler Pin-Up of the Year." Gorgeous girl. So anyway, she's laying down and laughing, and guys are taking pictures of her. She wasn't naked. This chick had been following the band around for probably a month and a half at that time, literally, every show. She was a fan. I said, "Eric, make her fuck me." And he said, "No man! You've got to do that shit on your own. I'm not going to do that for you." I dismissed it and didn't hit up on her. As the room was emptying out, Kulick came up to me and said, "Scott, this one's for you ... you owe me." I start walking out, and that girl taps me on the shoulder and says, *"You stay here."* Well, you can take it from there. But, yeah, as far as partying with the girls and having a good time, Eric was ... if anyone wasn't going to be doing that, it was him, because of this girl he was seeing at the time. He was kind of over all that shit. He was looking at a new direction for his life at that time.

WAYNE SHARP: Theresa was Eric's girlfriend during that tour that I was on. She was always with him during that tour, and he was madly in love with her. She definitely broke his heart, because she broke up with him to go out with Steven Adler. She was married to David Gahan from Depeche Mode. She's a life coach out here in L.A. That's the other thing. Eric was such a romantic. When he fell in love, man, I just remember him *falling in love* with Theresa, and he was just so crazy about her.

AJ PERO: We hung out and talked about the whole thing with Kiss, how he was always treated like a second-class citizen. And I always talked about Twisted, and when I got in the band, I was the fifth drummer. I was always accepted, but there was always that air of like they were together, and I stepped in. So we kind of had that thing in common, and we joked a lot about it.

CHRISTINA HARRISON: Eric and Bruce were in much more of an "employee" role. Employer/employee. I'm sure you know that whole story. Eric was in the band longer, but I think they were still in the "appreciative mode." I know Bruce loved his job. Bruce never complained about money as far as I know until years later, especially when they were doing well. They had their ups and downs. Sometimes, they'd be selling out Madison Square Garden, and then a few years later, they were doing gigs with just 3,000 people there. I know there was one year Gene and Paul very politely told Bruce, "We're going to lower your salary for one year, and then we promise we'll put it up the following year, to save money." Bruce wasn't happy about it, but Bruce is a team-player, and he said, "That's fine." And sure enough, on their word, 365 days later, they increased it, and I think they gave him a raise. But, back then, Bruce was just so happy to be in it, and I'm sure Eric was, too, because Eric I think so mentally thought that he was "a stove repairman." I know he appreciated his job. Come on, *he's in Kiss,* plus playing in Madison Square Garden. In '85/'86, he was one happy little camper.

Gene and Paul were like the "king and queen." [Laughs] And then Eric and Bruce were definitely their "loyal subjects." They were paid employees. And you know what? I'm a businesswoman, and I think if I was Gene and Paul—after the brouhaha with Ace and Peter and their drinking and their drugs, and Gene and Paul are so straight-laced—if I were them, I would have done the same thing. And I told Bruce that, when he was like, "Oh, the sky is falling, the sky is falling. One day, I won't be in Kiss." And I'm like, "Yep, *that's right*. One day you won't be. But at the same time ... it's such a good gig." If you had a band and four equal partners with Ace and Peter, and those two guys are druggies, and then you finally can get rid of them, I would have just had hired hands, too.

And, believe me, I would see Bruce's side, too. It would help with the camaraderie if you did make it all equal, but, of course, you'd have less money. So which way do you go? I get both sides. Of course, especially being with Bruce for twelve years, I understood Bruce's side more, because it really was unequal. He made a decent living, we lived in a beautiful condo. But it's funny, I remember Shannon one time—I don't know how that conversation started—but she thought that Bruce was a millionaire. I'm like, "Why would you think Bruce is a millionaire?" And she's like, "Isn't he?" I said, "No! Not by any stretch of the imagination." Of course, she's not going to talk money with Gene. So for six years, we're sharing a Honda—not that we couldn't go and buy another car, but we were thrifty, like, "Why do we need another car when I'm not working and you're always on the road?" But then there are other times where I'd go over to Paul's new house, and it has an elevator it, and it's five stories. I'd get a little jealous, to be honest. But it is what it is. I would just think positive, like, "You guys have a good gig."

1986

JAIME ST. JAMES: We played in Las Vegas with Kiss [on January 2]. W.A.S.P. was doing the tour at that time, but for some reason, W.A.S.P. was banned from Las Vegas. So they asked us to come to Las Vegas and open. So we did that, and at that show, I remember talking to Tommy and saying, "Let's go up to Gene and talk about producing the next record." Because at the time, we wanted to have a little more control than the record company did. We figured if Gene was on our side, he understands where we're coming from, so it would be a good match. So we asked him, and he said, "Yeah, I'd be a fool not to. Let's do it."

WAYNE SHARP: After the *Asylum* tour, I moved to L.A., and Bruce and I were roommates in Shannon's old apartment. Because that's when Shannon moved in with Gene—Gene bought a house. It's the same house they're still in now. But she moved in with Gene, and we rented out Shannon's house from her. Eric was looking for a place out here, but then he wound up moving into an apartment in New York. And when I got out to New York, we got to see him for lunch or dinner.

ADAM MITCHELL: Paul and I, back then in the '80s, were both single. And Paul and I used to go out a lot. In fact, at one point, we even dated roommates. Eric was living in New York most of the time, but he'd come out to L.A., and whenever he was in L.A. or I was in New York, we'd always hang out. The thing that I remember the most is just how much fun we had, how much we laughed. Because there would be times we'd be doing backgrounds in the studio if we were doing demos, and it would be hard to get through a take, because somebody would say something, and we'd just crack up.

JAIME ST. JAMES: I was up at Gene Simmons' house writing some songs once, and Eric came over. I know that Gene just loved him. He just did. He hung out with us for a little bit, and when Eric left, he said, "I just love that guy." He was like their little brother, that's the feeling that I got from Gene. He was a very sweet dude. Basically, I've always been in contact with Gene—Gene and I have done a lot of things together. I've always been close to Gene. And Eric was around, but I didn't hang out with him and stuff. I saw him when he was at Gene's.

[Gene] was a great producer. It was fun. We laughed a hell of a lot in the studio. We had a good time. He basically let us do what we do. But a lot of pre-production with Gene, and a lot of songs when I listen back to them now, have a little bit of Gene's stamp on them. They sound a bit "Gene-ish." But there's some good stuff there. And everybody thinks we ripped off "Domino" for "Nasty Nasty." "Nasty Nasty" was first. Gene ripped *us* off, and he'll freely admit it! We'll play "Nasty Nasty" live, and some jackass in the audience will yell out, "That's 'Domino!'" We were first, idiot! The standout memory that comes to mind is we wanted to put organ on a song. Anytime an organ came up, Gene would start "ice skating." It's the funniest damn thing I ever saw in my life. He goes, "It just goes with organ. I have to ice skate." So he does this little dance and starts ice skating.

SCOTT DAGGETT: I called Eric up one day, and Steve Riley—who was the drummer in W.A.S.P.—they had an important album out at the time, *Inside the Electric Circus*. He called me up, and they had done some opening shows with Kiss, and I had known Steve back from in Indiana—he was in a band called Roadmaster. Long story short, he called me up, and he wanted me to do the tour. I called up Eric, and Eric flipped. He said, "No, I'm not going to have you going to the other side." And I explained to him, "After the tour is done, I have to make money." And that's where the retainer thing came in. He paid me not to go on the road with any other bands. It was him paying me, not the band. I would spend two or three weeks at a time up at my house New York, and he would come down and visit me and my wife down in Chicago quite a bit. He wanted to get me involved. In hindsight, he talked to my wife, and she wanted me off the road. He had a company, and he put me under that umbrella—he retained me for a while—and wanted to fund a business for me, to be more or less a personal assistant for other rock n' roll artists. I would do it from home.

LORETTA CARAVELLO: He went to hear [the group Hari Kari] play, and he managed them with his company, Street Gang, which also handled [the group] New York. He also had the *Rockheads* [a cartoon]. That's how Street Gang began, and then he started to take different projects, and he managed Hari Kari, which was like a punk rock girls band. Charisse [Hari Kari's bassist] was his girlfriend. I think he started Street Gang in 1986.

BRUCE KULICK: I forget her name, Bambi or something? Or if it's not Bambi, that's another chick he had for a while there. I just remember he wanted to be involved with [Hari Kari] and tried doing some things with them. But it seemed like whenever he wanted to take a step forward, he had to take two back. It was a little frustrating for him. I was very supportive of him branching out and trying to work with other people or develop something in the same way ... which should lead us into talking about the *Rockheads*. But again, at times, I think he would hit a bit of a roadblock, where things just wouldn't work out for him. I remember when he started his own company, Street Gang Productions, he had the stationery printed up, and they had the wrong address on it, and he was really upset about it. Where I'd be upset, too ... now make it right. I know what it's like. I've had product where somebody fucks up a run of it, but just fix it. But I think with him, it was like, "Go figure. This always happens to me." That kind of thing.

LORETTA CARAVELLO: *Rockheads* was an animated cartoon creation he came up with. He started that in high school, and as the years went by, they progressed. In 1986, everything was really taking off, and he had his portfolio. That was when he was presenting it with Gene to Landmark and Hanna-Barbera, who did want it. But they wanted a little too much control for him, because those were like his babies. We actually have stories and all different kinds of drawings. It was a complete concept. It was not something that wasn't done. This whole thing, from promotional pieces to everything else, he had in his portfolio. And he had people looking at it from toy companies.

ADAM MITCHELL: We'd worked on *Rockheads*, which was a tremendous idea, which we almost got done. Hanna-Barbera was interested at one point, and there was a huge company in Toronto that was interested. We almost,

almost, almost got it done, because it was a great idea. He, Bruce, and I wrote all the songs. For one reason or another, it didn't get done. But it was a lot of fun to work on. I particularly liked working on it because it was Eric's own project. He controlled it, and it had nothing to do with Gene and Paul. It was really his baby. He had drawn the characters and had come up with the whole idea. So I was very pleased for him, because I really felt he deserved it. Unfortunately, it just never came to be. But we wrote, oh, at least four, five, maybe six songs. I can't remember.

BRUCE KULICK: I thought the *Rockheads* were brilliant. He had a real fantastic idea, extremely creative. It is hard to pitch where someone is going to invest, in those days, at least a hundred grand to make it a reality. Now, it would be like a quarter of a million dollars. And then he had Gene's help. Gene got really close with a strong contact for him. I remember Hanna-Barbera was interested. And then there was a company called Landmark Entertainment—I don't even know if they exist anymore. And I think whatever deal they offered Eric was probably very typical for a television-type animated development deal. And he just didn't like it. I had no experience in television—I understand some of that game now from some of my friends that are in the business. But back then, I couldn't help him.

I think it was a big mistake that he didn't try to take that deal. It was one of those offers where I guess he felt that he had to give up too much, where if he would have known what Mike Judge gave up for *Beavis and Butthead*, the guy who created that. So that was kind of disappointing ... but then again, maybe that was part of his personality, too, that he was afraid of the failure, and it's almost easier not to sign up and commit. I don't know. But I know it was very frustrating, because all of us were very supportive. I contributed time and effort into it. I loved the guy, so I had no problem with it. In fact, I always wanted to be busy doing other things, than just the Kiss thing. And when you're in the band, we weren't just free to go off and do whatever we wanted. So that was a really fun outlet for Eric and I. I recorded his demos. I thought he had some really catchy tunes.

ADAM MITCHELL: Eric and I had a tremendous vocal blend. My voice, as anyone's voice, doesn't necessarily blend with another singer. But Eric and I had a great vocal blend. And when it came time to do all the *Rockheads* stuff, he and I sang all the backgrounds.

BOB KULICK: It was one of those things that I don't know why it didn't happen, but I guess it was one of those other frustrations. At least he did try other things, other avenues of how to use what he had, to try to make something other than what it was. Because the guy could sing, and he could write, even though in the band structure, everybody had their "station," and his station was not that of the main writer.

BRUCE KULICK: Eric loved a couple of bands that he would refer to a lot, one being Van Halen, which of course, I loved as well. He thought Alex was a great drummer and Eddie was a great guitarist. And then he loved Metallica, too, who at the time, I wasn't really that hip to. This was before the *Black Album*. But he definitely had a lot of passion for the stuff he did like and would listen to it. We went to [Van Halen] shows a couple of times, and it was "cart blanche" for us backstage. They really liked Eric. It was very cool—they knew he was a real fan. It wasn't like, "You're just trying to meet chicks here" or something. Eric always had a lot of respect from the other groups. They knew he was really sincere and honest about who he was. Eric never came off like a poser. He might have had the iconic giant hair, but he was the real deal. I knew the Van Halen guys really liked him.

CHRISTINA HARRISON: I remember I met the lead singer from Guns N' Roses. This is before they were big. We were in L.A., walking backstage, but it was up the staircase. I remember Axl Rose saying, "Yeah, man, we're going to be huge!" His jeans were unbuttoned to pretty much his pubic hair, and I just remember thinking in my head, "Oh yeah ... *right*. What a loser!" And then fast forward a year, and they're like superstars, and they're selling out stadiums, and I'm like, "Oh my God, was that the same group?"

EDDIE TRUNK: I did radio right out of high school, and I ended up working in a record store that was right across the street from my local rock station in Jersey that I grew up with, WDHA. I had started to meet the owners of the radio station—they would come in the record store—and I just started pestering them to play music that I wasn't hearing on the station. They gave me that opportunity, and I started doing a radio show there. And that dove-tailed into the label gig, because I was playing what a lot of people consider to be one of—if not the first—hard rock/metal shows, a specialty show, on commercial radio. I was approached by a guy named Jonny Z, who owned Megaforce Records. I had gone to his flea-market store to buy records as a kid, and Jonny had this band that no one would play on the radio. And he drove the album to my show one night, knocked on the door, and said, "Hey man, I can't get arrested with this band. I need to get them on radio. Can you please help? Will you please give this a spin?" And I was like, "Well, what is it?" And it was Metallica, *Kill 'Em All*. I put that record on, and I gave him an opportunity to play it and let people hear it. And he's like, "I can't thank you enough. If I can ever get this band off the ground and get this record company off the ground, I want a guy with ears like yours to work for me." I was like, "Yeah, yeah, yeah. OK, whatever." That was it. And then, obviously, Metallica got off the ground, Jonny built the company, and he was true to his word in calling me up and saying, "Let's figure a way to get you to work over here with me." And then through the industry, I had a reputation, both on the label side and also on the radio side. So it all just came together.

I had always worked in radio, right out of high school. So I had always done a radio show, which I still do today, but at this point, in New Jersey at my local station. Eric knew a lot of the same people, and I think what happened was when I signed Ace to Megaforce—which would have been about '86/'87—Eric and Ace had a very good bond. They really had a friendship. They were only in the band for a brief time together, but I think Eric, being a young guy and new to the band, gravitated more towards Ace, who is more of the "fun party guy," obviously. Y'know, out for trouble and out to be "Mr. Rock n' Roll"—more so than Gene and Paul, who were/are all business. The one thing that I had found out is that Ace had a real love for Eric and vice versa. And it was probably through Ace that I had met him. He actually would come to rehearsals. He wanted to play in Ace's solo band, and Gene and Paul obviously weren't having it. But there was actually a day where Ace was auditioning rhythm guitar players for his band, and his drummer wasn't available, so Eric came to the rehearsal studio and played drums just to help him out.

LORETTA CARAVELLO: He was still working with Ace on stuff [after Ace left Kiss]. I know he went to his studio and recorded stuff. If it exists, hopefully one day it will come out. Ace was always good to him and encouraged him. Even Peter—he used to talk to Peter a lot. I'm not saying they were best of friends, but they really respected each other.

EDDIE TRUNK: So I got to know him through the business. We met on a number of occasions. And the other thing that had happened was that Eric never got to really do a lot of interviews. Interviews are always Gene and Paul, Gene and Paul, Gene and Paul. And whenever I did radio, I was open to and encouraged whoever was setting up the interview was to do Eric. I'd love to hear Eric's stories. And he really appreciated that. He loved the opportunity to be a more active voice in the band. So he came up and would do my radio show in Jersey at WDHA. He must have done it four or five times—he would drive out. One or two times, he came out with Gary Corbett [Kiss' subsequent touring keyboardist]. He's Italian, my mom's Italian, and I was living at home at the time. He'd stop over, my mom would cook an Italian meal, we'd have a great time, and then we'd go and do the radio show at night.

That's the thing—he was such an unassuming guy. He was in Kiss, but he never projected himself to be above anything. It was real easy with him. We really built a relationship, because he started to know me through the radio show. He knew me as a big Kiss fan. He knew me as someone that he could trust and talk to honestly about how he was feeling about things, and had his trust. I was kind of an ally of him on the business end, because he could throw things off of me, and I could give him some "Here's what I think" or "Here's what I think is going on." And he was a fan of some of the bands that I was working with at Megaforce—obviously Ace, and also King's X he was a fan of. We went to a King's X show together in L.A. We just built a friendship and a relationship through me interviewing him and him trusting me and knowing me through the business. It got to the point that we would talk regularly on the phone.

I remember the nights at the radio show when it would be freezing cold outside, and we'd leave, and there would be fans out on the front lawn, because it was in a suburban area. And he would sign and have drinks and just sit down on the front lawn, in the middle of the winter, and spend all this time with the fans. I'll never forget, one time we were doing that after the show, and this guy with this big monster truck came screaming down the highway. He was in such an effort to get to the studio to meet Eric before we were done with the interview and left, that he came rolling up off the highway—with these giant tires—right up onto the front lawn, not realizing that that's where we were all sitting. He almost wiped everybody out! We were all sitting there, and Eric's like, *"Run!"* You just see these giant headlights coming at us, and we all scattered. This guy screeched up on the front lawn and was like, "I just want to get an autograph, man!" Eric's like, "It's cool, man ... you don't have to kill everybody." That was Eric. He would sit there and take the time to sign autographs for the fans, talk to people, and get to know people. That was the type of guy he was.

BOBBY ROCK: I was touring the south and midwest with a band called Diamond Romeo. And another band on the circuit, Sweet Savage, had been coming out to the west coast, working with Dana Strum on their debut EP. So Joey C. Jones, the singer for the band, at some point, the band I was in disbanded, and I was looking forward to going out to the west coast, to have a shot out there. I contacted Joey, to see if he had any contacts or suggestions, and he said that Dana was working with Vinnie Vincent, who were putting a band together, which went on to become the Vinnie Vincent Invasion. He said I should call Dana and see if I could come out for an audition. So I, basically, from where I was living at the time—in Houston, Texas—left Dana Strum a rather brash message about how I was "the ultimate drummer for the band" and "Let me know when and where, and I'll be there." [Laughs] He and Vinnie decided to give me a shot, so I drove out to L.A. with my drums in the van and did the audition with Vinnie, Dana, and Robert Fleischman. Everything went great, and I was pretty much hired on the spot.

Vinnie, in general, had a very even-keeled kind of demeanor. I had heard some stories and some of the problems. At that point, it was kind of controversial how and why he left Kiss. But he seemed, again, very even-keeled, very friendly. I got along with him great. I thought he was very cool. He didn't really have much bad to say about Kiss. He just said it wasn't what he wanted to do. He had a different vision than what they were doing. It was all very cordial at that point.

The good news and the bad news that I say about that first Vinnie Vincent record [*The Vinnie Vincent Invasion*] is, the bad news is it was one of the most trying and difficult sessions that I've ever had to deal with. Just as far as how it went down—the pressure of it all and the lunacy that ultimately went down there. But that's also the good news, because I never in my career since had to deal with anything that treacherous. [Laughs] And I don't mean that necessarily as a criticism. The way the record was done, on the one hand, they wanted that "new, Mutt Lange, *Pyromania* type of mechanical-sounding drum vibe." They wanted that sound, but they wanted a live drummer to do it. So I think what happened was through the course of working on the record, what they would do is we had a drum machine that I was playing along with, and they would pan my drums to the right and the machine to the left, and everything I played was put under scrutiny to machines, note by note by note.

So the sessions for the first time or two that we did the record—because I ended up doing the record about three times, with no exaggeration—it became more of a game of accuracy. How *mechanical* could I play. So we ended up for the first two go-rounds emulating this mechanical thing, and it was just very arduous. It was my first major label recording, and it fucked with my head quite a bit, because I felt like I was failing them. Ultimately, when all the "brass" heard it—the manager, the label—they go, "Why did you use a machine on this? I thought you were going to go with live drums?" And then when they found out what happened, they basically sent us back to the drawing board, to do the record how we should have done it to begin with, with a click or a machine—but more of a live feel that it wound up with. Between Vinnie and Dana producing, it was a cluster-fuck. I don't want to paint a dark picture, because I don't think anybody was trying to be one way or another. It was a pretty dysfunctional band to begin with, and to endure a record like that was tough. But I'm glad to have had that experience out of the way early on.

MARK SLAUGHTER: A girlfriend didn't put the phone number on the demo tape [that Mark handed Vinnie a few years earlier]. That was the voice that Vinnie liked, and inevitably, he had Robert do the record, and inevitably, I ended up doing that tour [after Mark reconnected with Vinnie after the album's release]. It all worked out great.

BOBBY ROCK: I always liked Robert. I thought Robert was one of the better rock singers out there. We had always got along well, but it never worked out. There were business and contract issues that I never really was fully privy to. But beyond the initial sessions where I would see Robert, it was eventually decided that he was not going to be doing anything else with us besides recording. So when they brought Mark in, that was great for me, because me and Mark were the "young guys," so we immediately hit it off. We had a great brother-to-brother connection. We roomed together all of that first tour. And he had a real youthful exuberance of what he did, a very spontaneous, free-flowing vibe of his stage persona, as well as his vocals. Very fearless, you might say. It was the beginning of a life-long friendship.

MARK SLAUGHTER: Vinnie wanted a certain type of style of singer. I think Robert Fleischman was a great singer, but I don't think he was thinking about touring on an extensive basis, even when he recorded the record. Dana had contacted me in Las Vegas when I was working at a music store as a guitar teacher, and said, "Vinnie's ready. Let's do this." Basically, I put my guitar down and became a singer. So I was teaching, to all of a sudden being a frontman for Vinnie Vincent, which is obviously a part of Kiss and was a dream come true. We toured with Alice Cooper and Iron Maiden.

ADAM MITCHELL: Mark Slaughter and I are still really good friends. And Mark was part of that Vinnie Vincent Invasion. If you listen to the Vinnie Vincent Invasion record, *it's terrible.* And it bears no relation whatsoever to how Vinnie could actually play. He was just insecure, and he was trying to show everybody that he could shred. But it's terrible, it really is. But Vinnie actually is—or was—a really, really good guitar player. A really musical guy. I saw that in him, and I told Gene about it ... and I wasn't surprised when they didn't get along.

Vinnie is a perfect example of ... it's kind of like John Waite, who did a song that Vinnie and I wrote ["Tears"], and we had a big hit, and we made a lot of money. John Waite is a phenomenal singer ... but personality will defeat talent every time. John Waite is what I call "a natural singer." He has tone; he has everything. But he didn't have the career. Mark Slaughter told me just the other day, he saw John Waite playing in some little bar four streets off the strip in Las Vegas. This guy should have a career like Rod Stewart.

BOBBY ROCK: [The Vinnie Vincent Invasion's over-the-top glam look] is the kind of thing where if the record sold two million copies, then we would all would have been geniuses, because the basic concept was the band was a fairly serious band. Everybody could really play. Vinnie wanted great musicians in his band. My whole first audition was based around all this crazy drum solo shit I was doing. And, of course, Vinnie is an incredible technician, Robert was a world-class vocalist, and Dana was a really good bass player. So I think the idea was, "Here's a serious arena rock band that would appeal to the hardcore metal enthusiasts, who appreciated great playing, all the chops, and all the heavy duty arena rock shit. But now, let's combine that with what was currently going on in L.A. at that point, with bands like Poison, Mötley Crüe, and that whole glam thing." So the concept was, "Let's combine both. That will appeal to the Poison fan and the Iron Maiden fan, theoretically." And I think what wound up happening is it was always a little too heavy-edged for the Poison fan and the commercial outlets, but then the people who listened to music and liked good music were put off by the "transvestite thing." So I think we found ourselves in our weird sort of middle ground, where we alienated a lot of people that otherwise might have really dug it. An interesting thing also was Robert Fleischman was never able to embrace the whole transvestite look type thing. His thing was, "Why the fuck do we have to do this? We can really play and sing. We're not a bunch of posers." So, maybe he had a point. [Laughs] It's easy to go back, and knowing what we all know now, sure, it probably didn't serve us that well to go that extreme with it like we did.

ADAM MITCHELL: Terrible. In no way reflected the talent of the people in the band. Terrible, terrible record. Look, I knew all the people involved. Mark is one of the nicest, smartest people I've ever met in life. Mark Slaughter is really a talented guy. And Vinnie is talented. But that first record was just terrible. I mean, I knew how Vinnie could play. I sat there playing with the guy. But it was just terrible. The album is almost unlistenable. I thought, "Vinnie's doing his own record ... OK, we've had our own history, but I'm going to listen to this record," and I bought the record. *It's unlistenable.* He decided to show everybody that he could shred. It's like some thirteen year old jacking off. It is so beneath the level of his ability, it really is. Vinnie was a truly great guitar player. But as a human being ... people have questions,

OK? [Laughs] But as a guitar player, Vinnie was a real, honest-to-God talent. The fact that you look at his life history and his history with Kiss and so on, personality will rule talent. But as a guitar player, was Vinnie one of the best? Absolutely. He was a phenomenal talent. But personality will defeat talent, every time.

BOBBY ROCK: One of the things that I like to say about that [when the Vinnie Vincent Invasion broke up after their second album, 1988's *All Systems Go*] is it's kind of like that old parable about the six blind men standing around an elephant and asked to hold out their hand, touch the elephant, and describe what an elephant looks like. So the guy by the trunk says, "An elephant is long and thick like a snake." The guy by the tusks says, "An elephant is sharp and smooth like a spear." The man who stands by the side says, "An elephant is big and thick like a wall." And the man who stands by the legs says, "An elephant is like a tree trunk." The point being is that whatever their limited vantage point was or their particular bias based on where they were standing, that's what their recollection was going to be of an elephant.

    The fact is, there really is no set answer. If you talk to me, Mark, Vinnie, or Dana, we're all going to have our own perspective on what went down and what the issues were. Because there were many issues. At that point, it was three years of serious dysfunction, between band members and management and the record label and things that were going on internally with the band. Really, a lot of deep issues going on. So the short answer, from where I was sitting, it was accumulative dysfunction of several years, led to the inevitable. Where Vinnie saw things one way and thought one thing was going on, and maybe I saw things a different way than how everybody else saw things going on. It was just such a mess at that point. All you could really chalk it up to was an accumulation of all of this dysfunction over three years eventually led to us finally having to throw the towel in.

    I would say, yeah, Vinnie is difficult to work with to a certain degree. But I think he's been demonized quite a bit. There was a lot about what he did and how he did it that was very off-putting. In my opinion, I think he lacked a certain type of diplomacy that a great producer will have. The key to being a great producer—or for that matter, a great band leader—I think if you're a leader, your objective is to get the great performances out of your guys. To create an environment where everybody feels encouraged, and you could come out and speak your mind if something's not working or what you need, but there's a certain way to do it. Like Dana I thought had the knack for that, if he was expressing something in the studio. There is a certain way that people can put things to you. Not that they have to wear kid gloves, but there's just a certain way where you keep an encouraged environment happening while still getting done what you have to do. And I don't think Vinnie had that "filter." I think he would just blurt out or say whatever he felt, no matter how cutting it might be. A lot of times, that could get you overly self-conscious about things or worsen the problem that's happening. But, again, I don't think he did that intentionally. I think it was just part of the characteristics of his personality.

My experience with him is he was never intentionally a "bad person." He's definitely an eccentric character, there's no question about that. And for the most part, he and I got along really well. I never had any real issues with him as a person. I think he inherently was a nice guy. He was a good father. Him as a person, I always liked. I just thought that, in the professional realm, Vinnie needed the right kind of manager, or if George Sewitt was the right kind of manager, he really needed to place more trust in him. I thought Vinnie was the kind of artist that really needs to be managed, because he's such the proverbial "artist." And he wasn't, and as a result, there was this "loose canon thing" that would go down sometimes.

It must have been the early '90s or something [that Bobby last spoke to Vinnie]. This motherfucker just *vanished*. I've never seen anything like it. I've never heard of anybody who has legitimately had any kind of encounter with him since the mid to late '90s. I have heard no credible evidence of his existence in the last ten years, or longer. I think there might have been a few Kiss conventions that he popped out to do in the late '90s. But, basically, in the last decade, I have not heard of one sighting. [Laughs] Hopefully, the guy is still alive. I presume he is. So for that, that's impressive, to be that reclusive. I mean, how can you even do that these days with cell phones and Twitter?

1987

MARKY RAMONE: Eric Carr came to my show in New York City—he came backstage. He was a fan of mine when I was in a band called Dust, my first band, a heavy metal band. And he wanted to see the size of the sticks I used, because he was observing me from the audience. So, for some reason, he thought they were custom-made, but they weren't. They were military marching sticks that I used, which I don't anymore. But for the music I was doing, that's what I used. It wasn't the Ramones [that Eric met Marky at], it was a band that I had for a short time with the guitarist from the Plasmatics, Richie Stotts, called King Flux. Two of the guys were Tommy Hilfiger's brothers. We played at I think Irving Plaza or the Cat Club in New York City, and Eric came backstage with Little Steven Van Zandt and Michael Monroe. So he came backstage and said, "How do you play with those things?" I go, "Here," and he tried them. He goes, "I could never do that." I go, "Exercise. It's like a form of exercise." He was intrigued by that.

BRUCE KULICK: There we go once again [regarding the 1987 home video, *Exposed*]. Now, I'm not in the band that long to expect that I'm going to be featured equally like Gene and Paul. You've got to remember that videotapes and those long-form kind of things were a very new kind of a way for a band to promote themselves. But we weren't written in the script much. It was pretty pathetic. Again, I didn't expect much anyway, but Eric certainly felt like, "Hey, I've had some tenure here. What about me? Oh, we're with the monkey ... right." So was it funny? Yeah, we had a blast. We're up in Beverly Hills with a lot of naked women running around. I'm not saying we were partaking, but you know what I mean. Because it was like a crazy comedy/reality tape, pre-reality shows.

But I'm glad I had my camera. I grabbed that shot of Eric and I with the monkey. Some of the shots that I've seen, the ones from *Kisstory*, came from my camera. So we made the best of it, and I had my little silly scene, and Eric had some funny scenes. Eric would be very funny on camera. But, again, some of it was a little like, it fit more within the band's "inside jokes," not necessarily what they would want to present to the fans.   W h e n Gene and Paul present something to the fans, they're just very clever and crafted at how to do that, how to present themselves as the rock stars that they are. With Eric, it was more through humor and outrageousness. So that wouldn't always translate. But there's some YouTube stuff up there. I just saw something recently of us rehearsing for a Europe tour, and some French TV station is visiting us at rehearsal, and Eric is in that, being really funny. I'm playing "Forever" on the acoustic for a minute, but everybody's hilarious. The way we were joking around there was very typical of us. Great times.

With [*Exposed*], you audition a bunch of people, hot chicks to be running around. But we were a rock band that it was there for the taking if you wanted it. So when I was married, I didn't "eat at the buffet." And when I wasn't ... any and all of us could have anything we wanted, as much as you wanted. That comes with the territory. Kind of like, it's good to be king!

RON NEVISON: I was pretty hot at that time. In '87, I had done two gigantic albums, with Heart [1985's *Heart*] and Ozzy [1986's *The Ultimate Sin*]. They contacted my manager. I had some history going back a little bit, only because I had talked to Paul about doing the solo album that they all did in the late '70s. Ultimately, it didn't work out for one reason or another—I don't remember if I couldn't do it or he wanted somebody else to do it. But we did get to know each other at that point. In fact, at the end of '86, I had rented this house for two weeks in Aspen for Christmas. I broke up with my girlfriend around Halloween, so I asked Paul if he wanted to share the house with me. We had a great couple of weeks up in Aspen.

BRUCE KULICK: With *Crazy Nights*, it was Ron Nevison producing, and I knew he was the "hit engineer/producer guy." He knew how to pick songs. He had some success with Heart and Ozzy [and] other people. I remember that album was done out here in L.A., and I don't remember too much about Eric with the sessions. Here was maybe my first opportunity to watch the band be produced by a popular producer—an outside person, who had a real track record—which means respect from Gene and Paul, and myself, just to see how they work. So for me, it was a learning experience. I know that he made a kind of pop record out of us.

RON NEVISON: I was never, ever a Kiss fan. I think I did a really good job on the album, but I don't have to be a fan of the group to make an album. I have to be a fan of the music that I'm doing. So I was never a "devotee," let's say. I'm older—I'm 65 right now, so I was already in my 40s. I was 42 when I did that album. I worked at One on One, Can Am, and Rumbo. The time with Eric was One on One. From '86 to '90, I used several different places to cut rock n' roll tracks—I used the Record Plant, A&M, and One on One. Can Am and Rumbo I used for overdubs and mixing. Can Am mostly overdubs, I don't think I mixed many things at Can Am. I remember working with Paul and Bruce, I don't even remember working too much with Gene. But once the bass player does his part, just like the drummer, he's finished. Except for the fact that Gene sang a couple of songs, and that Gene was always hanging around in the back of the studio reading *Variety*. [Laughs]

ADAM MITCHELL: "When Your Walls Come Down" is really a good song. "I'll Fight Hell to Hold You" I don't remember that much. The thing I remember about "Crazy Crazy Nights" was Paul and I, we were not recording in my studio by this point. We had gone in and done pretty much a full demo on "Crazy Crazy Nights," and I don't feel that in any way what ended up being the record matched what we did on the demo. Principally because when we did the background vocals—the crowd singing along—it was *huge*. I mean, the crowd really was a participant. And that was the whole point of the song. By the time Ron Nevison had mixed it and done the recording "his style," the crowd was just not a part of it. So I did not care for it at all. I know Paul didn't care for it, although he wouldn't say so at the time.

Ron is certainly a hugely talented guy. He'd come off that Heart record, "These Dreams" and all that. Tremendous record. But I never felt Ron was the right producer for Kiss. His SSL/'80s/shiny sound was not warm enough or big enough ... in spite of his talents, I just felt he was misaligned for Kiss. And I was not happy with "Crazy Crazy Nights" in particular. I think "When Your Walls Come Down" turned out much, much better. It's a constant frustration I'm sure you heard before—demos are very often much better than what finished masters turn out to be, for one reason or another. They often have more sense of abandon, they're looser, [and] there's more life in them. And "Crazy Crazy Nights" just turned out to be too studied, not in the spirit of the original. They'd written an anthem ... but it didn't sound like an anthem on the record.

RON NEVISON: Paul submitted maybe six or eight songs to me, all really good songs. There was the song "Reason to Live," which I had high hopes for as a single, because it's tough to have a single for a group like Kiss. And Gene submitted 25 songs to me—all sorts of stuff. But the difference was Paul vetted the songs, I think Gene just sent me everything he had. So there was some good stuff, some bad stuff, and some amusing stuff. There was one song that Gene sent me called "I Want to Put My Log in Your Fireplace." *That's a typical Kiss sentiment.*

BRUCE KULICK: I think with that song ["No No No," which Eric co-wrote with Bruce and Gene], he had some idea for a fast riff. I know it was Gene and I that came up with that chord stuff—the descending chords—but I think some of the other riffs might have come from Eric. I know the first demo was just like a programmed drum thing. But it was fun to work on that one and make it happen. And then when we did it live, it became a little centerpiece for me to come out of the solo from Eric.

LORETTA CARAVELLO: When "No No No" was performed live, it was amazing.

RON NEVISON: They're all so different [the artists Ron worked with over the years]. For instance, Ozzy was hardly at the studio at all when I was doing work with the guitar player. Ozzy is just the lead singer, whereas Paul is one of the guitar players. Paul was always there. Bruce was always there, Gene was pretty much always there. Ozzy, I just had one guy there—Jake E. Lee. After Randy Castillo was finished, we finished all the bass parts. So that's different. With the Who, I was not the producer. I was just the engineer, and Pete Townshend was the producer [on 1973's *Quadrophenia*]. So that was a different situation. That was 15 years before that, too. That was the early days for me, my first big album. Keith Moon was just so unique—you can't compare anybody to Keith Moon, just like you can't compare anybody to John Bonham, who I worked with, too [1975's *Physical Graffiti*]. Those were guys that were both so unique—Bonham in his power and Keith's style. When I first tried to mic up Keith's drum kit, I couldn't find a place to put the snare mic. There was no room! Two hi-hats, one on each side. He had drums all around, a gong in the back. He had everything you could have in his drum kit. *And he used it all.* [Laughs]

SCOTT DAGGETT: When we were out here in L.A., doing the *Crazy Nights* album. Eric also hired me to tech for the album. So Ron Nevison was out here, and we were all sitting around the studio one day, because Eric's tracks were "come and go." Usually, they'll send a drummer in, he'll finish his tracks in a couple of days, and that's all you'll see. But Nevison was doing it different. So we were sitting around, doing our thing, and Gene calls a meeting, for everybody. Not just the band-members, but for everyone there that is dealing with the album.

We go to the upstairs lounge—I think it was at One on One Studios—he sits everyone down and put everyone at ease at first. He says, "I just want everyone to know that my mom is coming in tomorrow." Gene is very close to his mom, his family is very dear to him. I can't say enough good things about Gene as well, but that's a different book. He said, "Having said that, is anyone going to have a problem with that?" And everyone goes quiet, what seems like a pretty long time. Eric looks up, and he goes, "So ... *blow jobs for everybody?*" The room went dead. Everyone else did not know how the fuck this was going to go over. And what seemed like another long time, Gene started laughing, and it was all good. But only Eric Carr, y'know? He was so sick, but so funny. Who's going to tell Gene Simmons that to his face? And you would walk into the dressing room before the show, and Eric was famous for getting chalkboards into the dressing rooms, which were used by pro-basketball teams in these huge arenas. And you'd see something like, "Kiss is a pile of shit. They couldn't attract flies!" "These guys suck!" Things like that. I know Gene loved him to death.

RON NEVISON: I remember his great smile, and his wonderful personality. Tremendous drummer. They surrounded themselves with greatness, and that's one of the things that made them. I think Eric and Bruce were a couple of notches up from the original guys. Ace is a great guitar player, there's no doubting that. But I think that Eric and Bruce were a couple notches better than those guys, personally. That's from a person is not a gigantic devotee of the original Kiss, so I can say that as a producer who evaluates talent.

SCOTT DAGGETT: We had some funny times just hanging out. He had a bungalow out here in L.A. when they were doing *Crazy Nights*, and rehearsals were done out here, too. There's an insane story, about the guy down the hall from him was the chauffeur in *Arthur*, Bitterman [actor Ted Ross]. Well, Eric gave me a key to his place, so I'd be able to get in there and get stuff if he wasn't around, if he needed something. At any rate, I went over one day, and he was supposed to be there. I knocked, and nobody answered, so I used the key, and it turns out that my key worked on this guy's apartment. So I unlocked it, went in, and got about halfway to the living room, and here comes that guy—the actor—with a .45, pointing straight at my fucking head! I literally peed my pants. Eric, of course, laughed 'til he cried.

BRUCE KULICK: It had a lot of real tunes. I think Paul was really in a good place, and it was maybe more of a struggle for Gene to come to the party. But it was still a really good record. I thought the album artwork was great. And I think that one, as much as the *Asylum* one might have been Paul's cover art design, *Crazy Nights* was probably Paul's, too. It was more edgy in style and I think helped. Because of Nevison, everything was good, and we had a big hit in Europe with ["Crazy Crazy Nights"], so I can't complain. I think we started to get the look together, because *Asylum* was a disaster with how we all looked. I would have imagined that Eric would have been really fighting that, that glam kind of thing, because he seemed like such an Italian/Staten Island/Queens/New Yorker kind of guy. Like, why would he put up with that? But he kind of did. All the bands were looking like women then. But we got tougher with *Crazy Nights*.

RON NEVISON: I think "Crazy Crazy Nights" was too hard for CHR radio, whereas in England [where it was a hit], it didn't matter. That's why I had "Reason to Live." In fact, I had a big hit with Ozzy, called "Shot in the Dark." I had to talk Ozzy and Sharon into doing that. They did *not* want to do that song. They thought it was too soft. I said, "Well, it's only one song on the album." And then when it was a hit, they're going, "What do we follow it up with?" And I'm thinking like, "Well ... *you don't.*" I was lucky to get that one on! You could look at it like that—"Shot in the Dark" was for Ozzy like "Reason to Live" should have been for Kiss. I think what happened was once you put out a single and it doesn't do well, the second single is almost doomed. If they come with "Reason to Live" first, like they came with "Shot in the Dark," they could have had some success.

BRUCE KULICK: For me, the lead guitars were always featured in the ways they should be, but the record does sound a little thin. And I've actually worked at the Fantasy Camp with Ron Nevison, where he kind of apologized to me! He said, "I heard the record recently, and I should have EQ'd it differently." It's kind of funny how he was making a critique of his work from back then.

RON NEVISON: I would say that it was more in the mix than anything else. I agree. The mix of it was a little too "pop." I would love to remix that album. These days, with the technology, I could make that thing *rock.*

BOB GRAW: I remember getting the 45 of "Crazy Crazy Nights." It came out before the album, I think. The video was one of those big "MTV Premieres" for the video. I remember seeing the video and saying, "Oh my God ... this is even worse than *Asylum.*" It was so poppy. And I remember reading the coming attractions for that album, that Ron Nevison was producing, who had previously produced bands like Heart. I thought, "Wow, this is going to be even fruitier than that last Kiss album." And it absolutely was. But I remember reading in *Hit Parader* or one of those magazines, Gene and Paul saying, "It's the heaviest album we've done since *Love Gun*" or whatever. And I'll never forget the day I went to my friend's house and put it on the turntable. We just sat there and were like, "What the hell is this?" It's a very poppy album. You can definitely tell that Gene had very little to do with that album.

RON NEVISON: I think it's a great album. I thought that I missed the mark a little bit on the mixing. I think I didn't mix it as heavy ... it sounds a little lightweight when I listen back to it. I think I got caught up in that late '80s thing of synthesizer too much. You have to understand, I had to drag rock stars, kicking and screaming, onto the pop charts to have big album sales. In order to do that, I had to have something that was accessible to contemporary hit radio. They called it "CHR" in those days. And I had big success doing that. Looking back on it, I probably got a little too caught up in that, and I didn't make it "rock" enough. By that, I only mean in the mix. The guitar sounds, the drums—everything is great on that album. But I think I didn't make the mix as rugged as Kiss should be. So if I can say anything about that—maybe too much of reverb and too much of the '80s kind of stuff. Not exactly typical of other things I did in the same period. I didn't miss the mark on the recording, on the vocals, and all that stuff. But I did miss the mark on the mixing.

ADAM MITCHELL: Those Def Leppard records that Mutt Lange did are absolutely brilliant, there's no question about it. I mean, Mutt Lange is a total genius, maybe the single greatest rock producer who ever lived. But that '80s sound is just not Kiss. Now, understandably, from Gene and Paul's point of view—and Paul in particular—was concerned with staying relevant. And they felt the '80s sound was relevant. But I don't think that the mid-'80s stuff is their best stuff. And a large part of that was the sonic treatment.

BOB KULICK: You've got to realize, they were "kings of the forest" for a while, and then as with every band, things change. Styles change, the audience changes. In order to be successful and span decades, most bands have to do something to adapt to the change—i.e., Metallica cutting their hair and stuff like that. So they made that attempt, as with *The Elder*—"Let's do a concept record." As with Mark St. John—"Let's get a shredder like Steve Vai and

Eddie Van Halen." They tried to do those things, but the reality for them is really all they had to do was be themselves, because there was no competition for four guys wearing make-up. And when the make-up came off, the band was good enough without it. So all of the "Let's fix this and change that and adapt to this" really didn't work. And the "meat and potatoes" guitar player, which my brother is—more than he is Eddie Van Halen, although he can play some of that stuff—was more in keeping with what the audience wanted from them, than all of a sudden for them turning into something that they weren't.

Kiss was more "the Beatles" than they were "Van Halen." That is really the truth. More of a song-oriented band—not that Van Halen didn't have great songs—but more of a song-oriented band with an image for four guys. The Beatles. Like what Bill Aucoin tried to do for them—"Stand in the same order, so everybody recognizes Paul, Peter, stand next to him, and then Ace is standing next to him, and Gene is on the other end." All of that stuff—all of that concoction of how to be remembered, how to make it, how to get from point a to point b if you have a gimmick, an idea, or a talent. In their case, they had all of the above. They had a great gimmick, they had the talent, and they had a lot of luck and a lot of people who guided them. And with this gimmick, there was no competition. With our friend Michael Bolton, when he started singing R&B songs rather than singing rock songs, all of a sudden he wasn't competing with Robert Plant and every other rock singer in the world. He was unique unto himself; hence, he became a star. When he was one of 50 people vying for the one ride on the merry-go-round, it didn't work.

MARK WEISS: I feel Kiss in the '80s were trying to fit in, where the other bands were creating something kind of new, I guess. I think they were trying too hard. They had fashion people doing their videos. They had good songs, but it wasn't as raw as it used to be, which I liked better.

BOBBY BLOTZER: I'd say it was competitive on sound level and song level. I think they were trying to write more commercial, radio, hook-heavy songs, like the rest of us were doing. They did a great job at what they did. I loved that stuff.

AJ PERO: Kiss always had the "Kiss sound." I'm just doing comparisons [to Twisted Sister]—*Under the Blade* and *You Can't Stop Rock N' Roll* was more raw, and then, all of a sudden, we were told to ... not "bubble gum" ourselves, but we had to be a little more commercial. And *Stay Hungry* sold millions. It's *still* selling. I don't listen to the album at all. As a matter of fact, when we rerecorded it recently [2004's *Still Hungry*], we did it monstrous, and we played it the way we wanted to play it. And I thought it was ten times better, but the public said, "How can you do that? You have a classic album." Just like with Kiss, looking back at "Strutter," and then the albums to follow were very raw. And then they come out and try to lighten it up to be more commercial.

Give them a lot of credit, because Gene Simmons and Paul Stanley said, "Let's go along with the times," and they did. I thought it was a good move, but you've got to contend with the general public. Sometimes they don't like change. It would be like if Metallica came out with a top-40 hit. You've got bands like Bon Jovi that always sounded the same, Def Leppard always sounded the same. But bands like Kiss and Twisted and Alice Cooper that had to conform from what the '70s was all about, because the '70s, you know how we sounded in the '70s. And then you had to go to the '80s, which was a little bit more "1-2, 1-2." That's how you had to conform. So everybody made a change. I thought Kiss did the right thing, I thought we did the right thing. Sometimes, this is how the music business is.

EDDIE TRUNK: I certainly think they were spinning their wheels a little bit, trying to just get their following back, their fanbase back. Find something that was going to connect with a rock audience. But I don't think that what they went through is any different than what a lot of bands from the '70s went through in the '80s. I think all the bands of the '70s tried to find an image, a sound, something that was going to connect with the new breed of bands that were coming out at the time. You could look at Ozzy and the "Shot in the Dark" video. He's wearing eyeliner and a sequined robe. So it certainly wasn't unique to them, but I think they were just trying to relate to the times. You look at some of the pictures from the *Asylum* period or the *Crazy Nights* period. Kiss looks more ridiculous and has more make-up on then they probably had on when they wore make-up! It was just like, "What are we doing here?" But I think that, at the end of the day, there's some great records there. And, yeah, clearly there's stuff like Def Leppard meets Bon Jovi. Really produced stuff, the *Crazy Nights* stuff. It was definitely reactionary to what was going on, without question.

GERRI MILLER: I liked some of it. Songs like "Lick It Up" were great. Those were more of the "following the trend" type of songs. When you have a career that's that long, you can't be expected to stick to one ... I mean, I guess AC/DC would be the one exception. [Laughs] But most bands really do evolve and go with the times to stay relevant, so you can't fault them for that. They still stayed true to their core. They still were Kiss. I can't fault them for going with the prevailing trend.

BOB GRAW: Some people say, "They sold out," or whatever. Well, you know what? They stayed relevant. They were on MTV constantly, [and] they were on magazine covers again. People were starting to care about them, because their songs were easily accessible. They cleaned up their sound. So I didn't have a problem what that—I still loved them.

MARK WEISS: I started getting hired by a lot [of rock groups] in the '80s, because I did Bon Jovi's *Slippery When Wet*, and all these bands that started selling millions of records—Twisted Sister, Cinderella—I did all their album covers. So they started hiring me, and I read somewhere later on that they kinda followed what Bon Jovi did. They hired the same video directors, hired the same photographers. And I'm like, "Alright ... that was me!" I actually did the photo shoots for Kiss' *Crazy Nights* tour book, and I shot each of them in a theme. It was a "girl theme." Eric was in a jail theme with handcuffs, Bruce had a motorcycle, Gene had like 20 girls—all Playmates. Paul had a couple of nurses. I did the cover for that, and I did all that conceptual stuff. I think it was Paul's idea, as far as the jail cell, and Eric just kinda went along with it. He was like, "Alright, it's cool, man. I can think of worse things to do than be in a jail with two almost naked women." He had fun. I did Mötley Crüe in a gangster theme, with tommy guns, Rolls Royces, girls, and the whole deal. I think that's where they got the idea from, because I shot each guy in their own little motif, and then did the group shot. I do remember during that whole set-up, I did a couple of different sets. And I did this whole elaborate set for the band to go on, and Gene's like, "Nah, I don't like that." And I spent *days* on it. We went right to something else.

GARY CORBETT: I was working at a studio in New York called Electric Lady, and the guy who plays keyboards on the *Crazy Nights* record is a guy named Phil Ashley. We were friends from the studio, and he was going out on tour with Mick Jagger at the time. They wanted to have a keyboard player, and they asked him to recommend somebody. So he recommended me, because we knew each other at Electric Lady. I went up to the office and had an interview with Paul and Chris Lendt, part of Kiss' management team at the time. I was playing with Lou Gramm, the singer from Foreigner, at the time. So I basically got the gig, and then I had to leave to go do a tour in Europe with Lou.

They were starting rehearsals out in L.A., and I wasn't going to be back in the country. I missed the first week of rehearsals, and then flew straight from Germany to L.A., and started rehearsing with those guys. I got picked up at the airport and driven to a TV studio—they were taping a TV show. So I met everybody basically when they were "on." It wasn't a very personal feeling at that point. Everybody was being polite, but everybody seemed to get along.

They had been rehearsing for about a week when I got there, so my first day of rehearsal wasn't theirs. They had this studio in San Bernardino, I think, and they had half of the stage set. I got there, and everyone was off in their own corners, working on their guitars or dealing with the drums. It was very relaxed, very casual. And from the first note of actually rehearsing, they were 100% like they were on stage. I remember being really shocked that they went from zero to full speed and took the rehearsals really seriously. I mean, they worked really hard at rehearsals to get ready for those shows. It was very physically draining.

SCOTT DAGGETT: We had discussed before *Crazy Nights*, he wanted to take lessons again, which is common. Many drummers that I deal with—I worked with "Sugarfoot," Jonathan Moffett, who was Michael Jackson's drummer. He's an incredible technician, but he still goes and takes [lessons]. There are a few monster drum teachers. We discussed that a few times, but he was afraid that the fans would get a hold of that, and he didn't know if he wanted that out there. Every night, he would ask me how his solo went, because he could gauge his playing. He and Bruce were the two "players" in the band. And they still use that formula—Gene and Paul do. He would ask about how the solo went, and if it didn't go too good. Because of my schooling, I was able to say, "It kind of sucked tonight ... here's why." I think he really appreciated that, where most people would tell him what they think he wants to hear.

I know that Eric was a lot happier with [the band's look circa] *Crazy Nights*. He was getting tired of the tights. He felt that it was almost a little bit too much make-up with *Asylum*—he was wearing this stretch leotard type of thing. I don't remember the show being that much different content-wise. But content is not what they're really known for. I think there was probably more bombs and pyro in the *Asylum* tour ... no, because *Crazy Nights*, that was where the set I think exploded. It "spring-loaded" parts of the actual set, and during one of the explosions, they all popped up. They called it the "Scott swatter." It was a big piece of metal grating behind the drums that would snap up during the explosion. And if the safety device had ever slipped or broke, that thing would have clean swatted right down on top of me.

GARY CORBETT: That tour was a little strange. It wasn't a really successful tour at the beginning. As a matter of fact, ticket sales were kind of not so great, to the point where they actually let me go and sent me home after the first three weeks, because they felt they couldn't afford to pay me, because they weren't selling enough tickets. I went home, they did maybe two or three weeks of shows, and then called me back and said, "We really need the keyboards back," and asked if I could come back. Which I did. So the *Crazy Nights* tour was a little strange, and it was the first time I had ever been in the situation of playing off-stage before with anyone. It was a lot of fun. It was still a big tour, and it was still Kiss.

SCOTT DAGGETT: I fell apart. I self-imploded on *Crazy Nights* with cocaine. That's the reason why I left. Our tour manager talked to me a couple of times. Eric was doing his best to cover for me, but after a while, he couldn't. It was just getting too obvious and too crazy. So I left at that point. The last real thing that Eric told me was as I was leaving the tour, literally walking off the bus to go home, because my wife had threatened me with separation, he came from the hotel over to the buses, just to see me. I said to him, "Look, I'm fucking my life up." And he said, "Yes. *You are.*" I've never seen him look at me quite like that. He was very angry and hurt. I think he felt like I let him down. He felt bad for me, because I suspect at that time she already told him that she was going to divorce me if I didn't get my shit together, and he knew I wouldn't.

GARY CORBETT: He had those drum pads above the cymbals, and he had six, seven, or eight of them. And what they were there for primarily was so that at the end of songs—whatever key the song was in, when we were bashing the last chord—he had a synth that was hooked up to those pads. He had this low, really nasty sounds, and he would just bash along, whatever key we were in. I've always been into the synthesizers and samplers and stuff. When I came along and was able to help him program it, I was the one that actually programmed all the stuff for his electronic drum rig. He ended up buying a sampler. If I remember correctly, one of the solos, we sampled a bunch of Metallica guitar riffs, where it would just be the guitar by itself playing something. We sampled about five or six different things. He'd hit the loop, get the audience to do something, and then hit another one and stop it. He got the whole audience to participate a little bit. And then he'd incorporate his soloing over the loops. It was really new technology at the time. It was pretty cool.

BOB GRAW: It's got to be *Asylum* or *Crazy Nights*, and he made all those funky sounds with it. He had one that I think sounded like a guitar. He always had one of the best drum solos anyway, even without that malarkey, because he was fast and played with a lot of rhythm. His drum solos were always good. People would always go out and get a beer, but I always loved watching him play and doing his drum solos.

GERRI MILLER: I do remember a picture, and I think I still have it. I think this was at a Florida show. Everybody was kind of goofing around, and Eric puts this giant garbage pail over his head, and you couldn't see him. He was just walking around with this giant, inverted trash can. It looked really funny, because it was like feet ... and a trash can, walking!

BRUCE KULICK: Well, my favorite [of Eric's girlfriends] was really Carrie Stevens. Even though they would sometimes fight, I know they loved each other.

CARRIE STEVENS: Yes, I was a fan of Kiss. When I was ten years old—in fifth grade—my girlfriends and I actually dressed up as Kiss for Halloween. I was Peter Criss. That was starting real young. And I remember my first Kiss concert—I was 16 years old, and that was in Springfield, Massachusetts. I always thought Eric was the cutest guy in the band. I had their posters on my walls and all that. When I was 18, I was now living in Memphis, Tennessee, and that's where I met Eric. I was at the Kiss concert in Memphis [on November 15], and then a couple of their concert dates had been cancelled right after Memphis, so I'd heard from the grapevine ... Gene and Paul went back to wherever they lived, and Bruce and Eric stayed in town until their next gig, wherever that was. Ron Wood from the Rolling Stones was having an art exhibit at the Peabody Hotel, and my girlfriends and I went to the art exhibit. Then we recognized Eric ... well, I think we thought it was Paul Stanley from the back of his head, down in the lobby bar. And there were some other rocker-looking guys in there. We were sitting near them and overheard them talking about getting a cab and going to see a band play. I interrupted and said, "I have a car. I'll take you." And that's how we met. They said yes, they came with us, and the rest is history.

He was very soft-spoken, very sweet voice, very gentle. Sexy. Kind. He was fun. He wrecked my car the night we met, though! There was this girl that was with me. They said, "Do you want to go see a band play?" And we did. We went and saw the band play—the Willies, they were called—and it was at the Midway Cafe in Memphis. We all got drunk, [and] we were having a good time. He was driving my car. How he ended up driving, I do not remember. They were staying at the Peabody, and the parking lot there ... there was like a big, thick chain blocking the entrance, and he drove through it. And it went over my car and slammed into the back, the chain smashed out the backlights of my car. At the time, we were all not really even noticing, we were all just drunk.

And then we went back to his room, me and the other girl I was friends with and him. But in my mind, I was just completely *with him,* you know? No threesome stuff going on, nothing like that. I went to the bathroom, and when I came out, I noticed her making a move on him and trying to kiss him. I started screaming at her—"You slimy slut!" And keep in mind, I'm 18 years old, so I'm a little immature. I got in a fight with her and was screaming at her. He told me, "Why don't you take her home and come back?" I really can't believe that I was out drinking and driving like this, now that I'm a mom and I'm talking about this. But whatever—young, stupid. So I took her home, which was a really far drive away from the hotel, and then I came back. Why I did this, I don't know, but I came back. I can't believe that was the start of our relationship, but it was. He was like 37 or something, and I was 18, but he was ageless, because he was a rock star. You didn't think of him as someone so much older than me. And then after that, we kept in touch. We became really good friends. I would actually be his "ear." He had a girlfriend at the time, Charisse, and I was the one that kind of gave him advice and listened. Not just her, there were other girls, too. I think when I started seeing him, after Charisse, there was, at one point, four people he was seeing. I was just so in love with him—as only young love can be—and I just made him more comfortable around me than he was around anyone else. And, eventually, he just wanted to be with me.

GARY CORBETT: That was instant love. He was so crazy about her, and she was a really sweet girl. We were really close. My wife was really good friends with her—because I was so close with Eric—so the four of us would go out a lot together. Go out to dinner and spent a lot of time together.

BRUCE KULICK: Carrie was really young when he met her. And there she is, suddenly. I mean, she's still gorgeous, years on. But she was just like ... the sea parts when she walks. Back then, it was just wild. In some ways, I know that he would share with me some of their fights, because we were buddies. And there were times that I could understand it, and there were times that I was like, "How are you going to perceive this? How are you going to handle it? Do you love her? Well, then work it out." But she was the one that I knew the best. I know there was a Bambi and a Charisse. Charisse was the other one that was around a lot. Bambi was the one that I used to hear some really bad things about from the past, before me. Because I remember there was one around before that, that I didn't know too much about. But Charisse, I didn't know what was going on with that. I just didn't sense a real healthy, supportive relationship. Even if Carrie and him would have some fights, they seemed to talk it out.

CARRIE STEVENS: It happened pretty slow. It wasn't like one day we met and we were serious boyfriend and girlfriend. It probably took a year of knowing him until we were boyfriend and girlfriend. He didn't want to be my boyfriend—I had to *make him* be my boyfriend. I argued with him about it all the time. We would be together like 24 hours a day, and he'd say he wasn't my boyfriend. I'd say, "Whether you like it or not, you're my boyfriend!" I'll never forget it, one day we were at his place in New York, and he was on the phone talking to someone about something, and I heard him say, "Well, my girlfriend and I ... " He got off the phone, and I said, "See? I *am* your girlfriend."

CHRISTINA HARRISON: And then Eric ends up having this drop-dead gorgeous girlfriend, Carrie. He always probably told Carrie, "You can do better than me." She's gorgeous to this day. But he would always say things like that. That's where his insecurities would come in. And then Bruce would tell him—and I would even tell him—"She loves you *so* much." He was just insecure constantly. But I don't know. People who are insecure maybe seem a little more real. They're not as cocky.

EDDIE TRUNK: Eric was fairly insecure about stuff. He was fairly insecure about his standing in the band. Insecure if he was going to remain in the band. I think he was a little bit "on an island." With Ace, he had his real ally there in the beginning. Maybe it wasn't the best influence on him, but he connected with Ace a little bit. And then through the various other changes that went on, he kind of connected with Bruce. But Eric was the kind of guy that he was more comfortable hanging out with the fans or the road crew, or something like that. Or a guy like Gary, who was an off-stage keyboard player. Much more so than he would be getting caught up in all the "pageantry" or whatever that goes with Gene or Paul. I think that's just the kind of person he was. What led to the disagreements and issues, I don't know. But it's pretty well known that whenever a line-up change happens in any band, the whole dynamic—both personal and professional in the business end—shifts and changes. And Eric was an employee. He was an employee of the Kiss company. I don't know if it had anything to do with his deal or his business arrangement, but clearly, there was some head-butting that went on.

JACK SAWYERS: I was in Texas. I had moved out to San Diego, and I was driving back to Jersey, by way of the 40, and we caught wind that Kiss was playing. Ted Nugent and Kiss were playing in Texas [in November]. I forget exactly what city it was. It was the *Crazy Nights* tour. So, obviously, we made a detour, and it was that night that they were playing. We went to the place where they were playing, and I was trying to find where all the buses were, trying to find him, and couldn't find him. So we watched the show—it was a great show. And then after the show, we went back out there when they were leaving, and I caught a glimpse of Eric. I was waving at him, and he just starts laughing. He's like, "What are *you* doing here?" I said, "We were traveling through," and he's like, "Cool! Nice to see you." Nice five-minute conversation, and that was it.

1988

BOB GRAW: The first time on that tour was at the Meadowlands [on December 20 in 1987], with Ted Nugent, and that show was really big. As the years went on, the shows got bigger and bigger and bigger again, which was something I always looked forward to. Then I saw them again on the *Crazy Nights* tour at Nassau Coliseum [January 29], once again, with our friend Ted Nugent opening up. I saw that show front-row. It was general admission. I almost died that night—it was the closest I'd ever been for them. I remember thinking just how great it was to be up that close—I got all their guitar picks that night—and how great it was to see my heroes basically like a foot away. My friend took pictures. That was a great show.

CHARLIE BENANTE: I think that tour went for five or six weeks [Anthrax opened for Kiss from March to April]. I remember the first show we played with them, we were really intimidated, because most of us in the band were diehard Kiss fans. We were just shaking because it was so exciting. We knew Eric, so Eric was kind of the "conduit," and Gene came over, and he immediately warmed up to us. So we had that every day. Paul was a little weird in the beginning, and then it was great. We just got along. It was a really good time on that tour. I remember Eric had some problems on that tour—health-related problems—but we didn't know exactly what it was. I remember he had a problem with some numbness on the left side of his body.

It was different, a totally different animal. They transformed themselves into an "'80s hair metal band." And it didn't have the "Kiss vibe" at all. They were still playing certain tunes and trying to do it. I understood it, I wasn't a fan of it. I wanted to hear "100,000 Years" and crap like that. But at the end of the day, it was still the Kiss name. I just think it was a sign of the times. They were trying to compete with these other bands. The easiest thing for them to do was just conform to what was viewed as popular. You have to remember, MTV at that time was *huge,* and they were just trying to play the game.

I remember hanging out with Eric quite a bit on that tour. He would come in the dressing room, hang out, and we would just shoot the shit about anything, from pizza to drum stuff. And people used to say at the time that we resembled each other, that we looked like brothers—when I had the long curly hair and he had it, too. We actually did a little skit on one of our live home DVDs with Eric. I couldn't tell you what it's on, I don't remember. But I always remember Eric being a nice guy. I thought [Eric's drum solo] was awesome, I loved the way he incorporated the pads into it and created this really cool drum solo. I thought it was really creative and ahead of its time. I would watch it every night.

LORETTA CARAVELLO: On the *Crazy Nights* tour, do you remember the chikara ["力"] cymbals he had? When he was in the States, they had those made as a silkscreen, and those were put onto the silver drum kit. So what happened was when they wanted to go down to Japan, my brother wanted to take that set with him, because he loved those chikara satin whatever they were. Gene and Paul said, "We can't do it. It's too expensive. It can't go." For some reason, they got another set down there, or they couldn't make them. It was too late. I think he found out a week or so before he was going to take off for the tour. So there was no time to make those cymbals again to take to Japan and get a duplicate kit down there. At the time, I was doing graphic arts. I was working in Manhattan. He said, "Could you help me? Can you find a place where I could print them?" I said, "Well, I'll try."

I went to my job, and they couldn't do it. So I said to myself, "I don't want to disappoint my brother." He wanted *so much* to do this. So I had this brainstorm, and I went to a wallpaper store, and I bought this orange contact paper, white, and black. So what I did was I took the logo that was on the back of the *Crazy Nights* tour book, and of course, I snuck it at work, when nobody was looking, I would stick it into the stat camera. It would shoot like 20 or 30 of them, because they were on a glossier type of paper. So what I did was when I went there, I said, "Let me do a little more of these, and I'll make extras." I went home, and I said, "How am I going to make these big circles?" I went out and got a garbage can top, took the first garbage can top, made the large one ... you know Italians, how they are, we have a big sauce pot. That was the center. And I took a little pot. So I carefully pulled off each piece, put them all on, and then I took the stats, cut them out, sprayed them, stuck that on. And then I took that crystal stuff, and I sprayed the whole thing. So I said, "Hey, I'm on to something good here." So I made him like 25 of them and then had all these leftover colors, and I made all these variations.

The day comes when I have to meet him in the city, at the Kiss office. I have this big box, and he goes, "How did you make out?" I open it up, and he almost fell on the floor. "I can't believe it. This is great!" It was one of the best feelings I ever had for my brother. So he took those, and when he went to Japan, he put those onto the kit there. But all I could think about the whole time, was, "Oh my God ... are these going to melt from the lighting?" And then I'm going to see my brother screaming, "They melted when I was on stage!" But as history turns out, it didn't happen. So those cymbals that you see, I made all of those. What happened was Gene and Paul liked them so much that at certain shows, they took the extra ones and put them on the amps and all over the place in different colors. My brother only got charged 300 bucks for that, because I needed some money coming in, too.

CARRIE STEVENS: I went to somewhere in New Hampshire. It was an outdoor music festival [on July 4 at the Cheshire Fairgrounds]. I was in school—I went to Memphis State University—and he went off to tour Europe after we met. I was off school and staying with my sister in upstate New York. So some friends and I drove up to New Hampshire and went to this outdoor music festival they were playing at. I hadn't even seen Eric yet, but I was in the audience, and first, the roadie came out and told me that this guy, Romeo, was trying to get me to sit on the side of the stage, while the bands played. And I was like deathly afraid to meet Gene Simmons, especially Gene with that tongue, and he's such a big presence. I was like, "No no no, I can't!" And then Gene was pointing at me in the audience.

Then when I was backstage, Eric came out, and we were talking to him. Then Paul comes out and has no idea that I'm with Eric. So he starts flirting with me and hitting on me. Eric comes back, and Paul is in his seat, talking to me. Eric was so sweet and humble, that he just sat across from me. He was starving, and now his plate of food was sitting there, and he couldn't eat! The poor thing was probably nervous. I don't think Paul even figured out we were dating until much later. He just kind of got turned down and moved on, and then Eric and I went out the next night. He was staying at his parents' house in New Paltz, New York, and I was staying with my sister. We went out then, and from there, we started getting pretty close. Before that, it was kind of talking here and there.

He and Bruce were always close. Bruce and his ex-wife, Christina, and I hung out. The four of us would go out and hang out a lot, because they were both the "hired guns" of the band, and I think they related a lot. And Bruce is just an easygoing, great guy anyway. And I think his relationship with Gene was more ... it was less competitive than with his relationship with Paul. I think maybe because they were the single guys in the band or something. Paul's more to himself, in general. Gene's just a more friendly, talkative, outward kind of person, where Paul is more inward. I think it was mostly business—it was a very business relationship with Paul. Like, I don't think the two of them were going to go out and have cocktails, not that Paul drinks. With Gene, it was a little more warm, yet Gene was the "big boss." I think Eric was a little frustrated because it wasn't really his band. Creatively, he was limited, because they made all the decisions. He had some frustration about that. But I think he really liked Gene a lot. I don't know about Paul, honestly. I think, sometimes, he really liked him, and I think sometimes he was just confused by the hot and coldness of Paul.

BOB GRAW: I also saw them on that, the *Crazy Nights* tour when they played the Ritz in New York City [Kiss played two nights—August 12 and 13]. That was the "show of shows." It was all old material, songs I'd never heard them play before. That was one of the best shows I'd ever seen. I went with my buddy Rob, and I can't believe we got tickets. We got in, and I remember we worked our way to the front. I just remember how hot it was ... it was like death. It was a thousand degrees in that place, but that's what made it so cool, to see Kiss in a place that small, and be just jammed in with a couple of hundreds of your rock n' roll brothers. I remember people on shoulders and falling over the place and puking because it was so hot. My friend definitely has one of Eric's sticks from that night, because at the end of the show, Eric came out, threw his sticks out into the audience, and it bounced right off my head ... and into his hands! And then I remember we stood over by the side of the bar, and we took our shirts off and squeezed them out. I don't know how the band played that show. If it was that hot on the floor, I can't imagine how hot it was underneath the lights.

GARY CORBETT: Right after the *Crazy Nights* tour in the States, that summer, we ended up going over to Europe to do the Monsters of Rock tour there, which was a lot of fun. When we did Europe, they started breaking out some of the stuff that the fans would always request, that they hadn't been playing. I remember we did a bunch of stuff that I hadn't learned previously for that tour. And what I remember the most about that tour was the audiences were huge. In England, in Donington, it was like 110,000 people, and each show was 70-80,000 people.

BRUCE KULICK: The problem with the festival tours are sometimes you get a lot of days off. Really, the story that stands out is clearly the "Amsterdam story." Y'know, Eric definitely could drink, OK? But he never smoked any pot or anything like that. In Amsterdam, obviously, it's legal. Myself having experience, and our keyboard player, Gary Corbett, having experience, because we did have a behind-the-scenes keyboard player, oops! I let that out. [Laughs] We had a couple of days off, and he was just like, "Maybe I should try one of those space cakes or something." I have enough experience about people that don't know about getting high that when they get high for the first time, that the reactions can be very varied. And, sadly, Eric's wasn't a good one.

He ate one of the space cakes from the Bulldog place and didn't feel anything. Which is not that unusual from what I understand. Usually, when you digest it, within a short period of time—within the hour—you're usually getting high. So then, the next thing you know, he figured, "Let me eat another one." And it was probably a bad idea. [Laughs] Because now, he can't feel his feet. And instead of it being like, "Wow, I feel like I'm floating. I can't feel my feet," it's like, *"What the hell is going on?"* And Gary, I, and one of the road crew guys, we ended up babysitting him for the rest of the night. It was terrible. He basically ruined our evening, but we loved the guy. What are we, going to abandon him? Weed like that, I don't care how strong it is, has never killed anybody. So we knew we didn't have to take him to the hospital, even though we had to reassure him that he was going to be OK.

It was such a bummer. And I'll tell you, it's nothing like when everybody has a buzz, and then somebody's bumming. That brings down everybody. And you know, nobody in the band was like ... even though then I would indulge in something like having some fun in Amsterdam with weed, it would never be on a show day. It would be on a day off. But I have to admit that the weed there is kind of strong. That was kind of stressful for us, but we got him through it. I doubt if he ever even thought about touching it again after that. It was just him sitting, petrified to do anything. He was extremely uncomfortable with it. And you know, whatever it is about the chemical in marijuana kind of thing and all that, that affects certain parts of your brain. It took him to a place that he didn't want to be. It was one of the worst reactions to pot that I've ever seen, I have to admit. I've heard things like Gene was tricked into a brownie one time, and he hated it, because he didn't feel like he was "in control," is the way he put it. You know, accidentally eating something at a party. Because clearly, I know Gene's never willingly wanted to be high. But I can see that, in the same way when I was young, once, even though I thought I was taking something else, it turned into some speedy acid thing, and I didn't think I was taking that. And then I was not happy. But, again, I'm talking about those were more "chemical." Here it was just weed, and he was completely paranoid, completely immobilized from it, thinking that he'd stop breathing or something. Very strange. But he got through it.

GARY CORBETT: I got the blame for that one with everybody else ... and I was actually responsible! What happened with that was Eric was upset with Gene and Paul, because they took his drum solo away for the Monsters of Rock tour. They weren't headlining. They were second to Iron Maiden on that Monsters of Rock tour. And Eric loved doing his drum solo, so he was really upset with the fact that they pulled his drum solo. The Monsters of Rock tour, I guess we did like seven or eight shows, and then Kiss was doing their own tour through the rest of Europe. Word came down that even when we went out on our own, they still didn't want the drum solo in the show. And that really upset Eric. So we were in Amsterdam. The Monsters shows were only on weekends, so wherever we played, we had the week prior to or after in that town, or a few days. So we do the Amsterdam show and had three or four days off there.

Eric had never smoked weed in his life. He'd never gotten high or anything, and I was a big fan of the coffee shops over there. What happened was Eric came to me and said, "I want to try smoking weed." He was really upset about the drum solo, really mad at them and hurt. He said, "I want to get high." So we go down to the local cafe, and he ate a couple of brownies and really didn't feel it. The next day, Bruce was out shopping, and he came across some less tourist-y, "more for the locals" coffee shop, on a little side street. And I guess they made their space cakes a little more potent. He calls me up and told me about the place. I called Eric and said, "Hey, if you want to go and try it again, this place, you should definitely feel it." So we did. He ended up eating up a little bit more than he should, I think. He took a couple of hits. I rolled a big spliff with hash, [and] he took a couple of hits of that. Chocolate bonbons—he was eating up a storm.

Then we left, and we went walking around the streets. We even bumped into Gene and Paul. So at that point, we're sitting with everybody, and everybody was hanging out at an outdoor cafe. We were there for a little while, and Eric said to me, "I think I need to get out of here. I'm feeling really strange." Being around them made him really paranoid, so we split. We got back to the hotel. I call up Bruce and told him what happened and what's going on. And him and Nitebob, who was our front house engineer at the time, came to my room, so the three of us could keep Eric calm. He was really not doing well, to the point where I said to him, "Why don't you try taking a nap? You'll probably wake up feeling a lot better." He's like, "No, no, I don't want to go to sleep. I'm afraid if I go to sleep, I'm not going to wake up." He was really paranoid about everything. I go, "OK, what about eating some food? That will usually bring down your head a bit." So we ordered food, he took one bite of the food and couldn't eat it. He thought he was going to choke. I mean, he was just really not doing too well.

And, of course, I had a video camera with me. I have a lot of the time we spent in the room together documented on videotape, which is really hilarious to watch. It's like one of those bad '70s hippie movies, y'know? He just was basically frozen—he couldn't function. He didn't handle it well. Well, I left town the next day, because at the time, my sister was living in Switzerland, and we had another three days, and then we had to meet up in Italy. He went to bed that night, and I left early the next morning and didn't see him again. Three days later, when I showed up in Italy, I was sitting down in a restaurant, and Paul came into the restaurant. He comes over to me and says, "Ohhh, *it's the pusher-man.*" And I went, "What do you mean?" He goes, "I heard you got Eric all screwed up." So for the next few weeks, he called me "the pusher-man." It turns out that Eric was so high, that he didn't come out of his room for the last three days that we were there. He did not handle it well, and I don't think he did it again after that.

BRUCE KULICK: I thought we played well. I've seen some footage of it, and Eric had the huge kit and everything. We had a good record to play off of—*Crazy Nights*.

GARY CORBETT: That was basically anywhere they could find a spot to set it up [where Gary's keyboards were set up on stage]. They didn't really think about it ahead of time. And the fact that they didn't want me to be seen, they should have thought about it a little bit, because Kiss fans are diehard fans, and a lot of them show up at more than one show. And they find out things about our schedules before we did—they knew everything about everything. So it didn't take long before the "Kiss Army guys" knew what I was there for. They'd see me and want to ask me questions about what I was doing. I wasn't really supposed to be talking about it, so I'd keep a low profile about it. But there were times when it just couldn't be hidden.

As a matter of fact, when we did the Monsters of Rock show in Germany, I was off on the side of the stage, kind of behind the stack of PAs. And they had the huge JumboTron screens on each side of the stage. They had three cameramen roaming around the stage, filming all of this stuff. Nobody told them that I wasn't supposed to be known to be there. And during "Rock and Roll All Nite," one of the cameramen came wandering back on the side and started filming me playing, which now winds up on the screens in front of 60,000 people! Of course, that was long before YouTube or anything, but somebody did run a VHS tape of whatever the cameras were shooting, and that became a really hot bootleg to have for a while. [Laughs] Because of the fact that I was "exposed." Yeah, Gene and Paul were not real happy about that. Now, you can go on YouTube, look it up, and see it. But back then, it was just the underground Kiss Army network guys would swap videos and stuff. It made its way around quite a bit.

Those guys didn't really socialize much, to be honest. Gene was very business-minded at the time. He had a label [Simmons Records]. He would pretty much, from the time that we finished a show, he'd go back to his room, and you'd really never see him again until the next day when we'd leave. He'd be in this room, doing business. It wasn't really a sociable thing. Paul, pretty much the same thing. We didn't see Paul that much. At the time, Paul was dating Samantha Fox, so she was around Europe a little bit at that point. As far as socializing, I don't really remember much socializing. See, that's how come Eric and I got so close, because he and I were really the only two people that wanted to go hang out and walk around whatever city we were in. I had my video camera. I have hours and hours of footage of Eric and I all throughout Europe. Some great stuff.

One of the funniest things was the day before the Donington show, Eric and I went down to the site. Guns N' Roses was a brand new band at the time. As a matter of a fact, "Paradise City," which was their third video, part of it was shot at Donington. Eric and I really liked the band, so when they soundchecked the day before in the afternoon, Eric had to go and deal with some drum stuff, so we were there. When they started to soundcheck, we went out to the middle of the field, sat down on the grass, and watched their soundcheck. I had my video camera, so I was like, "I'm going to videotape the soundcheck." So it's just the two of us that are on this field that holds 100,000 people. I'm videotaping, and these two guys up on stage—who are up looking out at where we're sitting—one of them is pointing at us. Eric leans up to me and says, "Dude, they're pointing at us. You better turn the video camera off, because they're probably not too happy about that." I didn't turn it off. I put it down on the ground and tried to aim it at the stage.

Well, nobody ever came and said anything to us, but when we got back to the hotel that night, Paul calls me up and says, "Y'know, I was watching the news tonight. They were talking about the concert tomorrow, and the news person says, 'Guns N' Roses played for a very small audience today,' and the camera turns around and shows Eric and I sitting in the middle of the field! [Laughs] So that's why the guy was pointing at us. It wasn't because of my videotaping. We ended up on the news that night in England. We had a lot of fun together doing stuff like that. And we'd go out on the streets. Eric had no problem walking up to strangers and interviewing them. Or the fans would be following us around, and I would videotape everything.

This one fan in France shows up at the hotel in Paris, and he had done these miniature recreations of every instrument that those guys used on that tour. I don't know how he did it—every guitar that Paul [played], every guitar Bruce played, every bass Gene played ... they probably were eight or nine inches long, and the detail on them was unbelievable. Every little thing about those instruments was done exactly right. And he'd done Eric's drum kit, which if you remember, was a pretty large drum kit. Each kick drum was like double. It was two kick drums stuck together, so they were really long. He used three kick drums. He had probably nine, ten, or twelve toms, plus all the pads, plus all the cymbals. And this guy recreated that drum kit to the tee. Every pad, every cymbal, every decal that was on Eric's drums was on this little drum kit.

We had come down to the lobby of the hotel we were staying at in Paris, and the guy was in the lobby, waiting for any of the band members to come down, to show them what he had done. So Eric came down. Eric was great with the fans. He would sit and talk to fans until the very last one was gone— he never blew anybody off. So he goes over and sees what this guy had done, and he was floored. And the guy gave it to him to keep as a gift. He was *so* touched. And his plan for it was he was going to put it in a plexiglass box and put it on his coffee table. He really carefully boxed it up, and somehow, in the process of shipping it back from Europe, it never made it. Again, that's something I have on videotape. The guy found me on Facebook or MySpace not too long ago, and was asking me for a copy of the videotape of him giving Eric the drum kit.

CARRIE STEVENS: I never saw Gene with anybody. Maybe he was. If he was, he kept it awfully under wraps. I know he likes to brag about it, which is kind of weird, because I don't understand how Shannon ... I don't get it.

Because I don't think they have an open relationship. I have no idea. No, I never did physically see Gene with anybody. Paul, there's a couple of times. One time, he was in a bathroom backstage, in this old locker room-looking thing. He was with some girl, and me and Eric were taking pennies and throwing them over the top at them and trying to hit them and run! Then one time we were in the tour bus, riding in the bus, [and] there were some girls riding in the back of us, clearly following the bus, and Paul told the bus driver to stop, [and he] got out, and rode with them! So those girls must have gotten the biggest thrill. I don't know that he did anything with them. I just know that he got off the bus, got in the car, and rode behind us. None of the guys drank, besides Eric. They weren't a party band. They weren't like Mötley Crüe was. They were serious about making the money and the music. If there was any partying—meaning drinking, Eric never did drugs—it would have been Eric and I at the bar by ourselves, at a restaurant. It never happened backstage.

GARY CORBETT: There were always a ton of women around them. And because that was a known thing I guess, it kind of perpetuated itself, because the more women that were around, the more it was talked about it, the more women wanted to be around. There was always a lot. As far as who participated in anything, that I don't really know. At the time, I remember hearing Gene supposedly sleeping with 20,000 women [Note: The exact figure Gene has been quoted as saying is 5,000 ... but who's counting?]. There were supposedly Polaroids of quite a few of them, that he was going to do a book. I guess this is long before *Girls Gone Wild*. He was going to do a book of Polaroid pictures, and unfortunately, the folder that was full of the Polaroids was stolen from the manager's office, so the book never got done. I mean, I used to walk out on the stage during set change with my video camera, just to film the audience. Just by doing that, you'd see 20 pairs of breasts. Yeah, there was always a large amount of women around. It was the '80s, and that was all part of the scene, I guess. But the "participation" factor—not as much as they made it out to be, I would say.

CARRIE STEVENS: Eric was a big slut before he was with me. He admitted to me that he was with five girls at a time on the road. I was always paranoid that he was going to cheat on me, because of the past. He told me he cheated on every girlfriend he had, and he was very sexual on the road. It always meant a lot to him that I believed him that he wasn't going to cheat on me. I wasn't sure I ever believed it, because I thought, "Well, if he cheated on everybody else, why wouldn't he cheat on me?" I never caught him. Of course, there was always girls sending him cards and phone numbers, but I never really caught him. But, yes, he told me he did it to everyone else. He lived his "rock star life," for sure.

MIKE PORTNOY: I first met him ... it was about 1988. Dream Theater had just finished recording our debut album, *When Dream and Day Unite*, and our manager at the time was working at the Kiss company. I guess he played Eric our album, before it was even released, and Eric immediately liked it and came to a whole bunch of our shows in about '88 and '89, when we were just playing locally in New York. That was the first time I met him, coming out to the shows. At that point, we were complete unknowns, so I was very starstruck by him, being such a Kiss fan. We were still young kids starting out, so it was awesome to have his support at such an early stage of our career.

He saw us several times, and I also hung out with him several times, outside of Dream Theater shows. He was just always the sweetest, nicest guy, and I'm sure anybody you're interviewing is telling you the same thing. He was such a nice, sweet-hearted guy. And like I said earlier, we were kids and just starting out, with no success behind us. So there was no reason for him to cling to me and be nice to me, except for the fact that he was a nice guy, and I guess he liked my drumming. It was an honor to have been befriended by him at such an early stage of our career. I have a couple of pictures of me and him, just hanging out.

JACK SAWYERS: I went back home to Jersey, packed up all my stuff, and moved to Hollywood, California, in September of '88, which I guess they were just wrapping up the *Smashes, Thrashes & Hits* album. I got a job at Guitar Center, working right there at the front door. It's funny [because], a week later, who walks in? Eric Carr. [Laughs] He walks in, and I said, "Hey!" He looks over at me and starts cracking up. He says, "What are *you* doing here?" It was like a whole big joke. I said, "I moved out here. I'm in L.A. now." So he would come in from time to time. We got to know each other and became friends. And then I remember all of a sudden, he was like, "Hey, I'm going to be hanging out at the Rainbow tonight. Come on. Come and hang out at the Cat & Fiddle."

BRUCE KULICK: I know that Eric wasn't happy about it [rerecording the vocals for "Beth" for *Smashes, Thrashes & Hits*]. Of course, he wasn't a complete nut where he was going to say, "No!" But he wasn't happy. I knew he'd sing it great, because Eric had a great voice that could have been used even more with Kiss. I was kind of excited for him. You're wondering, they're obviously revisiting it because there's something contractual about Peter's version, from what I think I understood. But it was also nice to say, "Hey, we don't need you Peter. We've got Eric to sing it." But I think it was a good opportunity for Eric. And if I did talk to him about it, I'm sure I would have told him that. Even though, "Yeah, you're stepping on some holy ground, blah blah blah, but you're a great singer. Take the opportunity to be featured on a record." And I thought he did a fine job, and I think he did like doing it in the end, and Paul helped produce and guide him. And there it is.

LORETTA CARAVELLO: I think it's pretty well known that he thought Peter knew about it [being redone]. And then he found out he didn't. He was embarrassed and felt bad.

BOB GRAW: With all due respect to Eric, and I know he didn't want to do it, [and] I remember reading that he was totally against it, but he was on the payroll, so he had to do it. *I hated it.* I thought it was the ultimate slap in the face to Peter Criss. It was very, very disappointing. I still wish they hadn't of done it. It had nothing to do with Eric, because I loved Eric Carr. I loved him as a member of Kiss, and I thought he was a great replacement for Peter Criss. He always fit in, and he looked great on stage and played great. He definitely looked like he belonged in Kiss. But when I heard that ... I never listen to that song. I always skip it.

Young Paul Caravello [Photo by Loretta Caravello]

Teen Paul Caravello [Photo by Loretta Caravello]

Paul Caravello keeps the beat
[Photo by Loretta Caravello]

Paul Caravello shortly before joining Kiss
[Photo by Loretta Caravello]

Kiss in the 1970s: L-R: Gene Simmons, Paul Stanley, and Ace Frehley
[Photo by Richard Galbraith—myspace.com/richardgalbraith]

Kiss' original drummer, Peter Criss
[Photo by Richard Galbraith—
myspace.com/richardgalbraith]

Eric's debut with Kiss, at New York's Palladium, 1980
[Photo by Lydia Criss—lydiacriss.com,
from the book *Sealed with a Kiss*]

E-ric! E-ric! [Photo by Lydia Criss—lydiacriss.com, from the book *Sealed with a Kiss*]

Eric, Paul, and Gene meet the people, 1983
[Photo by Donn Young—donnyoung.com]

Kiss rock Oklahoma, *Creatures of the Night* tour, 1983
[Photo by Richard Galbraith—myspace.com/richardgalbraith]

Vinnie Vincent, Ace's first replacement
[Photo by Richard Galbraith—myspace.com/richardgalbraith]

Eric stands tall
[Photo by Richard Galbraith—myspace.com/richardgalbraith]

One mean tank [Photo by Richard Galbraith—myspace.com/richardgalbraith]

WE WANT KISS! WE WANT KISS!
[Photo by Richard Galbraith—myspace.com/richardgalbraith]

Unmasked at last. Eric snaps a photo of Vinnie, Paul,
and Gene at Radio City Music Hall, 1984
[Photo by Loretta Caravello]

Kiss on the *Animalize* tour, 1985: L-R: Eric, Gene, new guitarist Bruce Kulick, and Paul [Photo by Bev Davies—bevdavies.com & flickr.com/people/bevdavies]

Gene licks it up
[Photo by Bev Davies—bevdavies.com & flickr.com/people/bevdavies]

Pointing Paul
[Photo by Bev Davies—bevdavies.com & flickr.com/people/bevdavies]

Eric goes back for more [Photo by Loretta Caravello]

Gene's snazzy stage duds, *Asylum* tour, 1986 (Eric in background)
[Photo by Richard Galbraith—myspace.com/richardgalbraith]

Eric's massive drum set-up
[Photo by Richard Galbraith—myspace.com/richardgalbraith]

Bruuuce [Photo by Richard Galbraith—
myspace.com/richardgalbraith]

Pouting Paul [Photo by Richard Galbraith—
myspace.com/richardgalbraith]

Paul and Bruce share the mic
[Photo by Richard Galbraith—myspace.com/richardgalbraith]

Black N' Blue's Tommy Thayer (Kiss' future guitarist!) and Jaime St. James [Photo by Richard Galbraith— myspace.com/richardgalbraith]

Eric and Carrie Stevens, shortly after their first meeting in 1987
[Photo by Carrie Stevens]

Eric gets ready to rock, 1988 [Photo by Carrie Stevens]]

Bruce and Eric, 1990 [Photo by Carrie Stevens]

Carrie and Christina Harrison (Bruce's then-wife)
[Photo by Carrie Stevens]

Carrie's mother, Eric, and Carrie backstage
[Photo by Carrie Stevens]

Slaughter's Blas Elias, Carrie, and Eric
[Photo by Carrie Stevens]

1. SLOW FLOOR TOMS w/ SMALL TOMS
2. HAND & FOOT AROUND KIT
3. TIME w/ FILLS
4. LEFT KICKS w/ COWBELL
5. LONG ROLL DOWN TOMS
6. DOUBLE KICK w/ FILLS
7. STOP
8. SINGLE FOOT w/ TOM ROLLS
9. SLOW DOWN
10. VOICES w/ KICKS ON 4th OR TIME FILLS
11. AUDIENCE CHANT / E-RIC, "E-RIC"
12. SPEED UP
13. CHORD END
14. JUMP BOW
15. SEQUENCER JUMP DOWN
16. "WHO ARE YOU" DRUM RIFFS
17. SNARE ROLL
18. DOUBLE KICK END w/ CHORDS

Eric's written notes for his drum solo on the *Hot in the Shade* tour
[Photo by Greg Prato]

Eric and Carrie in Massachusetts [Photo by Carrie Stevens]

Eric on the set of a video shoot
[Photo by Carrie Stevens]

Eric with his father, Albert Caravello,
and mother, Connie Caravello
[Photo by Loretta Caravello]

Eric backstage with his niece, Sara-Jean,
and his mother
[Photo by Carrie Stevens]

#1 Kiss fan Bob Graw, 2010
[Photo by Greg Prato]

Eric's drum tech, John Walsh,
displaying Eric's *Hot in the Shade* stage
outfit and sticks Eric used for his
drum solo, 2010 [Photo by Greg Prato]

Paul Charles Caravello/Eric Carr: 1950-1991
[Photo by Angela Simon]

1989

BOB KULICK: [Eric's] frustration level really reached its height when I did Paul's tour [Paul did a short solo tour of clubs in 1989]. Because instead of *him* playing those songs, it was Eric Singer, and Paul allowed Eric Singer to take liberties he would never allow Eric Carr to take. And this created animosity, because Eric Carr could not understand why that was so, even though it was as plain as the nose on my face. "We're not Kiss, so we can get away with playing a whole bunch of different stuff." Although having said that, every time I asked Paul, "Can I do a longer solo at the end?" "*No!*" "Can I extend the solo at the middle of this one?" "*No!*" He never gave me any room. And there were times he barked about, "Can you play it closer to what Ace was playing?" They did bust chops, not only Eric Carr's, but mine as well ... and I wasn't even in Kiss! Forget about what they did to my brother.

But what I'm saying to you is that in a way, he had become a tortured soul, and this is part of the program that to me was sad, because you've got a hit band. You shouldn't be a tortured soul. But he took it too seriously, and so I think that is where the grey area came in—the drummer in a mega-star band but feeling less than what he should have about it. I would say to my brother sometimes, "Whatever the reality may be—I stood on stage with Alice Cooper, Diana Ross, Meat Loaf, Michael Bolton, and big stars—no matter what may have happened, the perception of that audience is you're standing there with those people. *You're* a star. Never forget that." Eric took all of this too seriously, I fear. And hence, some of what went on—the times where he drank too much or whatever—I think was a byproduct of what people do when they're tortured and they're trying to cope with their reality.

GARY CORBETT: Eric Singer and I are still very close friends, because we did Paul Stanley's solo tour together, that Paul did in '89. And the really strange thing about that is when we played the New York show, Eric Carr came to the show, and he came backstage after the show and said to me,

"That guy is going to get my gig." And I'm like, "What are you talking about? They're not going to fire you." And he goes, "No man, I'm telling you. That guy is going to have my gig." And there was no basis for feeling that way at that point, other than the fact that Eric Singer was such a great drummer. But he was in Badlands at the time, and there was nothing about that that was based on anything in reality. After the tour, when Paul would do demos—he would be writing for the next record—he did use Eric Singer to play drums on the demos. A few of the demo drum tracks ended up actually being the drum tracks they ended up using on the record. So Eric Singer actually is on *Hot in the Shade*, although he's not credited. There were one or two songs that they used the demos of.

BRUCE KULICK: Not a great experience [the recording of *Hot in the Shade*]. Gene and Paul found this studio with this guy, Pat Regan, where we were demoing up ideas. Back then, I think what was kind of hip were drum pads that you didn't have to mic up a whole kit. You could have your samples. I remember that we worked up a lot of the songs, and then once they were ready to do the record, we started actually using the demos, because they didn't sound half-bad. But they sound "half," if you know what I mean. I wish we would have started all over in a big studio and just go for it. But they wanted to do the "less is more/let's keep this more organic." So some of that was the right approach. But I think what was wrong was we certainly had the budget, and could have done everything better and bigger, and maybe even used a producer. And then there were a few tracks that Eric's drums don't even appear—it's really a drum machine. I found that really kind of a bit of a blasphemy. And it didn't help Eric's feelings.

CARRIE STEVENS: I was in the studio with him while he recorded [*Hot in the Shade*]. It was right across the street from this restaurant, Genghis Cohen, and I remember the first day I walked in, Gene looked at me, looked at Eric, and goes, "You should marry her." Gene, who is so against marriage, was telling Eric to marry me! It was a thrill for me to be there, but I was more "the girlfriend." It's not like I was paying attention to which notes were being played. Having sex in the bathroom at the recording studio—I was the girlfriend, I wasn't a musician! We were always having fun together. Going out to eat and hanging out. I was still so young. Eric didn't want to go out to clubs or do anything like that. I would go out and come home afterwards and tell him all about it. There was a huge age difference.

BRUCE KULICK: I thought the "Little Caesar" sessions were fun [a song Eric sang lead on and co-wrote with Gene and Adam Mitchell]. I was very excited to be a part of that, and the fact that Gene and Paul said, "You know, this is a good song," and Gene jumped in and helped finish it. But originally, it was just Adam Mitchell and Eric. I don't think I was even involved in the writing of that, but I helped out with the guitar playing. So overall, it was kind of a bittersweet experience. Here's Eric singing a really good song, and the demo was not that much different than the final version. But overall, that record I felt was stained because of the fact that you're going to take your demos and make them your masters and just fix them up a little bit. Although the album has its highlights, too. I just kind of was a little surprised at how we handled that record, that's all. I didn't mind the artwork, and our look was kinda cool.

ADAM MITCHELL: We did ["Little Caesar"] at his apartment in New York. The thing I remember is when we were doing the demo for that, as I said, I had a drum machine, and the biggest difference I remember—and this is true when we did the songs for the *Rockheads*—I had originally started out as a drummer, but the difference between me programming a drum machine for a demo and Eric programming the same thing was night and day. I mean, it just hit me so vividly at the time, and Bruce, too. And Bruce is a hugely talented musician, but when we were doing the demos for the *Rockheads* stuff and Bruce would be up there programming, Eric would come over, change everything, and it would just be tremendous. So much better. It felt suddenly like a real drum track, and it was rocking. That's what I remember mostly about writing "Little Caesar." He'd moved way up on the east side. He was up in the 80s and Second or something like that. It was a big thing for Eric to have a song on a Kiss record, because that was hard to do. Normally, it was all Gene and Paul with co-writers. It was hard for a band member to get a song on the record. So I was really pleased for him. It didn't turn out to be a hugely successful record, but it was good for him.

EDDIE TRUNK: The one thing that I do know, too, [is that] he was immensely proud of having had the opportunity to sing lead vocal on a Kiss record, on that song "Little Caesar" on *Hot in the Shade*. He was not so excited about singing "Beth" for the greatest hits record, because he knew that it was sacred ground. But he did that, and after a while, I think he liked what he did with it. It was what it was. He never did it live or anything like that. But he really, really wanted to sing lead on a record. Anytime we got together and did radio, he always made me play "Little Caesar." He was always proud to tell people that he did everything on the song. He played drums, bass, sang, [and] I think he even played guitar. He told me once that it's basically him and Bruce on the whole song, with Paul on some backing vocals or something. That was something that was really important to him, and [he] was really proud of being able to do that. And that's the other thing that people who don't follow Kiss might not know. Eric did play bass on some songs. I think he played bass on "I Still Love You" on *Creatures*. So he did a lot more than just sit down and play the drums as however he was told. He sang, [and] he wrote "Breakout" on Ace's record [1987's *Frehley's Comet*]. There's that connection, because that's one of the songs that he wrote. "All Hell's Breakin' Loose" on *Lick It Up*. So the guy brought a lot more to the table if you really dig a little deeper, than what he's really given credit for.

LORETTA CARAVELLO: He always wanted to write more. If you look at *Rockology* and all that stuff, he had tons of music. There are tons of demos that haven't been released. I'm going to release a few things coming next year. Those songs, even though they were written for the *Rockheads*, they also were written for Kiss. The song "Somebody's Waiting" was questionable to go on *Hot in the Shade*, but "Forever" got on, instead. My personal opinion—if you listen to "Somebody's Waiting," you get chills down your back. "Forever" is a good song, too, but there is no reason why that couldn't have been on, either. It's the same. Gene and Paul write most of the stuff, and any member of Kiss wants more of their songs on, but it doesn't usually end up that way.

BOB KULICK: Sure, he could have done more. But the perimeters of the band were always set up so that in any given show, Peter or Eric or whoever it was would sing one song, and Ace would sing one song. It was like the

Beatles—George Harrison would do a song, and then Ringo would do his song. It was not that dissimilar. Could he have done more? Yes. Should he have done more? Yes. But as I said, when you join a band, you have to accept the arrangement that was made, and Paul and Gene were the main songwriters. And, again, music is a matter of personal opinion and taste. Could he have had a song that they missed that would have worked for them? Of course. I couldn't say for sure, but is it possible? Of course. But it's music. It's a matter of personal opinion and taste. The good thing for him was that, let's face it, there were a million people that would have killed to be him. So he was the lucky one. It's so hard to walk into a band like that. Bear that in mind—*he walked into a successful band.* Just the pressure of that alone, you have to give it to the guy. That's a lot of pressure. No matter what we think of Peter Criss, those are huge shoes to fill, for a crowd that is fanatical.

ADAM MITCHELL: I think on *Hot in the Shade*, it was nice to hear Eric's voice, but it was like, "How many songs did Ringo have on the record?" Eric was "the Ringo" in some respects. The fans basically wanted to hear Gene or Paul. I didn't realize until I'd actually been in the studio with Paul [that] Paul is ... I always knew he was a great singer, but it's not until you stand there and sing with him that you realize what a *phenomenal* voice he has. Paul has the most bulletproof voice I've ever heard, and believe me, I've sung with a lot of great singers—Linda Ronstadt and I did a lot of singing together. Paul could sing higher, longer, and harder and still keep his quality, still sing in tune, better than anybody else I'd ever heard. He has an absolutely bulletproof voice.

BOB GRAW: I thought they were starting to go in the right direction. There was a lot more rockin' songs on it. I loved "Hide Your Heart." It was a big hit for them on MTV. I remember the first time I heard that song, I absolutely loved it. I thought, "This is a great sound for Kiss." That album probably was starting to bring them back to their heavier '70s sound. It might not have been all the way there yet, but it was definitely working its way back in. "Rise to It"—great song, great video. But other than that, it's very poppy. But like I said, there's certain songs. Eric's song is probably the best song on the album.

EDDIE TRUNK: Even though the record I think is pretty poorly produced, the material on it, the direction, the way they looked, and everything they tried to be at that point seemed to be much more natural and kind of comfortable.

BRUCE KULICK: There's no doubt that Eric, if need be, he could have contributed more. When you look at the reality of what Kiss was about and how it was put together and how it's run ... what you heard is how it fit for Eric. Meaning could he have sung a song? Sure. But Gene and Paul were very competitive about giving those things up. How I got one on *Carnival of Souls* is a miracle ["I Walk Alone"]. But, again, he certainly did his thing, and he was great at it. I think what he contributed and his talent was always obvious in the band. If you're a real fan of him, you could complain and say, "Some of the songs on *Rockology* could have been finished. They could have been on Kiss albums." All true. But what are you going to do?

CARRIE STEVENS: He was frustrated. He was happy that "Little Caesar" was on the album. He was proud of that. Every musician wants their songs to be [on albums] for financial reasons. But for him, creatively, he did want to do more. I was so young and immature, and I just wanted to have fun. He used to express to me that when he was with me, I'd fly to New York, or he'd be in L.A., and we'd spend weeks together, and then he'd be like, "When I'm with you, I get nothing done." And I was like, "Well, what do you have to do? You're in Kiss. You don't have to do anything." But he had a lot he wanted to do, creatively.

CHRISTINA HARRISON: Carrie said we met at the Palladium. They weren't playing there, but we went to see a bunch of bands, and she said she saw me at the top of the stairs. She said it was either '89 or '90. I was already married to Bruce. I thought I had met Carrie before at a shed show in New Hampshire [in 1988]. She said she moved to L.A. in February of '89 and that Eric kind of kept her on the down-low then, maybe because he was kind of dating somebody else, or he didn't know "Do I love her? Do I not love her?" And I said, "I could have sworn that I met you before that." My first recollection of meeting Carrie was a shed show. She seemed so young and gorgeous. I remember her being heavier—not fat by any stretch of the imagination—but more a country girl body and wearing a flower-print dress.

He was always insecure, because he started out as the range repairman. He knew he was a good drummer, but he couldn't believe he was in Kiss, because he was just an average, wonderful, normal guy. But yet at the same time, he was so insecure. And his relationship with Carrie was on-and-off, on-and-off, on-and-off. "I love her ... I don't know ... I love her ... I don't know." They would argue a lot. I would always say, "Oh, it's young love, arguing and make up, arguing and make up." Bruce would always tell him, "Why don't you just schedule the flight ahead of time, two weeks or a month ahead of time, so you can save money? You guys fight, and then you fly her out the next day." But what couple doesn't fight, though? Couples do.

BRUCE KULICK: My ex-wife Christina [and Eric] were friends. And then at times, they would fight. He wouldn't want to talk to her. I probably saved these letters. I remember him writing a very long letter to her, talking about whatever he was going through with Carrie at the time, and trying to make Christina understand why he was being so, maybe, difficult to the situation. And I just thought it was interesting that he would write it, instead of saying it.

CHRISTINA HARRISON: [Bruce and Christina] got married on September 24, 1989. You know who was the most genuinely excited—which is funny, because he's so anti-marriage—when we drove up to the house to tell Gene we were getting married, his eyes lit up, and he was like, "Mazel Tov!" He hugged me and was shaking Bruce's hand. He knew we were a good couple. So the day of the wedding, it was a super gorgeous day, and everyone was in amazing high spirits. It just goes to show you, I didn't know Carrie that well, and I found out quite a long time later that Eric was really insecure, he didn't know if "Should I call Carrie my full-time girlfriend or not?" She had actually flown out and was in his hotel room, and he didn't bring her to the wedding. But at the same time, we were trying to keep the cost down. I had even told Paul, "You can't bring a date." I didn't want all the single friends to bring dates, because that would double the wedding. I mean, the wedding was small. I think there was like 66 people there. So I didn't let any single friends bringing a date unless it was like their significant girlfriend or boyfriend. So I even told Paul, "You can't bring a date," and he's like, "I don't care." I was pretty verbal about it—"We've got to keep it small." But it was a fun day. They were really genuinely happy for us.

LARRY MAZER: I was managing Cinderella at the time, which was a multi-platinum band. And I had met Gene and Paul prior, just, "Hello, how are you?" at different shows that we were both at. When Cinderella played the Forum in L.A., Gene was there, and I met him there, and Paul was once in Sweden when Cinderella played, and we brought him out to do the encore with us. So they knew who I was, I knew who they were, and out of the blue one day, in '89 I guess it was, they called me. They had been working prior with Danny Goldberg, I guess, in a consultant role, and they had ended that relationship. They called me, because I had a lot of strength at Mercury, because of Cinderella's success, and said, "Would you be interested in working with Kiss?" I was in New York the next day, and we made a deal in five seconds. That started the seven-year relationship. I got involved about a month before *Hot in the Shade* came out.

My biggest concern was from the point when they took the make-up off, Kiss really became "Paul Stanley's band." Gene had his Simmons Records. He was working with Liza Minnelli [as her manager], [and] he was doing his acting thing. And Kiss became a very one-dimensional band from *Lick It Up* through—and including—*Hot in the Shade*, where it was pretty much Paul's band. Every single track that went to radio during that period were "Paul tracks." "I Love It Loud" was the prior Gene track, which was on the *Creatures of the Night* record. I made it clear that I felt they were losing a whole side of them by not having Gene be more visible in the band. What I demanded when I got involved was that he had to stop with Simmons Records, he had to stop managing Liza Minnelli, he had to stop with all this other stuff, and he had to get back into Kiss. Which he did.

Unfortunately, *Hot in the Shade* had already been done, but if you look at the *Revenge* record, *Revenge* was really the return of Gene Simmons. As a matter of fact, the first track I went to radio with was a Gene track ["Unholy"]. The third track I went to radio with was a Gene track ["Domino"]. And he toughened up his image. That was what, to me, brought back Gene Simmons into Kiss. He's a very important part of the band, especially during the make-up years. I mean, Gene had as many hit songs as Paul did, but for whatever reason—for him having his outside activities—he let Paul take over the band. Not to take anything away from Paul, but Kiss was built upon the duality of Gene and Paul, and that's what was missing. So that was something that I made clear had to happen, and it did.

At that point, I had to work with the record at hand, which was *Hot in the Shade*, which was a very average record as far as material. There were fifteen songs, of which maybe six were good and the rest were pretty terrible. But there was the song "Forever" on there, that I was lucky enough, with my ability to work radio, to get them their first top-ten single since "I Was Made for Lovin' You." The record ended up doing I think 800,000 copies, and we did a very mega, mega tour [in 1990], which I think looking back was probably one of the best live stage-shows they ever did. We had a big sphinx on stage. I think if you look back at all the tours in history, I think that was the more interesting Kiss show there ever was, because we just did so many things with that sphinx that was cool. I'm very proud of that tour.

JACK SAWYERS: I would go and hang out with Eric at a few of these different places. We'd get to talking, and we became friends. He kept asking me, "What do you want to do with your life?" And I told him the basics of it was, "I'm a filmmaker and want to get into filmmaking and music videos." So we'd call each other and have lunch. So I get a call from him one day, and he was like, "Hey, that company that did that 'Exposed' video with us, they're going to be doing a couple more music videos with us. You should come down to the set." And at that point, I had been working at SIR Studios already. I had got a job working in production. I'm like, "Where are you guys shooting?" And he's like, "I think it's at SIR Studios." I'm like, "Cool. I work on the lot there." So I got the dates of when he was going to be doing it. I go to the Kiss set for I believe it was "Rise to It." Eric gets me in, and he walks right up to the director, Mark Rezyka. Eric's like, "Hey, this is my friend Jack ... *give him a job on the video.*" It was really funny—that's exactly how it happened!

I found out later, the directors aren't usually the people that hire on music videos—it's usually the producers and the production people. But anyway, it was almost like Mark sat and thought about it for a second, and then said, "OK." And then Eric's like, "Cool. You're in," and then walks off. So the director's like, "Here," he gives me 20 bucks and some car keys. He's like, "My car, the black Jaguar convertible parked outside, go down to the liquor store and get me a bottle of Scotch ... and don't tell anybody." So I did it, I got back, and I was there for the whole thing, the whole video shoot. And I remember that they were trying to get an audience to come in for the last part of the video. Everybody was making suggestions, and somebody suggested to just call KNAC and say the first hundred people that can get to SIR Studios can get into a Kiss concert. So that was cool.

It was also cool to see Gene and Paul put [on] the make-up that day [The opening segment of the video includes a bit of Gene and Paul back in make-up]. I wish I would have had a camera with me to take pictures. So that was the very first Kiss music video I got to work on. I'd worked on a few other videos before that, through SIR. I basically blew SIR off when the Kiss train rolled into town, and [I] worked on set all day, all 15 hours. So after that, the director told the producer to consider me for working on other stuff. And immediately, the following week, we were doing the "Forever" video. The "Forever" shoot was a very cool shoot. They had acoustic guitars, and in between sets, they were doing old Beatles songs. Just a really cool vibe on that set—that was a very long day, too. But like I said, Eric was very instrumental in helping me get my foot in the door with that production company that I really wanted to get into. Basically, Eric just walked me in the door. That was very cool, and I was always very grateful to him for that.

TY TABOR: We met at first at the Santa Monica Civic Center—King's X was doing a show with Mr. Big and Winger. This was probably '89. It just so happened that, between all three bands, the amount of people that came out from other bands that happened to be a fan of this or that musician turned out to be this huge crowd of people, of musicians. We even took a picture together, this whole group of people from all these different bands. I've lost the picture. I haven't seen it in a long time, but I know it exists. But that was the night I'd met Eric for the first time. He just came up and said he was a big fan, and I couldn't believe it. I was just like, *"You've got to be joking."* Every time he was [at King's X shows], I was excited he was there. We had exchanged phone numbers and kept up with each other. He was just a super cool guy that I dug. We kept in contact. Every time he came, we hung out.

1990

JACK SAWYERS: It's funny, because I remember telling Gene, "We should just get a couple of cameras and follow Kiss around, just everyday stuff." And I remember Gene going, "Who would be interested in that? Who would be interested in seeing everyday life stuff?" Basically, reality television. And I said, "I'm telling you, the fans would dig it. There's nothing like that out there, if we followed you guys around with a couple of cameras. Everything from getting up in the morning and this and that." They were like, "We'll just shoot stuff, and we'll see what we can use." It was supposed to be *Kiss Exposed Part Two*, and we were going to shoot the entire *Hot in the Shade* concert, as well. But from my understanding, Gene didn't like the way his hair looked. It was something funny like that. And we never ended up shooting the concert professionally. We went to Texas, saw the rehearsals, were shooting all behind the scenes, and following them around with cameras. It's funny, because somebody's got the footage—it's all over YouTube.

JOHN WALSH: I go back 32 years in this business. I started out working as a drum tech for the Good Rats. Eventually, Bruce Kulick got in the band, and I knew Bruce for several years before he got into Kiss. And then years later, when the drum tech job came up [for Kiss], both Bruce and Gary Corbett, who I had known before that as well, they both said to Eric, "This is the guy for you." And that's pretty much it. It was because Bruce and Gary together telling Eric, "OK, you don't have to worry. We have a drum tech that's not only capable of doing the drum tech job, but whose personality will fit in very well with Eric." Obviously, you've heard a million people tell you what a great guy he was and what a sweet man at the same time. And that's exactly how I was introduced to Kiss and how I got the job. [*Hot in the Shade*] was already in the can, and then I was hired on for the tour. Of course, at the time, I thought, "OK, this will be a ten-year job, probably."

It didn't take me long to figure out what I'd heard about Eric was true. When it comes to personalities, the thing I heard about him was he was a really nice guy, because that was important to me. Regardless of the job, if the people that you work with aren't nice, it's just not fun. And it didn't take long to realize Eric was a real good guy, and I enjoyed his personality, and eventually, "being in the trenches" with Eric. It was always an uphill battle, and sometimes, it was him and me against the world. [Laughs] But it was a very easy transition for me to get in with it. Paul and Gene have always been really good to me. If I run into those guys at the NAMM show convention or here or there, whenever I see them—I'm sure other people will tell you that they've had different relationships with those guys—they were always nice to me. Even back then and to this day when I cross paths with them, it's always a very positive thing. I have to give them credit. At least with me, they were always very good.

The pyrotechnics [for the tour] were going to be done by the guy who did *Star Wars*. Do you remember when the Death Star exploded? They were very excited. "We're going to have this pyro guy do the Kiss tour!" When we were in Texas doing the rehearsals, everybody was excited that "We are going to see the pyro for the first time." Myself and a few other techs went to the front of the house to watch some of the pyro stuff and, "Here comes the part of the song where there's going to be big pyro." And it was like, *"Pop, pop, pop."* We realized this guy did this stuff for *movies*—it's not going to work out for the Kiss show. So he was let go, and they in turn went out with some other company. I forget them right now, but the bombs were big. These guys were so proud of themselves. If they knocked four or five shingles out of the ceiling in an arena every night ... it had to be big for those guys. Since it all went so well—the buses were great, the gigs went well so much of the time—overall, Eric was always happy. We were a happy bunch.

GARY CORBETT: That was a really successful tour for them. Things were a lot better. The stage set was a lot bigger. By this point, I was off stage, and in the beginning, they never gave it much thought as to where they put me. I'd be down on the floor, but then I would still be visible to certain parts of the audience. By the time the *Hot in the Shade* tour came around and they were designing the stage, they decided to build a little ... we used to call it "the condo." That was where my keyboards were. It was basically stage right. It was on the side of the stage, but it had curtains all around it, so nobody in the audience could see in. It was great. Because of being off stage, I decided on that tour that I was going to do stuff in the condo every night, that would be stuff I wouldn't be able to do if I was on stage.

All of the opening acts were guys like Slaughter, and those guys were all huge Kiss fans. So I used to let them come into the condo during the show, and they'd all stand behind me while I was playing. But when it came time for the choruses, I did a lot of background singing. They would all join in on the microphone and sing background with me. We had a lot of fun doing that. One night before the show, I ordered a Domino's pizza. I told all the security guys between the back door and my condo that I did it, and the guy was going to show up during the show. And I wanted him to deliver the pizza to the condo. I didn't want them to take it from him and bring it to me. I wanted the guy walking *into* the condo! It was awesome. I had the money on my rack, which was right next to my keyboards. I'm standing there playing, and this guy pokes his head in, looks, and he doesn't know what to think. I motion him to come on in, [and] I pointed where the money was. He stood there for about five minutes or so. He was just mesmerized. And we had a little pizza party in the condo!

JOHN WALSH: I remember seeing in a magazine or a fanzine that Gene was saying early on in the tour, "Things are going surprisingly well." My insight is that, originally, I didn't know if there was going to be a *Hot in the Shade* tour, if not for the video "Forever." Because when that went through the roof on MTV, that big hit made the difference of "Is there going to be a big tour or not?" And that song ... we did very well. I'd say the arenas were pretty much full all the time. It was rock n' roll, but it was very business-like. If you look at the itinerary for *Hot in the Shade*, quite often, it was five days on and two days off. Just like a 9-to-5 job. And the business part of it I think went very well. Since most of it was in America, it was run very well. And because of that, everything was very smooth. I think when you're on a tour like that, there's not a lot of conflict. And when the crowd is good and there's money coming in, there's never a problem with equipment. We were always told, "You've got to have back-ups for back-ups." They didn't hold back on spending money for making sure that everything looked great and all the equipment was great. There wasn't a whole lot of hanging out on days off, because the band stayed in a different hotel. Which was OK—we preferred to be near the venue. That was always better for us, we stayed in nice hotels. But when we did get together, it was fairly mellow. Eric wasn't a party animal, although we had a good time. There was no drugs as far as he and I were concerned. Nothing stronger than a few drinks here and there. Eric was always in control.

EDDIE TRUNK: It was the best line-up, with Bruce and Eric. I think it's the best non-original Kiss line-up to date, in terms of everybody found their own footing. Eric had been really entrenched at that time and done a number of records. Although if you dig deeper, I think people will tell you that that's one of the tours that Eric and Paul didn't even talk the whole tour, because there were some "wars" that went on back then. But as far as from a fan standpoint, I thought the line-up was great. Bruce started to come into his own.

I thought that was Kiss in their most natural form, in the sense that I don't think Kiss was ever a pop band, and I don't think Kiss was ever a metal band. I think they made great records on both sides of those equations, but I think Kiss is more comfortable as a hard rock band. With *Hot in the Shade*, that was them in their most natural skin—the way they dressed, the way they looked, the line-up ... it had gelled and really come together.

The set list was a good amount of old stuff and more recent stuff, no extended solos, just 20 great songs. The coolest stage set they ever had without the make-up. That was the first time for me in a long time that it really felt like *a band*. They had went through the Vinnie thing, that was on again/off again. Did he play on the record ... does he have make-up ... does he not? They went through the whole Mark St. John thing. This finally felt like, "Alright, we've got a drummer that's been here for a good six or seven years at this point. We've gone though all these phases." This is really what "Kiss Phase Two" felt like to me as a fan. Visually, stage-show, the performances, the members—it just all really came together the best there.

BOB GRAW: I remember the stage they had was amazing. They had a big sphinx head, and the sphinx shot lasers out of its eyes. They had a lot of pyro. That was the tour where they brought back a lot more of the classic material. I was very happy about that.

BRUCE KULICK: By the time I got in the band, they were using a business manager, which was the Howard Marks Agency, which was an advertising agency, too. That fell apart. Some shenanigans went down by the time *Crazy Nights* was put out. Here I was in this huge band, and I was wondering why we didn't have this huge manager that also would handle other really big bands. But again, I wasn't driving the car. And Larry Mazer, I loved his vision and personality. I thought he was the best guy for the band, and I know he still has a lot of respect from Gene and Paul, and he's still very successful. As much as I knew that Eric liked him, as soon as he convinced them not to do a drum solo, he didn't like him. [Laughs]

LARRY MAZER: What was interesting in regards to Eric was after I got hired ... I had known Bruce for a long time, so I had called Bruce, and he was very excited about me getting involved. I had never met Eric. And immediately, the very first phone call to Eric Carr, I told him I hated drum solos! And it really didn't start the relationship well. As a matter of fact, I don't even think we spoke for the first couple of months that I was managing the band. During that period of time, all those drummers in those bands—Cinderella, Poison, all the "hair bands"—they all did the same drum solo. It was pretty much "boom, boom," then put your hands to the audience to scream. I hated it. To me, it was the time when people wanted to take a piss was when drummers did solos.

I told him, "Eric, I love you. I'm a huge fan of your playing. But I have to be honest with you. *I hate drum solos.*" And there was this deathly silence on the phone. And like I said, I don't think it started our relationship off well at all. It got better over time, but unfortunately, at that point in time, I don't think Eric was too happy with his lot in the band at all, because of his relationship with Gene and Paul. I can say truthfully, looking back on it, that in that period of time of *Hot in the Shade*, compared to the other three, I really didn't become that close to him as I did the other three. And it probably started out bad with my comment about drum solos but then expanded because I think, at that point, he was not really happy with how he was being treated overall, financially or whatever. I was just looked upon as "Gene and Paul's new manager," not "Kiss' manager," because he and Bruce were really hired guns. Although they were involved, it was really Gene and

Paul's band. I think Eric was probably hoping that I was going to be more of the "band manager," and I was. I gave everybody the time of day—Bruce will tell you. But I think he still looked upon anybody in that job as an employee of Gene and Paul, not an employee of the band Kiss.

I mean, they got along, but there was definitely tension. There was tension with Bruce, also. Kiss is Gene and Paul. So there was definitely tension. There was constant—I think—money disagreements. I wasn't involved in any of that. The band had a business manager, and I wasn't really involved. I would just pick up vibes. But you could get a vibe that it wasn't like a normal band where I was used to—with Cinderella or any of the bands I managed since then—where it was really "all-for-one-and-one-for-all." Bruce and Eric "knew their place," so to speak. And their place was that they were employees, basically.

BRUCE KULICK: There were times he was in a great mood and pretty cool with everything. And there were times when he was really not happy. I think his low point came in *Hot in the Shade*, as soon as his drum solo was taken away. Which was really Larry Mazer's idea, to put more songs in the set. Eric felt emasculated by that, or castrated. He harbored a real grudge with Gene and Paul about that. And I understood again why that felt weird. But I was excited about, "Hey, now we can do over 20 songs and not have a drum solo. There's so much to represent from the history of this band." So he would act that frustration out by not socializing with anybody. It was a really stressful time at times with him. And finally, Paul and him had a talk, because it seemed like it was almost more just between Paul and him. That was when he told me that I'm on their side. I was uncomfortable with that. He wasn't handling the situation well, and he just seemed [to think] I was with Gene and Paul. There was no sides to take. And I'm like, "Can't we all just get along?" Or, shall I say, I was more like I'm not going to beat them that way ... and again, there were times that I had my frustrations, too. I didn't want to take it to a level of not wanting to talk to anybody or socialize. It wasn't healthy for him, clearly.

There was a big change in attitude once Paul did talk to him, and they had a good heart-to-heart about, like, "Come on." I can't tell you exactly what he said, but it's pretty obvious that either get along and play well and be happy, or we'll get someone else, and I'm sure Paul clearly could remind him, "Do you realize how lucky you are?" The whole thing was remarkable to me. You get jaded when you're in a really great situation, even if it's a great situation with some limitations. And it's real easy how your mind can fool you to be absolutely miserable, when if it was taken away, you would be devastated. So you don't know what you've got sometimes until it's gone. But that was kind of hard for me to watch. It was stressful. I didn't always understand it, even though certainly because I was around, to get what was frustrating to him. I also didn't think that being really stressed about it to that degree was going to make it better.

LARRY MAZER: That would be the logical thing, which is instead of ten minutes [or a drum solo], you can play three more songs. Again, I told him, and I did talk to Gene and Paul about it, and I think they then agreed with me. I tell everybody this—in 40 years of being a manager, the most fun I ever had was managing Kiss. As painful as it was certain times with Gene's point of view with money and this and that, as far as fun and as far as cooperation, there wasn't one idea that I brought to them in seven years that they said no to. They said yes to every single idea I had, which I really appreciate, that they gave me the latitude creatively to basically run the show. And that I really appreciated. I'm still friendly with Paul to this day. If I see Gene, I'll be friendly, but Paul still I talk to semi-regularly.

CHRISTINA HARRISON: Eric would go down to the bar and have a couple of drinks, and he'd be super-friendly with the fans. He'd be sitting down there drinking with fans, and then he would bitch about Gene and Paul, which didn't go over. Fans are of course going to run back to Gene and Paul, because they want to be able to talk to Gene and Paul and have the inside scoop. Which I thought was pretty crummy as fans to do that. If some guy is drinking in a bar, and you complain about your boss, like if you worked for IBM and you're bitching about your boss, and you're having a beer, who runs and tells the boss? I used to get really mad when I'd find out that fans would run and tell Gene and Paul. I'm like, "He's just crying in his beer." What person in this country doesn't complain about their boss?

He did realize he had a good gig, but he was bitter because he was a paid, salaried employee who wasn't getting a cut of anything. I think he and Bruce complained a lot pretty early on, even when we moved to L.A.—but not where they were like seething. They really had a good relationship with Gene and Paul. Bruce always treated Gene and Paul like, "They're my bosses," and he'd talk to them very respectfully. It's like, yeah, you're in the band, and you're on the bus. But at the same time, you will always know that they're your employer.

I didn't see it [Eric upset about his drum solo taken away], but I sure heard about it. It wasn't good. In the end, Eric was absolutely PO'd, bewildered, and angry. He was livid. So how do you work like that? And Paul was sick of hearing things come back to him, so Paul's PO'd. But then he had to have some sort of empathy. I mean, he did have sincere empathy, but I think the empathy was being overridden about hearing things come back to him. So he's pissed.

BOB GRAW: To be honest with you, I had no problem with it. I think they took Bruce's guitar solo out of that show, too—I don't think anybody did a solo. Gene didn't, Paul didn't. They all had their moments in the show before that, but I had no problem with them taking guitar solos and drum solos out of the show to play more songs. I prefer it.

JOHN WALSH: I wouldn't say he was hurt by it, because he knows the business, and of course, he's a good guy. I think, originally, there wasn't going to be one, and he was like, "There should be one." He would say it kind of in confidence. And then when they decided, "Maybe there will be one," he was like, "Well ... I don't know." They tried to maybe put him under their thumb a little bit, and he said, "Maybe there *won't* be one." Ultimately, we knew he wanted to do one, so he constructed one, and there was a big drum solo on the *Hot in the Shade* tour. I was very proud to say that I had a part in that, because I was very interactive in that solo. I controlled the electronic drums that Eric was playing. So if you ever saw that solo, I'm there for every note, because I'm doing something behind the scenes, as well.

The whole thing for me was just so much fun, because we really sunk our teeth into this. This was not the kind of gig where you just kind of set up the equipment and, "OK, in two and a half hours, we'll take it down." You were really part of this. I was "plugged in," because with that kind of show, anything could happen at any time. We had fire, we had lasers, we had smoke. We had an electrical storm knock everything out in Kansas City. With Eric, we had a rack of electronics, and these things just started doing whatever they wanted to do. It really was something that you had to pay attention to. There was blood, sweat, and tears over that drum riser every night—it was a very intense gig. But at the same time, it was so much fun. We were on tour with Winger and Slaughter. The music was great, and I say it was more fun than I should be allowed to have on a job, because I really enjoy the job itself, being a drum tech.

BRUCE KULICK: We toured with two popular bands at the time, so it was one of my favorite tours, actually. Even though for Eric, it was disappointing about the drum solo. We had the lasers and the big sphinx. It was a huge show. It really looked great. Those were two bands Eric got close to—Winger and Slaughter. Overall, that was a good tour for us in many ways, but I know that it was still a hard tour for Eric in many ways.

MARK SLAUGHTER: Here's the funniest part of it. Carrie is the one who gave Eric the product [Slaughter's music]. Eric heard the *Stick It to Ya* record prior to the release, went to Gene and Paul and said, "You're not going to believe this. The guys from Vinnie Vincent Invasion put out a real smoking record here." And Eric Carr was the responsible party for taking it to Gene. As they were putting the tour together, they said, "Yeah, let's put them on." Inevitably, Eric Carr was the responsible party in that, that made it to where we actually got that tour. Our very first tour was with Kiss, and the very first show we did was in Lubbock, Texas, on May 4, 1990. When we came off the stage, in front of 11,000 people, there were gold records waiting in our dressing room. So it was a really Cinderella story.

BLAS ELIAS: All of us in the band were huge Kiss fans. I think Carrie helped us to get that tour by contacting Eric. We had just put out our first record, and Mark was going out with this girl who was friends with Carrie, so just hanging around with them, we all got to be friends. And Carrie, as far as I can remember, she may have taken our demo to Eric, who played it for Gene. So through that relationship, I think we owe a great deal of our success, because that first tour with Kiss was very important for us, as far as getting out there in front of a lot of people. So if it hadn't have been for Eric hearing the music and digging it, I don't think we would have been nearly as successful as we were. We were stoked just being out there, as fans of Kiss. And me in particular, playing with one of my heroes. Almost every night of that tour, I was on the side of the stage, watching the show. I'd sometimes put my hair up in a baseball hat, sneak out in the audience, and watch from the front. It was just a dream come true being on that tour—it was kind of surreal.

MARK SLAUGHTER: It was a very happy, cool time for us. Even for Kiss. They were just digging doing it. It was a lot of fun. And the key is they really were a class act. And it stems all the way into their production and the people that work with them. It was all "A-class" people. I think if anything I really learned—and I had already toured with Alice Cooper and Iron Maiden at that point—but going into Kiss' camp, there's just an element of class to it. It was just really cool to be a part of. It was the integrity of the show. It was the show being run right with pyro and all the other things that they do.

You know what was really cool to me? The soundchecks. I dug the soundchecks, because they'd get up there, and instead of just running through songs, they would actually play around with old material that they listened to when they were younger. Some Grand Funk stuff, and they'd play some of the older '60s songs that, quite honestly, some of the stuff I didn't know. But it was kind of cool, just the fact that Gene would go, "No, I think it goes to 'a' there." And they'd sit around and tinker, tinker, tinker. Gene would throw picks at me. I'm riding my bike in the arena, and he'd throw picks at me and hit me. It was just a really cool time.

BLAS ELIAS: It had a huge impact on all of us musically. I think being it was my first major tour, especially as a drummer, I learned so much from [Eric] about playing to a big audience. Where I had been playing in smaller clubs, I had learned from him that you don't have to fill every space with lots of notes, because the people in the back of the audience aren't really going to read that. So he played big in his selections of notes, and also the way that he played. He played to people in the back. And he just looked larger than life. His sound was larger than life. His kit was larger than life. I learned a lot about playing arenas from him.

ROD MORGENSTEIN: I'm probably one of the only people that never saw Kiss in concert. I was not really part of the "heavy metal rock world." For many years, I was in the "rock-jazz/fusion world," playing with Steve Morse and the Dixie Dregs. And then, through an interesting set of circumstances, found my way to the guys in Winger, who were doing demos and were getting rejected over and over. I met them right within a couple of months before they hooked up with Atlantic Records. They asked me to do the record, we became really good friends, and then it became a band. When we did our second record, *In the Heart of the Young*, one of the first tours we did was the Kiss tour. I believe it was October/November of 1990, the *Hot in the Shade* tour. So that's where I met Eric. We started hanging out at the meals prior to the shows in catering.

They're an amazing live band. I've never seen them with the make-up. I'm told that took it to a whole other level—total fantasy. On the *Hot in the Shade* tour, the make-up was off, and I don't know that they were doing some of the bigger-than-life things that they had done on previous tours, and on future tours when the make-up came back. But they're total pros, what can you say? This whole thing was really foreign to me. I hadn't gone to rock shows in years—I was a jazz-fusion snob, and suddenly thrust into this world. I remember when we got the Kiss tour, the other guys in the band going, "Oh my God ... *we're going to tour with Kiss!*" And Reb Beach, our lead guitarist, said, "Kiss is the first band I ever saw live," when he was thirteen or something. He said he was almost scared when he went to the concert, because here they are dressed in these costumes, and Gene is the lizard, breathing fire. He said it was so overwhelming and unbelievable.

I remember Gene always walking around backstage in his bathrobe with his name on it. There was a funny story—my wife, Michelle, was out on tour at one point. I forget what the circumstances were, but she knew that Gene liked Jewish jokes. Both of us are Jewish, also. I can't remember the joke itself ... I remember her telling it to him, and he had that "Gene Simmons grin" on his face, and he shook his head up and down. Apparently, he never really laughs out loud or has a hearty laugh. He found the joke to be really funny. So then, about three weeks later, Michelle was back out on tour with us, and Gene walked in our dressing room and proceeded to tell us that joke! Michelle said, "Gene, don't you remember I told you that joke when I was out a few weeks back?" And he waited for her to be finished speaking, and then proceeded to continue telling the joke.

BLAS ELIAS: We didn't hang out too much with Paul. He wasn't around as much as Eric, Bruce, and Gene. But Gene is a great guy. He's funny, too. We'd share stories—we got to hang out on his bus with him. A funny story for me was asking him about his old days with Kiss when he was wearing the make-up, when he met girls, if he would keep his make-up and his costume on when he was with a groupie. And he said he didn't want to, but he learned quickly that the girls would rather have him in full costume. [Laughs]

MARK SLAUGHTER: One of the first times I met Eric, it was another opening act before Kiss, and I was hanging out on the side of the stage, looking through the curtain, waiting for the other band to come on. And Eric comes up behind me, and he's got this big squirt gun. And he says, "Hey man, do you want to 'shoot' some people?" So through the curtains, we're shooting people in the audience! He was always a practical joker like that. We got to be friends, and he was a really down-to-earth guy. He didn't have any air of being better than you or being a rock star. He was just a good guy, someone you could hang out with, be comfortable with, and not be intimidated. Which to me was huge, because like I said, I was such a big fan. I was always intimidated around the rest of the guys and some of the other bands we toured with. But him, I never felt that way. He was just really easy to hang with.

EDDIE TRUNK: The last couple of tours, the *Hot in the Shade* tour, he would send me a couple of laminates in the mail and the tour book, and say, "Here's the alias that I'm under and our tour routing. Just call any time you want to come and hang out." And I did that a few times. I introduced them at the Meadowlands [on June 30], and he gave me a shot before I went up, and threw drumsticks at me from behind the curtain while I was out there. We would go to the mall together. Just a fun-loving, real, great person. Look, we all have our favorite rock stars, but when you get to know them as people, sometimes they're not really what you think they are. With Eric, he was a great asset to Kiss and a great musician. But he was a great, fun person that never put himself above the fans. I think that's really why he was so loved and respected so quickly by the Kiss fanbase.

I was real nervous going up on stage at the Meadowlands—my hometown of New Jersey—and introducing my favorite band. Eric knew how nervous I was, so he was really pranking me backstage, saying, "Don't blow it Trunk, don't blow it! You've got to do this good. You don't want to screw this up!" Just making it worse for me. He kept walking with me to the stairs to the stage, and I was like, "What are you doing? Don't you have a show to get ready for?" We walked up the stairs, and he gave me this cup just before I had my cue to go out onstage, and he said, "Just drink this. You need to make sure your throat is opened up for when you talk on the mic." He gives me this red plastic cup, and he's like, "Just knock that back." I did, and it was like Chivas or whatever, some sort of booze. Just a total head rush, and then boom, he pushes me out to the curtain and says, "Go ahead, go!" Stumbling out there, I had no idea what I just drank, and he's behind the curtain. As I walk up to the mic, he cracked the curtain just enough, and he had a handful of drumsticks that he was throwing at me from the curtain, while I'm addressing the crowd, trying to hit me. You just saw this arm coming out through the gap in the curtain, with drumsticks, hitting my back or hitting my feet! And it was him, just to mess with me. That was Eric—a prankster, a fun guy, a ball-buster, and [he] didn't take it all too seriously. That's one of the many reasons why I loved the guy.

ROD MORGENSTEIN: I do remember watching and enjoying Eric's drum solo, because he knew all the things that an arena band was supposed to do, to get the best out of an audience. It was a very audience-participation kind of solo, very visual. He had really good ideas in there, also. But for me, I grew up like the typical rock kid and was into the Beatles, the Stones,

Led Zeppelin, and Jethro Tull. And then when I hit my late teens and went away to college, I totally left all that and was fully immersed in the jazz and fusion scene. Mahavishnu Orchestra had just turned my head around. I sort of became a bit of a "musician snob," where I kind of looked down my nose at rock music and that whole genre for a number of years, until I came back to it when I did the Winger record and entered this whole other world again.

Having been a schooled musician that had a little bit of a different perspective in terms of, "What are the important things as a musician?" And not really paying any attention of, "What are some of the important things that go along with being a musician *and* an entertainer?" These are things I never really considered. And here, I found myself with Winger, playing to 10,000-15,000 people a night. So in my drum solo, I was still kind of doing the things that I do in the Dixie Dregs and the fusion world, which doesn't necessarily translate in a gigantic hall. A lot of it gets lost. I never learned how to twirl my sticks. I wouldn't say I'm a shy person, but I never had the nerve to stand up on my drum seat or engage the audience. So all of these things were swirling in my head when I would watch Eric have his moment during their show. I was really impressed by it. But the best part of all was just getting to know him during those two months that we were on tour with them. Just a genuinely good guy.

CARRIE STEVENS: That's the tour that I was mostly on—*Crazy Nights* is just where I met him. It's kind of a nightmare dating a rock star. It's all thrilling in the beginning, but then once you're in love with them, it was like the only thing about him that I didn't like, because it's hard to be together and then not be together. The distance. It's fun when you go see him, but then you have to leave. It's hard. I went to see him a lot—one time in Virginia, Gary Corbett's wife and I were friends, and Gary's and Eric's birthdays are at the same time, like a day apart or something. So Lenora and I planned a surprise trip to surprise them. She was coming from New York, and I was coming from L.A., and we bought tickets and planned the times. We both had laminates, so we could just show up.

So I showed up at the venue, and I ended up surprising him. JW, his drum tech, always handed him a glass of water at the same time during every song. So when Eric turned around to get the water, I gave it to him and said, "Happy Birthday!" And then I found out that the band had hired some stripper to come on stage and give him a cake and sing "Happy Birthday." I got livid and started a fight, and then the whole night of his birthday we ended up fighting, and he slept on the floor ... which I still feel bad about today. Now, at the age I am, I'd be like, "Who cares. It's harmless." But at the time, it was some horrible, threatening thing. When everyone got wind that I was there, they quickly cancelled the stripper. But somehow, I found out about it. So it didn't even happen, but just the notion that it was going to happen.

CHRISTINA HARRISON: Eric and Bruce were two peas in a pod, because Bruce is really insecure in many ways. I would always tell Bruce, "You're a typical Jewish guy. You're so neurotic." And he's like, "Thank you, Christina ... *thank you very much!*" He's like your typical Jew, y'know? They would always say, "Did you watch the show?" They'd both be beating themselves up—"Oh, I could have done this better." But we wouldn't be watching the show, because we'd seen it a million times. So we'd be backstage talking to the wardrobe girl, or helping the wardrobe girl pack up the make-up and stuff, just to have something to do. Or walking into Kip Winger's dressing room and stealing M&Ms. We would just be doing stuff, because we couldn't watch the show every bloody night. I mean, I wasn't even a Kiss fan. Of course, I grew to be a Kiss fan, but I wasn't a Kiss fan. It wasn't like all of a sudden I married someone *in Sting,* y'know what I mean? [Laughs] We'd say, "Oh, it was great!" But we didn't watch any of the show.

CARRIE STEVENS: Christina and I used to pretend we were watching the band. Oh God, if Bruce learns this, he may be pissed! We had it down to a science. We knew when their solos were, and we were backstage hanging out with Slaughter and Winger. There wouldn't have been anything inappropriate that ever went on with them, but we'd go out, eat their M&Ms with them, and talk to them. And then Kiss went straight off the stage onto the bus after the show, and we were always perched there like little angels when they got off. "Oh, great solo, honey!"

CHRISTINA HARRISON: [Eric and Carrie's relationship was] up and down. They really did fight a lot. I think it was in Massachusetts—it was after the show, and we were at some ... of course, they tried to stay at nice hotels, but you can't do that at every city. There's not a Four Seasons in every city. So we're at some hotel, and I could hear Eric and Carrie arguing. [Laughs] To be a goofball, I took a glass and held it against the wall, and I remember saying, "Bruce, come listen!" I remember Bruce laying on the bed, playing his guitar, saying, "Oh my God, I'm *so* not going to do that." And I'm like, "Come on, let's see if this works!" And I'm holding the glass, and maybe because the walls were so thin, it actually did work. I could kind of hear what Carrie what saying, but I couldn't hear what Eric was saying. She told me later that Eric was saying, "Don't talk so loud. They're probably listening!" They fought a lot, but when they were together, they seemed like the cutest, perfect couple. I just think they both had short fuses, and Eric was far more insecure. I keep going back to the range repairman who is with this drop-dead gorgeous girl, and he thinks he's not good enough. But, of course, he is good enough, because he was a good person.

CARRIE STEVENS: One time, Eric and I wrecked a hotel. Why we did this, I have no idea. Were we in Maine? We were in somewhere like that. Shows got cancelled for some reason again, and I don't know, I guess this is just what you do. There was a banquet room set up for this banquet, and Eric and I went in and trashed it. We threw silverware, plates, the table cloths. And then we did the "rock star thing" of having sex in the elevator. We had sex under the podium in there. Just craziness. And then there was some weird lady who was convinced she was Eric's wife. Just some crazy, crazy fan. And she was threatening to kill me, and that she had a knife. She was telling security that Eric was cheating on her, and she was his wife, and he was upstairs with some girl. Then the tour security had to start walking me separately than Eric onto the bus. She even made up an ID with his last name on it! *Crazy.*

We had a very active, healthy sex life. He was energetic. Yeah, there's no complaints. He took me to this sex hotel, it was called Sybaris. I wonder if it's still around. It was in Chicago. Nothing seedy—it wasn't some sleazy hotel—but they make it seem like it's a romantic place for people having anniversaries and stuff like that. It's like its own little house, different "houses" with a jacuzzi in it, a swimming pool, an indoor waterfall, and a waterbed. And there was this hook on the ceiling, and both of us were like, "What the heck is that for?" Then we opened up the closet, and there's this swing! We were both pretty innocent. Now, I'm a little more wise to the world—I'm not shocked about something like that. But at the time, we were both like, *"What do you do with this?"* A swing with a hole in the bottom. But he wanted to take me somewhere special, so we didn't stay at the band's hotel. We went there—somebody had told him about it.

Eric liked to take naked pictures, and we had so many "naughty" pictures of us. I think there was video, but I'm hoping we deleted it. He bought me a video camera when they first came out for Christmas one year. He used to love to take pictures on the road, even when I wasn't with him, and he'd give them to some random PA, and they were just like college kids that worked in whatever city they were in. It wasn't like a member of the tour. He would give them the roll of film to go develop, then bring back to him, and he'd send them to me. I was like, "Eric, don't be giving strangers these pictures. I'm naked in some of them!" I'm shocked to this day nobody ever stole the pictures and they didn't come out anywhere.

I remember one time, we were naked, as usual, on his bed. He had these mirrored ceilings and walls. We looked up, and he said, "You know, you've got one of those bodies like those girls in the magazines." And I'm like, "What magazines?" And he's like, "*Playboy*" I said, "Really?" It's like I never thought of myself that way. And he said, "I'd be really proud of you if you were one of those girls." But still, it took me way after that to have the confidence to think I would actually do that. So I think he would be proud. If it wasn't for him, I wouldn't be doing it, because I never thought of myself as special or pretty. And where I come from, a small town, nobody does stuff like that. You don't even say you want to do anything like that, or you're laughed at. So he was a wonderful boyfriend. I remember exactly where I was sitting at Teru Sushi, when he said to me, "Is there anything I can do to help you with your career?" And that was followed by, "What do you want to do?" It was so embarrassing for me to say I wanted to be a model and an actress, but I managed to get the words out, and then he said, "What can I do to help your career?" That brought me to tears, even back then, because that's something I didn't even get from my parents. He was so supportive and loving and encouraging.

BLAS ELIAS: They seemed like a great couple. She would come out on tour all the time. She was one of the first people I met when I moved to Los Angeles, and we got to be friends. That was how I met Eric. We'd hang out just like friends would. Like I said, it was surreal for me, because he was someone that I watched on TV and listened to records, and to be hanging out with him was kind of surreal. They seemed like a great couple. She's a great girl.

CARRIE STEVENS: I'd say he was always the same person. He was super sweet to his fans. He was always joking, and he was the same way with his parents that he would be with his fans. Except for when we were fighting, he was always the same with me. He didn't have an ego, he didn't have a rock star attitude—just really a normal person with his own insecurities. Very great sense of humor, very thoughtful. I still have all the cards that he used to send me. He used to buy me stupid little gifts on the road, at truck stops. Just the most random, stupid gifts. Postcards from every city, a ton of them, just to show he was thinking of me all the time. For my twenty-first birthday, he sent me this giant arrangement of flowers, and the card said, "All of your goals and dreams will come true." And I still keep that on my refrigerator, as a reminder that all my goals and dreams will come true. It was thanks to him that I got the courage to be a model and an actress. He was very supportive of that. It was almost like he picked up where my parents left off. When he was on the road with Kiss—this is before fax machines—when I had an audition, he would write down my lines. I'd tell him what my lines were, and he'd write them down. And he'd practice with me for my auditions over the phone. On my first audition, I think it was on the Sony lot for *Parker Lewis Can't Lose*, I mean ... I showed up with Eric Carr from Kiss! He came everywhere with me. When he was staying with me and I had to work, he'd pack my lunch and make my lunch. He was just really a down-to-earth guy.

JOHN WALSH: She was young at the time. She might have been 21 or so. She was very nice and very sweet, and Eric, you'll hear it, was a very loving guy and a sweet person. Whenever she was around, it was nice.

BOB GRAW: It was the first Kiss tour that I think they didn't use the logo behind them. I saw them on the first leg at Nassau Coliseum [on June 28]. I was I think sixth row for that show. But the defining show of that tour was the last night of the tour, at Madison Square Garden [on November 9], when Winger and Slaughter opened up the show. I was front row for that show, and I remember how great Eric Carr was that night. The band sounded so great at that show—it was the best-sounding Kiss show I had ever seen, by far. They were so into the show. I'm pretty sure that show was completely sold out. I remember being in the front row that night and how great and just clear they sounded, how booming Eric's drums were that night. That's really something that I'll never forget. In fact, I hang out with Rod Morgenstein from Winger a lot—he's become a pretty good friend of mine—and I got into a big conversation with him about that night, and he remembers the same thing that I do, about how good Eric's drums sounded that night and how everything was just mic'd perfect that night, and how sonically good Kiss sounded that night. He said it was probably the best sounding show of that entire tour. Who knew it was the last time we would ever see him live?

BLAS ELIAS: Playing Madison Square Garden just by itself was something you always dreamt about doing but never thought you would actually do. I watched *The Song Remains the Same* and watched Led Zeppelin ride the limo up to that place, and it just seemed surreal. And playing there with one of your favorite bands—your idols—was just amazing. Something that none of us will ever forget. We got to go to the after-tour party with them and hang out and meet people [like] Aerosmith. It was New York, so everybody was there. It was an amazing experience meeting all those cool people, just being there.

MARK SLAUGHTER: I remember Gene had his mom there, and Eric had his family. It wasn't like your typical "ending of a tour." It was really cool, a lot of families, and then we had a party afterwards. The whole cake and ice cream and everybody having a good old time. Y'know ... Madison Square Garden, you can't ask for a better venue. It's *the* venue. That's what I remember the most. Everybody was very, very happy. There wasn't any issues. There wasn't any headaches. Right at that moment was a great pinnacle to leave it at, especially for Eric's last run.

JOHN WALSH: For me, I'm a local boy, and this is my home arena. To be on the stage there, I had worked there before with Cyndi Lauper—it wasn't my first time working there. But I was so excited, because once again, I'm standing on stage at Madison Square Garden, and I have family that's in the audience, and this is the last show of the tour. It was really exciting. I felt so proud that I was with a New York band. Even though a couple of them may have lived in L.A., they were local guys. I really felt it went so well, that it would continue ultimately with another record and another tour. I really felt like we were all locked into this now. This went so well that these guys are going to want to do it again. And I remember when the last note of the last song was over, I was tearing down the drums, and I had drumsticks in my hand, and I threw out a bunch of drumsticks [into the audience], just because I was so excited. It was such a great thing because they played so well. They always played well, but when the chips were down or there was a lot of pressure, they really excelled even more. But it was just so much fun to be there at Madison Square Garden, and it meant so much. Of course, we didn't know what the future was going to bring, so it wasn't like, "This is over, and now, I'm going to work for somebody else." I really felt that this was a great way to end the tour and that it would continue.

LYDIA CRISS: I was at Eric's first show and Eric's last show, and nothing in between. It's so odd. And it wasn't planned that way, it just happened that way. It's so weird. A friend of mine was into the opening act for Kiss at the last show, Winger. She had asked me if I could get tickets, so I called the record company and got tickets. I did talk to the band after the show—I went to the party. There was a party in one of the restaurants in the Garden.

I met him three times. I met him at the China Club and the Cat Club. I was with Ace and Ace's girlfriend at the time. But it was just basically, "Hello. How are you?" The time at the [post-MSG] party, I did get to speak to him.

They had put out *Smashes, Thrashes & Hits*, and he sings "Beth" on it. So I'm talking with a bunch of my girlfriends, and he walks by. I say, "Eric, come here. I have a question for you. When you sang 'Beth,' did you think of me?" He said, "Of course I did," and I said, "That's the right answer!" I didn't have many conversations with Eric, but I just always felt that he was a sweetheart. At one point, a lot of people used to ask me, "Who is your favorite member of Kiss?" and I used to say, *"Eric."* [Laughs]

CARRIE STEVENS: I didn't go to that show. I think we got in a fight, and I left. He wanted me to leave, then he wanted me to stay. I was pissed off because he did this to me all the time. I'd fly all the way somewhere to see him, then we get in a fight, and then he'd want me to leave. I'd be like, "I'm not leaving, I'm staying!" And then we just wouldn't speak to each other. We wouldn't in public. Everybody else would think everything's OK, and then we'd be in bed at night with a pillow between us. Normal couple stuff, y'know? We fought. So I think that's why I didn't go to that one.

LORETTA CARAVELLO: That probably to me was the best show he did, because it incorporated all the shows that I've ever seen with him. I didn't know too much about the '70s, but there were parts that they took from the '70s that they incorporated, like the ball that would go around. That was one that my niece [attended]. She was sitting on the soundboard in the middle of the auditorium. It was unforgettable, because he was so happy. He was taking her around backstage—"This is my niece." And he would take her out through where the people walk out, like where you would walk out on the ice, and kids were there, and he was holding her up, and they were high-fiving her. Maybe it was so good because it was the last. Maybe it was so good because it was the end. It was something we didn't know.

But that to me was the most unforgettable, between the solo and everything that went on. And the fact that he was sick at that point—he was ill—just to be able to play the way he did and perform the way he did was to me just amazing now, when I'm reflecting back on everything, and I notice more things. "Oh, this is why he felt like this. That's why he said this." It's 20/20 hindsight. My parents were really happy, and it was just a great show. As a matter of fact, I just emailed Bruce something from backstage—him with his father, because he just lost his father. I found a picture of him with my father and his father. It was a really sweet picture, so I emailed it over to him. But it was the best Kiss show in my opinion, of all the years my brother was with Kiss. It was everything rolled into one, and it was quite fitting for the way it ended. My niece still remembers him. He adored her. There's tons of pictures. She used to go to the shows, and she used to sit on the soundboard. Somebody once put her on their shoulders—I think a roadie—and she was right in the middle of the audience. And the volume didn't bother her. She kept taking the earplugs out and throwing them. This is like a four-year-old kid! My brother adored her. It was the love of his life.

BRUCE KULICK: Like most Italians, it was the usual drama kinda thing. And yet, similar to Jewish people, you love your parents so much. He loved his folks. He spent a lot of time with them. He would pick on their idiosyncrasies, of course. I was always flipped out by how much his father looked like him. In some ways, Loretta does, too, [and] sounds very much like him. It was kind of funny. But there sometimes were aunts and other people that would show up, and look, I grew up in New York, and I'm Jewish. I had so many Italian friends growing up, and I love them. And they're characters. Everything is loud and wild and over-the-top and full of life and love and drama and craziness. And that's his family—I loved them. I welcomed it, it was great. It was always wonderful to see his folks. His sister was a trip, and still is. There was one young cousin I remember that meant a lot to Eric, which I thought was interesting, because I think she had kind of reddish hair. I don't know if she was pure Italian or not. I might be wrong. I think it was the other sister got married and had a kid. I don't know. He was the uncle I guess and was really great with all of them. And then like a typical Italian, [he] would complain about all of them. [Laughs]

CHRISTINA HARRISON: Tight. Very proud of their son, that's for darn sure. Bruce would always say, before he made it, he was giving guitar lessons at his parents' house, and they were always saying, "Why don't you cut your hair?" And then he makes it, and they're like, "Oh ... *my son!*" I think that's how it was with Eric. They were so proud. They'd come to the shows. How could you not be proud?

LORETTA CARAVELLO: When my brother was home, he was just "my brother." He rarely talked about anything that was going on. Once in a while, he'd make a comment. He more confided with my parents. He didn't want to be "Eric Carr" when he was with us. He wanted to be Paulie, which I think was good, because when things upset him, you might be able to see something on his face, but at least, he didn't bring it into the family. It was a job.

CARRIE STEVENS: He was very close with his family. He loved his niece, and she was just a little thing back then. Can't believe she's grown up. We went to stay with his parents quite a bit up in the country. They were always very sweet and welcoming to me. I still talk to them. He liked to go up there, and we'd do normal things. We took walks in the woods, skipped stones in the water, and cooked. Really normal stuff.

SCOTT DAGGETT: At that time in his life, I think he was closer to 40 or in his 40s. He was kind of over that whole "thing." He was very aware of what kind of a star he was. He was always preaching about never leaving the place without his hairspray and having his image right there. But as a person, he was kind of over that and was ready to get married. He was looking at some different places to be other than getting loaded, because he was a big drinker. He was changing.

BLAS ELIAS: I think he was planning on moving to Vegas, actually. All of the guys from Slaughter are from Vegas, and he came out, and me and Mark were showing him around the area that we lived, on Henderson. He had planned on possibly moving out there. He seemed like a great guy who wanted a normal life, didn't want to be around the Hollywood craziness and all that.

ROD MORGENSTEIN: It was very funny—it turned out that both of us at that time were living on 37th Street on the east side in Manhattan. Right as you got out of the Midtown Tunnel, I was a little closer to Lexington and Park Avenue. But it was funny to find that you live on the same street, even though you're separated by probably 50,000 people. He and I exchanged numbers and had talked about getting together when our tours wound down. Since we lived so close and we're both drummers, we both really struck up a nice camaraderie. He really struck me as just a very down-to-earth, gentle, sweet, nice human being. Which not everybody that you meet in the music business—I'd imagine just life in general—is that kind of a person. So when I meet somebody like that, I like to keep in touch. I remember him telling me how, during his time off, he had gotten involved in wanting to work with new, up-and-coming bands and do production deals with them. Get in the studio and work with them on a production level, and then also try and get involved where he would shop deals at the label for them. It was like a whole other sideline that he was very pumped about.

LORETTA CARAVELLO: He went back and forth, because Carrie lived in Los Angeles, but then she came down here. He had apartments. When he first joined Kiss, he lived in the Village. Then he moved to I think the west side, and then he came home. In the beginning of his Kiss career, he lived in our house for about a year, and then he moved to the Village. He came back around '85 or '86 and stayed with us for about two years in Queens. That was Ozone Park. I'd say around '89 he came back home again, and then he finally got a nice apartment in '90. And then everything was downhill from there.

1991 [Part One]

CARRIE STEVENS: He was just fine [health-wise during the *Hot in the Shade* tour]. Sometimes, I wonder if the cancer wasn't already in his brain, because of the way he was so erratic with me. I mean, literally, I'm not exaggerating, one time I flew all the way to Maine, 3,000 miles from L.A. I got there, we had sex, he jumped up, got in the shower, came out, was toweling his hair, and he goes, "You know ... I think I want to break up." My jaw just dropped. I'm like, *"What?* I just flew all the way here, there's been no fighting, we just had great sex ... and now you want to break up?" It was craziness. Sometimes, I do wonder. I don't know—was it already there and we didn't know it? He could change that fast. Like the time I wouldn't leave, and I was like, "I'm not leaving. You're going to break up with me this time? I'm not getting right back on a plane. I'm not leaving." I thought maybe he was going to try and see his ex-girlfriend, so I was not leaving.

The week was over, and he's like, "Do you want to go to my parents with me this weekend? Do you want to spend the weekend with my parents?" And I'm like, "What? After I cried all week and pretended we were together when we're not, and you broke my heart?" I was like laying underneath the covers with tears just streaming down my face. He peeled the covers back gently from my eyes and said, "Do you want to go to my parents this weekend?" I'm like, "Are you crazy? We're going to pretend everything is OK some more, when everything isn't?" And then so many times we'd fight and break up, and then I'd wake up in the morning, and he'd be kneeling on the floor, looking up at me with those big eyes, and he'd say, "I don't want you to go away. I don't want you to be gone. Please don't go away." And then, of course, I always stayed, because he was literally on his knees next to the bed when I woke up in the morning. He was always very sorry. I'm sure it wasn't all his fault. I don't even remember what we fought about, but I'm sure every couple fights.

I had finally just had it with him. I finally broke up with him. It was the last week of the tour, and he did it to me again. I forget where. It was the last week, and they were going to be all through upstate New York ... I think it was Maine. And he did it to me again, and I was like, "You know what? I'm not leaving this time. I'm staying on the tour." And he always acted in front of everyone like everything was perfect. He'd have his arm around me. And then at night, we'd be like not talking. I always kissed his ass. It was always me chasing him all those years. And, finally, the tables turned. I think I changed my phone number, put "return to sender" on all of his cards. I did this because you know how many times he broke up with me over and over for no reason? Finally, I just wasn't having it anymore. And he went crazy, as most guys do when they can't have something.

ROD MORGENSTEIN: He was telling me at one of the last gigs, "I just don't feel right. I think I'm going to go get a check-up when the tour winds down."

GARY CORBETT: All I remember was towards the end of the tour, he started to have these weird cramps in his leg. And after the show, he looked really drained. He didn't know he was sick yet, and there really wasn't anything definite he said he felt, other than feeling drained. I think it was just one of his legs—it was his thigh—that had really intense cramps.

JOHN WALSH: I remember him getting a cortisone shot in his knee somewhere along the tour. But if he was sick or ill in any way, I would know, and he was not. The very last show, I have a CD of it somewhere. If you hear the way he played ... I would know. Absolutely not. He played as strong as he ever could, all the way until the end. He was not sick.

BOB EZRIN: I kept in touch with Gene during that period of time. Ace had left the band, and Paul was very angry with me over *The Elder*. I'm sure he would tell you that. When it was time to go back and we decided to talk about doing *Revenge* together, we had to have a little "therapy session," with Paul, Gene, and me. Paul was angry, and he needed to express his anger.

And Paul is a kind of guy who never forgets and carries everything with him forever. I think he was angry with me for steering them in the direction that I did on *The Elder* and also for not being on my game during the making of the record. And I apologized. I said he was right.

We came back together for "God Gave Rock n' Roll to You," to do the song for the film [*Bill and Ted's Bogus Journey*]. Eric was in the band. Actually, let me think about this ... we attempted some stuff with Eric. We did a first run, so no, we didn't come back together for "God Gave Rock n' Roll to You." We did come back together to do an album. We started with Eric, and we started in Canada, at Phase One Studios. We had I think four or maybe five songs. We didn't do a lot. We just had some original ideas. We were really just trying to find a new direction for Kiss. A new sound.

And then Eric got sick. He had to start his treatments, which made it impossible for him to play and have the energy to do it. So we had a hiatus until "God Gave Rock n' Roll to You." Eric Singer played on "God Gave Rock n' Roll to You." We started this project—Eric was in there, and we were working at this studio in Toronto, starting to work on some new material. Eric was an integral part of it. We cut a certain amount. It was a good session, everybody had a really good time.

We set the console on fire in the studio! That was one interesting evening. [Laughs] We didn't *set it* on fire—we broke for dinner, [and] we ordered pizza or something like that. We were out front in the studio, and I smelled smoke. I thought, "Is somebody's pizza burning or something?" So I went back to the control room, opened the door, and it was filled with smoke. Then it was a mad scramble. We grabbed all the tapes and got everything out of there. And then the console burst into flames! I don't know what happened—there was a transformer or something within the console that had blown. The fire department was there. The fire department couldn't believe Kiss was there, I think they were so distracted by the Kiss guys that they were hardly doing their jobs, in a way. That brought the session to a close. We decided we'd reconvene, but then Eric got sick.

GARY CORBETT: When Eric found out he was sick, I think it was around May. He wasn't really sure what it was. He had gone in and had a bunch of tests done. The doctors said to him, "You have an infection in the fluid sac around your heart. We're going to put you on some medication that will clear it up." They did, and it did clear it up enough that the next time they did an x-ray, they actually were able to see there was a growth, an actual tumor, on his heart. At that point, they needed to do open heart surgery on him. So he was getting ready to go in for the surgery, and needless to say, he was pretty upset.

CARRIE STEVENS: He started calling my family—my mother, my sister, my father—just went crazy because I wouldn't go back to him this time. And then that's when my mom called me one day and said, "You should really talk to him. He's really sick." And I'm like, "Well, what's wrong with him?" And she's like, "He has the flu," and I'm like, "Whatever. It's the flu." And then [I] found out that it wasn't the flu, and we started talking.

BRUCE KULICK: I remember I was at a movie theater in Hollywood, and he was back in New York. In fact, I was at that Cinerama Dome. I'm calling him on a pay phone—that's how long ago that was—just because he left me a message and said, "I'm going to the doctor. I've got some sort of infection, I don't know what it is. He's got to do some tests. They think it's this or that, but they don't know." And I was pretty stressed just hearing that. Then by the time they did some bigger tests, they found out he had a tumor on his heart, which is extremely rare. But that's why he was having the infection thing going on. Gene and Paul were there when he had his open-heart surgery to correct that, but before he had the surgery, I asked him, "Do you want me to be there?" He said, "Don't bother. Don't worry about it. I've got plenty of people here." And I kind of appreciated that, because I had just bought a new house, and it was very expensive, and I was still settling in and everything. It's funny—it was in the same building that he looked at one of the condos in. We could have been neighbors. The news fluctuated for a while after that surgery, but by then, they realized it was cancer.

CARRIE STEVENS: When I found out that it turned out not to be a flu, we thought it was a tumor, and he just needed open-heart surgery. And I wasn't there for that surgery, because by then, we were back together, but barely. And he said he didn't want me to see him like that.

ROD MORGENSTEIN: The way he explained it was that the doctors said that through the pumping action of his heart, it was sending cancer cells throughout his body. Now, I don't think I had confided in him about my own life, because at that time, my wife had already been battling breast cancer since 1983. And she, Michelle, had from the very beginning made the decision that she wanted it to be a private affair. So here I was, out and about living this life and traveling around, and the nature of cancer is you might buy some good years, and then all of a sudden, it can come back. And when it comes back, it's at an even more intense level. You live your life through looking at the calendar for when is the next set of tests coming up. You kind of live in a silent agony, and I wasn't out to share this whole secret life we were living with most people in our life. So when I had this conversation with Eric when he was telling me this, my heart was breaking, because we had been living this for eight years. My wife subsequently passed away four and a half years ago.

ADAM MITCHELL: This is just my opinion. He used so much hairspray, and between that and the fog machines ... I think it contributed to his cancer. Because he was constantly breathing in all those fumes from hairspray. And then in the shows, the smoke machines would go off. Again, it's my opinion.

WAYNE SHARP: I went to visit him in the hospital once. He was actually up and walking and was so optimistic. He wouldn't say what was wrong, but he had a heart operation. To get cancer in your heart ... I've just never heard of that before. He looked good.

JOHN WALSH: I saw him in the hospital. It was interesting to me because it was the hospital that my mother had been in when she had a heart problem, as well. At the time, he was in great spirits.

GERRI MILLER: He was scared. He was trying to be positive. Any time that you're facing a really serious health problem, you don't know. So, yeah, it was scary. We spoke from the hospital a couple of times. I felt really bad for him. What can you do? I didn't visit in the hospital. Looking back, I wish I had seen him one more time. We did speak on the phone a couple of times, and I'd say, "Hang in there. Hopefully, everything will work out." I didn't really realize at that time how dire the situation was.

CARRIE STEVENS: He flew out to L.A. to see me right after the surgery. He was very proud of his scar. He would, like, show it to a cashier at a 7-Eleven. He was always showing off that scar. At the time, we didn't think there was going to be anything else, or else I'm sure he wouldn't be showing it off. I was with him when he got the results. He used to stay at this place on Larabee in Hollywood. The band always put him up in this hotel/apartment thing. He got the call that pieces of the tumor had been breaking off and going into his lungs. So they took a biopsy of it and found out that it was malignant. I think it was even too hard for me to grasp. I remember being distraught about it. When he went back to New York and more doctors' appointments, I remember staying with a girlfriend and sitting on the floor, on the phone with him, crying. But it never occurred to me what would lie ahead.

BILL AUCOIN: Eric and I always kept in touch. When he got ill, he called me. I think he had a rough time talking to Gene and Paul during that period. They were having a rough time as well. Here Eric was sick, he was in the hospital, [and] he had to get an operation. They weren't making money. It was a tough time. I think they kind of separated themselves from Eric.

GARY CORBETT: I was just trying to be a friend and console him a bit, and if I remember correctly, Carrie came into New York to stay with him. They actually went to Great Adventure, just to try to have a nice day. Even at Great Adventure, he called me from a pay phone. He goes, "They're going to fire me." I'm like, "No, they're not going to fire you. Don't worry. You don't need to be thinking about any of this stuff. Just do what you need to do, and everything will be OK."

EDDIE TRUNK: He was very concerned about his standing in that band, and even if he did get healthy, if he would still be in that band. I remember having many conversations with him along those lines and trying to keep him positive and encouraged—not only to get healthy, but also to reassure him that, "Hey man, there's *no way* if you're healthy and active and playing, that Kiss is possibly going to move on from you, because the fans would revolt. You're too loved." It's ironic saying that at that time, because obviously in retrospect, we've seen from Kiss they will—and can—do anything. And there's a portion of their fanbase that will accept it. I never in my wildest dreams would have thought that Kiss fans would accept someone impersonating Ace [when Tommy Thayer joined Kiss in 2002]. And a lot of them have.

GARY CORBETT: I couldn't completely believe it, because he was always paranoid. He didn't have a good relationship with Paul at all. Paul would always fuck with Eric, and he knew how to push the buttons to do it, and he knew how to get to Eric. And he would. For the first three months of the *Hot in the Shade* tour, Eric didn't talk to Gene or Paul on the bus. It was really uncomfortable, because he would get on the bus with his sunglasses on and his Walkman, and he'd basically sit in the front lounge where everybody was sitting, looking anywhere but in their direction. Again, with the sunglasses and headphones on. So there was no communication. They didn't talk. And that's the way he was—he took that stuff really to heart. And Paul, like I said, knew exactly how to push his buttons. And did.

So when Eric would say stuff like that to me, I had to take it from where it was coming and go, "Nah, come on. That's not really possible. That's not going to happen." But I can't remember who it was that told me. It came from a few places, but primarily, a lot of it came from Eric. And it was because of things that were going on between them and him. Well, one way was taking away the drum solo. Things like that. Anything that lessened Eric feeling like being part of the band or the rock star that he was. That was who Eric was. Once he was the drummer in Kiss, that is who he was. He loved being the drummer in Kiss—it was the only thing that mattered to him. So when you mess with that, you were really messing with him. And, of course, those two guys were the only two guys that could really do it. Gene wouldn't do it just for the sake of doing it, whereas Paul took some pleasure in it.

TY TABOR: It got serious instantly of course, when he let me know what was going on. He came to a show, and I was unaware that he was there. Somebody like Doug in my band said, "Eric is downstairs in the private area and wants to talk to you." So I ran down. He looked his normal self, but I could tell something heavy was on his mind. So we went over somewhere private and talked about it. He just spilled his guts and let me know what was up. That first night, it was just about his health. But we talked many, many more times after that night, of him letting me know what was up [about Eric's status in Kiss].

CHRISTINA HARRISON: That's exactly what they should have done [told Eric they would get a fill-in, and he could come back if/when his condition improved]. But if they had done that, then they'd be obligated, because there was a chance he could have gotten better. People do get better. Because I know that Paul was investigating it a lot—what does he exactly have [and] can he get better? I know that they were looking into it a lot. I don't know this for sure, but maybe even talking to his doctor or a doctor.

CARRIE STEVENS: That's what they should have done, even though Christina doesn't know what I know, and that's that they talked to Eric's doctors, and Eric's doctors told them basically, "He's going to die." They were basing their decisions on that very negative prognosis, where other people go, "I was given two to five years, and I'm still alive 20 years later." I think I would have been one of those people to say, "Who's to say the doctors are right? Some of these people survive." And, yeah, I think in hindsight, even though Gene and Paul thought they knew that he was going to die, they should have said that anyway, just to spare Eric. They should have said, "We want you to sit out this year. But after that, if you're well, we're going to take you back." That's what they should have done. Why that didn't occur to them at the time, how do we know what goes on in their heads? Maybe all these years later, they're going, "We were shitheads, and that's what we should have done." Maybe people advised them to do that.

I know for a fact—and I can't speak for Paul, because I'm not close with Paul—but Gene and I over the years developed a friendship. I consider him a friend. I consider Shannon a friend. Gene in 2002 ... have you seen it—

Tongue magazine? He put me on the cover of the magazine. We weren't that close actually. Since I was a Playmate, he came back in my life, and I'd see him around the Playboy Mansion with Shannon, when I hadn't seen him in all those years and had no contact between '91 and '97. And then I started seeing him around because of the Playmate connection. He called out the blue and said, "I'm doing a magazine. I'd like you to be in it." We did the interview, which brought us close, because like I said, I was very honest with him and said, "I hated you guys." And he loved that I said it—he wanted to know more. Plus, I think he knows that controversy sells. He's not stupid, and he's not shy. And then he ended up putting me on the cover.

I felt—and I don't know, [as] I'm sure Gene and I will never discuss it—but I kind of thought that was something special that he did for me, to kind of show me ... like, Gene does things. He won't say why. But he's a pussycat—he's not a complete evil ogre. He cares about money a lot, but he's not evil. I think he did that for me as kind of a sweet thing to do for me and Eric. He didn't have to do that, let's put it that way. He didn't have to put me on the cover. It was really nice, and it kind of made up for a lot, for him to do that for me. And we had a party for it, and Paul came. Paul's never really chit-chatted with me much. I don't know him very well. He's very closed-off. They used to call him "Phyllis" on the road. [Laughs] That was his nickname. I hope I find the pictures. I have pictures of JW and Eric trying on Gene and Paul's wigs backstage. They're pretty funny.

CHRISTINA HARRISON: [Def Leppard's Rick Allen] became friends with Eric after he became sick. Rick Allen—maybe because he lost his arm or heard what happened to Eric—they became buddy/buddy. I think they went to lunch. I know Rick was really upset by Gene and Paul. They would get together and kind of bash Gene and Paul.

CARRIE STEVENS: I used to be friends with the girl that married Rick. I believe they're divorced now. But back before she even met him, I was friendly with her. Out of nowhere, she meets him, and they instantly get married. The four of us had breakfast one time—we met at Sunset Plaza, and we all had breakfast. Christina told me that, too, and I don't know if they ever had any conversations about quitting the band or getting fired. I didn't know any of that part of the conversation. I did remember that they got friendly, and we all went out for breakfast. I can't remember anything besides breakfast. So much went on back then.

CHRISTINA HARRISON: [Def Leppard] were *a true band.* They were there for Rick. I mean, come on, a drummer losing an arm? If that happened in Kiss, it would be like, "So sorry to hear that ... OK, we're having the auditions set up for tomorrow." Is that a bad thing? No, it's a business, so they treat it like a business, and they didn't treat it like how most band members do, where it's "all-for-one-and-one-for-all." They didn't treat it like that at all.

GARY CORBETT: After the open heart surgery, he went through the recuperation for that, and before he started his chemo, we were having a conversation about it, and he felt that he wouldn't be able to keep his job. At that point, he hadn't played the drums in months, and I said to him, "Listen, you're still the drummer in Kiss. Stop driving yourself nutty about this stuff. You've got to go for chemo. You've got more important things in front of you than whether or not you're the drummer in Kiss." Which to Eric really *was* the most important thing in his life. It meant a real lot to him. I was living in Brooklyn at the time and said, "I'm going to call a few friends of mine and book a rehearsal studio in Brooklyn. You're going to come, and we're going to jam. You're going to see that you're still the same drummer, and you can still play." And we did. We spent a really great, fun night, just jammed for three or four hours. And he played great. He played the same as he played.

CARRIE STEVENS: When he was getting admitted to chemotherapy, they told him that he might be sterile. The chemo can make you sterile, if the cancer didn't already. He had to, y'know, "do it" in a cup. And I wouldn't help him, because I was too embarrassed to go in there with him. [Laughs] I had to hold what was in the jar close to my stomach and hail a cab across town to this place where they could store it. I remember being like, *"Wow,"* like I was holding our baby next to me. Because I had to hold it next to my stomach to keep it warm, so it wouldn't die. I got there, gave it to them, and they did the count. They told me it was too late.

BOB EZRIN: Yes [Bob spoke to Eric during this time]. He was very upbeat. He was really downplaying it. He could have died, but he was OK now. He was going to be fine, and he was going to beat this thing. And that was that. We had to regroup—I was doing something in-between there. When it came time to get back together for "God Gave Rock n' Roll to You," we did it in Los Angeles. And by that time, Eric was now no longer able to play. Between the treatment and the illness, he was too weak to play. We started it without him. He wasn't even there, it was very sad. And I remember Singer being in a very difficult position, because he's filling in for a guy that everybody is so close to and feels such deep affection for. And Singer had to sit there and realize that this was going on, but at the same time, he really had to perform. He was great. He was sensitive, he was hard-working, he did a fantastic job. The drumming on the record is brilliant.

And I think Eric Carr appreciated it, because Singer and Carr were similar stylistically in a certain way, and I think Singer went out of his way to make sure that this lived up to the "Eric legacy." And then halfway through the making of that song, Eric Carr came and visited us, on the day that we were doing backing vocals. I had him sing very prominently—he sang the high part in the breakdown chorus. He came in, and he was sweet. And he looked OK. He didn't look like a guy who was going to pass away any minute. But he walked in and referred himself as "the dead guy," jokingly, to try and lighten the mood. I guess we put the melancholy behind us, [because] we had a great session doing all the vocals. We laughed, [and] we had a really good time. It was wonderful to see him.

TY TABOR: I always felt like he was trying to be positive and that he had an amazing amount of courage every time I ever talked to him. And at the same time, there was that undercurrent that you could tell he was scared, from some of the things that we were talking about. But as far as him, he never was "feel sorry for me" or anything like that, ever. He was always trying to be optimistic or hang onto any good idea or thoughts. Of course, he was also dealing with a whole lot of "darkness."

AJ PERO: I remember sitting in my kitchen, and he called me. Twisted Sister had broke up, and I was going through my own shit. I had a business, I got divorced, [and] I'd just gotten remarried and had a kid. I was kind of bitter. Eric heard it in my voice and said, "How's everything going?" And I poured my heart out. And then I said, "I didn't want to bring it up. Are you OK?" He was the healthiest person, even more than me. He said, "I'm going through the chemo. I'm a little weak, but I'm going to come back, and I'm going to do the rehearsals and start off the next album."

ADAM MITCHELL: When he got cancer, my wife and I had just gotten married ... we might not have even been married, but basically, we were living in Santa Monica, and we had two places. We had her place and my place that I had rented when I moved to Santa Monica myself. Eric came out there, and we let him stay at my place, and me and [Adam's wife] stayed at her place. He and I went out to this place on Main Street one day. And by this time, he'd had cancer treatments. He was on this special diet, where he was supposed to be eating a lot of broccoli and these healthy foods. He and I go out to dinner at this place called the Omelette Parlor, and he starts ordering burgers and french fries, all this terrible stuff! And I said, "Eric, what are you doing? You're supposed to be on this healthy diet." He looked at me dead-straight in the face and said, "Yeah, but you know ... *you don't want to over-do it.*" [Laughs]

EDDIE TRUNK: I'll tell you this. Eric was completely convinced that if he did get healthy that his place in the band was still very much in jeopardy. For whatever reason. He would call me and ask me, "Hey man, keep your ears open for me. Let me know if you hear of gigs. I heard that Whitesnake may be looking for someone—let me know." And I'd be like, "Eric, *are you crazy?* Stop worrying about this shit. First is your health, then you're healthy, your gig will be there. There's no way the fans will allow it." He's like, "No, man, I think it's over." And he was fully aware of Eric Singer. He was fully aware that Eric Singer played on "God Gave Rock n' Roll to You." He was fully aware that Eric Singer was being groomed as his successor, which was another thing that made him so uncomfortable at the time that he was sick. And it was also one of the huge reasons why he completely insisted on being in the video for "God Gave Rock n' Roll to You." That's not him on the track. He had a scar on his chest, he had surgery on his heart, he was not feeling great, but there was nothing that was going to stop him from being in that video, and at least visually, holding on to his turf.

BRUCE KULICK: He had twice the energy I had [on the video set]. It was unbelievable. There he was, wearing a wig to look like the way he looked, and he looked the same, believe me. He put so much hairspray in his real hair that it wouldn't have mattered. The wig looked the same. He played his heart out, and I was just thrilled that he was there. In fact, he was my ride that day—he picked me up. We were at the shoot 'til all hours of the morning, and [he] dropped me off when we were done. It was amazing how well he did. I was so happy for him, and he was so thrilled to do it. Although he wasn't on that recording, he played it like he *owned* the drum parts.

JACK SAWYERS: He would call. He was in New York most of the time he was sick, and I still lived in L.A. It was back in the time when you had answering machines. I'd come home from being out late, and I'd have a message, like, "Hey, it's Eric. Give me a call when you get a chance." I'd call him, and I remember when he told me. We'd have these conversations. My reaction to all of that was, "They'll take care of it. They'll fix it." More time goes on, and I'm still working at this production company, doing tons of music videos. And we were supposed to do three videos for the *Bill and Ted's Bogus Journey* soundtrack. But we only ended up doing one—the Kiss song. I remember Paul Stanley's assistant, I think her name was Hope ... I hadn't seen Eric in months, and it had been a while. She had said, "We're doing the video out there," and I remember she made some remark about Eric. And I was kind of like, *"Oh."*
    So I gave Eric a call, and I'm like, "Hey man, how are you doing? We're doing another video, so I'll get to see you." He's like, "Yeah, I'm going to fly out for that." And I'm like, "How are you feeling?" And he's like, "I'm good, man. I'm doing good." He was going through chemo, and he was recovering. I could just tell in his voice that he was going to give it everything he's got. And the rumors that were flying around were that they were replacing him with Eric Singer. But Eric put up such a fuss about everything, that he wanted to be in the video. He was going to be in the video, and he didn't care.

So he flew out to L.A., and he was in the video. He called me and said, "I'm going to be out there next week. Let's get together." So he got out there, and that's when I noticed he had gone through chemo, and he was trying different wigs. He was trying to keep "the image of Eric Carr." The image of Eric Carr to him was very important. He was very dedicated to how people perceived him. His whole thing was he didn't want to let anybody down. And him getting sick, he felt like he was letting people down by not getting well. He was just the greatest guy in the world. That's what he was thinking about—"I'm not going to let these people down. I'm going to get well. I'm going to get better." Which I thought was awesome.

He showed up just like everybody else, and it was a very long day. He was there the whole day. I took a ton of pictures that day. He played his heart out—he played harder I think than anybody else. Even on the takes when it was just close-ups or medium shots of Paul or Bruce or Gene, Eric still had to be in the background for those shots. He's basically playing on every take that we do. I just remember him playing his heart out, breaking stick after stick after stick. I thought he did amazing. I remember there was this little bit of him saying, *I'm going to show these guys.* I'm not sick. I can handle this. There's no way I'm getting kicked out of this band. I'm going to make it—I'm going to beat this thing." And then I remember at the end of the video shoot, some of the very last shots and takes were wraparounds of Eric's drum stuff. So when it was all over, Eric hands me the very last pair of sticks that he used that day, both of them. And I said, "Thanks! But you've got to sign them, so I can frame them and put them up on my wall." He was laughing, and he signed them. I actually have the last pair of sticks that Eric used for a Kiss project. Something that I will treasure.

CARRIE STEVENS: I was there with him on the set of that. I felt really bad for him. You can see it in the video. He was very pale and puffy from the chemotherapy. He had a wig on. Such courage. It meant everything for him to do that. And the band didn't want him to do it. He was really upset at the band. Now, looking back ... at the time, I was furious at the band—I was totally on Eric's side, of course, and furious at them. Because I wanted Eric to be able to feel alive, and I knew that playing would do that for him. I wanted him to have that motivation to get better. Him playing in that video made him really happy and gave him the will. That made him feel like he wasn't going to die. It made him feel like he'd get better, and eventually, he'd just be playing again. Like he was still a part of the band.

BOB GRAW: I read about it in one of the magazines, saying that he had cancer and that he was in the hospital, but he was recovering. I remember seeing the video for "God Gave Rock n' Roll to You." He was in that video. He's playing and looked great. I don't think anybody on the outside—other than people that were affiliated with the band or related to the band—knew how sick he really was.

CARRIE STEVENS: I was flying to New York to see Eric, and this was back in the day where you could walk people to the gate. So my friend Marie was walking me to the gate, [and] we stopped in the bar, and there was Zakk Wylde, waiting to get on the same flight as me. So we meet Zakk Wylde, we're chit-chatting with Zakk, and he was going to see his now-wife, Barbara. He was in first-class, and I was in coach, and he ends up giving up his seat in first-class to come sit with me in the back. And we get completely bombed on the plane. We were just drinking, laughing, talking loud. It was a red-eye or something. There was no hanky panky, but he was giving me a neck massage in the aisle, and I passed out drunk. The next thing I know, everyone's off the plane, except me. So I get off the plane, and Eric's standing there. He goes, "Hey, guess who was on your flight? Zakk Wylde!" I'm like, "Oh ... *really?*" [Laughs] And then I threw up all the way into Manhattan.

1991 [Part Two]

CARRIE STEVENS: Late at night at Eric's apartment when he was going through chemo, I remember answering the phone, and it was Paul, but I thought it was his friend Paul, so I gave him the phone, and he was like, *"Ugh,"* like rolling his eyes like he didn't want to talk to Paul Stanley. I was like, "Oh, sorry. I thought it was the other Paul." I know it wasn't pleasant with him [and Paul Stanley], but I don't think that he had the authority to call Eric and fire him. I think Gene would not have accepted Paul just firing Eric. It would have been "professional/contractual," and they would have had to have someone like the spokesperson do it. I don't remember them speaking to him very much at all during that time.

CHRISTINA HARRISON: He actually *was* fired. But then Gene and Paul tried to reword it. Of course they're empathetic, but at the same time, I felt that this gave them an excuse to get rid of him. And this was a good excuse. I even heard them talking to press, they said, "We care about him, we love him, [but] it's about his health now. It's not about the band—it's about his health, it's about life." Quite frankly, I thought it was BS. I thought it gave them an out. They definitely weren't not like, "Oh yay, he got sick!" No, nobody would do that in a million years. But it did give them an out. So they weren't going to be like, "We're going to stick by you. We're going to wait, or we'll postpone the tour."

JOHN WALSH: The theory could be that this was a way for Gene and Paul to part ways with Eric and make it easier. If they wanted to do that, I didn't know, but when Eric got sick, it was like, "OK, this is how we're going to do it. He's not going to be able to play, and we'll just say it's for health reasons, and we need to move on, because we want to do another record." It's just a theory, but I don't think they felt that way until after Eric got sick. And this was their way of saying, I believe Paul said it to Eric, "Eric, being in a band is kind of like being in a marriage. And, sometimes, the marriage ends." I can't say that's what he said, but I did hear that. And, again, I think they found this opportunity to go this way.

CARRIE STEVENS: I think Gene absolutely adored Eric and loved him, but he's a businessman. I think that definitely came first. They realized if Eric couldn't play, it was going to be losing a lot of money on a tour. And I think they talked to his doctors, and the doctor said, "No, he can't." And, basically, they wanted him to say he was quitting. They didn't want to fire him, and they never did, and he never quit.

EDDIE TRUNK: There was a very big pride thing, too. He didn't want to be viewed as a broken-down, sick, old man that couldn't do it anymore. Whatever issues that were going on with him and Kiss at the time, he wanted to get healthy and get right back out on that "horse" again and show people that he could still do it. And that was a lot of what was driving him. I remember when we would have those conversations, I would get mad at him about it, though. I could totally respect where he was coming from, but I wanted him and all of his energies and focus to be saved for getting healthy.

Because like I said to him, "I love you as a player, but I don't care if you never pick up sticks again. *I want you around.* That stuff will take care of itself. Get yourself healthy, put all this behind, and then, whether it's Kiss or anything I can help you with, I'm happy to help you." It bothered me so much that so much of his energy was based also ... and I understand it, because it was his gig and his life, and he had loved the fans and loved the gig. But it just sucked that whatever drama that was going on between him and them at the time was also taking some of his energy away from what should have been his sole focus. Not to say that he didn't do everything in his power to get healthy, [but] you know what I'm saying. I just wish his mindset could have been solely focused on his health.

LARRY MAZER: It was a terrible reality. It was hard to deal with. But, unfortunately, they had to make another record. Unfortunately, a record had to be supported by touring. And as much as Eric kept the brave face that everything was going to work out and he was going to recover, it was obvious that it wasn't going to be, that this was going to be a very serious illness. I sat there in the meeting, as we talked about—me, Gene, and Paul—it was, "What do we do? What do we do? What do we do?" A lot of people paint them as the bad guys—and Gary Corbett might also—but I have to tell you as a person that was there, absolutely, they did not do anything wrong. They did not do anything impassionately. They did not do anything negatively. The band had obligations that they had to fulfill. Eric was not going to recover, which obviously, he didn't. They had to move on and make a decision. It's a shame, and I feel terrible that it got to that, but unfortunately, we had to do it.

It's a situation faced by a lot of bands, whether it be Metallica, Blind Melon, Drowning Pool, or most recently, Avenged Sevenfold, who had to get a new drummer to replace a guy who died. Unfortunately, it happens sometimes, and there are some bands like Led Zeppelin that say, "We can't continue on," and then 99% of the other bands say, "We'll have our mourning period, and then we'll have to move on." It bothers me. I have my own personal criticisms of Gene Simmons on other things, but on the Eric Carr situation, Paul Stanley and Gene Simmons did nothing at all that should come under any criticism whatsoever on how they handled the decision to move on to Eric Singer to become the drummer in Kiss, and to move on with the *Revenge* album and the tour that followed.

I mean, I'll criticize Gene on things up and down, but everything I've read in different books that criticized him for this is totally unfounded. They in no way, shape, or form did anything with a bad heart on this one. It was a tough decision, but it had to be, and the bottom line is he didn't recover. He was upset because he was convinced that he was going to recover, and if they had just waited a bit, he was going to be fine to play. And look, I give it to him. That's how you have to be when you're in that position. But from the research we did talking to different people who had "inside baseball" so to speak, it was not going to be that way.

BILL AUCOIN: He called me and told me what was happening. It was a tough time, because once Eric went in for the operation, Kiss' insurance went sky-high. And I think that's the reason that Gene I think called him. [Eric's] parents talked to me about this afterwards, that Gene had called, to tell them they could no longer have him on the insurance because it was too expensive.

BRUCE KULICK: There was definitely some moments that were clearly awkward for them, as the band and Eric as a contracted member, and then of course just being a friend to him. So in one way, they were extremely supportive, and in another way ... I know there are a lot of rumors about weird things about the health insurance for him that I never understood. He was covered. We had amazing health insurance. And then at one point, I think they were very clear that they wanted to move on, realizing that this guy is in a place where he's really sick, and he needs to just get better, not be concerned with drumming with Kiss. The band wanted to move on and keep going. That was devastating news for Eric. It really was. And I kind of understand that. And certainly, there were some things, in retrospect, that could have been handled better. And there is some stuff that I'm still confused about, even though I was right in the thick of it. But I also know that I had a radiologist friend just like Paul did, and I knew that only a miracle would have saved Eric. The kind of cancer that he contracted has a 5% survival rate. And then the fact that it went into remission so quickly, my radiologist friend told me, "That's not a good sign." And I'm like, "What do you mean it's not a good sign?" "Those kind of cancers don't work like that." So I think Gene and Paul knew that they were going to lose him.

CARRIE STEVENS: A lot of people ask me about the health insurance issue. I don't know that to be the truth—I don't think it was. If you really think about it, he had Aetna health insurance. How expensive, if it's company health insurance, is it really anyway? I thought about this over and over. I don't think it was about, "I don't want to pay your health insurance." And everyone tries to make Gene and Paul sound evil, because they wanted to like, "Let the poor guy die without health insurance." I don't think it was that at all.

My educated guess was that they didn't want to risk the tour. I think there's some kind of insurance that goes with touring, and say they're touring somewhere, and they have to cancel a show because Eric suddenly gets ill, then my guess is that probably hundreds and hundreds of thousands of dollars they're going to lose and mess everything up. If I had to guess—and no, I don't know it for a fact—I did overhear conversations about insurance, but I don't know if it was health insurance. I don't know if it was tour insurance. I think quite possibly there was some manipulation going on to do with health insurance, some conversations in the hospital. It's a fuzzy memory now. But I think there was some kind of manipulation to try and get him to quit the band. It doesn't make any sense. Even if somebody is fired, don't they get to keep their health insurance for a certain amount of time? You can't just take it away.

BRUCE KULICK: It's all so confusing to me, for any of that to be going down. You know, your health insurance doesn't get cancelled in a day or a week even. I thought you're protected. So I could never really understand any of that. And if it was true, I don't know it. It could have been something that got out there or some awful rumor.

CHRISTINA HARRISON: I am pretty sure, because of the rumors, Gene and Paul heard that people were getting really disgusted, so I think they really did start doing a lot of backpedaling and clean up the story. And clean it up by saying, "Oh no, no, no. We're taking care of him." Which they did. They didn't cut off his insurance, I'm sure of it. Did they think that way or somebody was talking about that? Probably. They definitely heard rumors— and I don't know who they heard it from—but they knew the rumblings of some people's disgust. So I think they did a really good job of cleaning that up.

WAYNE SHARP: The last time I saw him was at the Clash of the Titans show [featuring Slayer, Megadeth, Anthrax, and Alice in Chains] at the Garden. He wanted to see the show, and he came down, and I saw him backstage [Sharp was "Vice President of Concerts at Madison Square Garden" at the time]. It just wasn't him—he had lost 30 or 40 pounds. He wasn't a big guy, so it really showed on him. He was wearing a wig and a hat on top of the wig. It was so sad to see him emaciated like that. He wanted to see the show. It was hard to talk to him, we only had a few minutes. I remember his girlfriend was with him, Carrie.

CHARLIE BENANTE: I remember when we played Madison Square Garden, he came to the show, and he came backstage. That was the last time I saw him, actually. It was a real hectic time, because it was packed back there. Eric did come in the dressing room, and we talked a bit. I asked him how he was feeling. He said he was feeling really good with the chemo, and everything was going great. It was just great to see him, and he was in good spirits.

MIKE PORTNOY: I had known what was going on from our mutual friend that was working at their management company, Derek Simon, who was working with them and working with us at the time. Derek was really close with Eric. Derek would fill me in on his progress and how it was going. The last time I saw him, he and I were in Manhattan, and we shared a cab together. We dropped him off where he had a place, down where the Twin Towers were, in the south end of Manhattan. I just remember him getting out and saying goodbye.

SCOTT DAGGETT: A couple of times [Scott spoke to Eric in 1991]. There was still a little bit of friction between us. There's some private stuff that went on between us, that drove a wedge between us. Me doing the cocaine and letting it get way out of hand—he was hurt by that, and he was also very mad at me. Because I know that he cared about my wife at the time. Since then, we've divorced. She was very concerned about it as well—they both loved me. When I talked to him in the hospital, it was all about being cheery and telling him I love him and all this other stuff.

BOBBY ROCK: I was on tour with Nelson, and we were playing in New York. Eric showed up as a guest, with Carrie. That was the first time after all those years that I had a chance to meet him. Vinnie always spoke highly of Eric and had a few stories here and there from the Kiss days. At that point, we had heard that Eric had been ill and was battling this thing. It would have been summer of '91. I think, at that point, it was still kind of touch-and-go. But it was heartbreaking to see him and meet him under those circumstances. He was a very friendly, gentle guy—we had a nice, immediate rapport. It was great to meet him and talk with him. But the undertone of our meeting was that this was going on. At that point, I think he had been making some progress, some headway. I believe he had been in the middle of the heavy treatment. He was optimistic about his recovery prospects.

It seems like there could have been some weirdness on the Kiss front. I don't know how the politics were playing out at that point there. It just seems like I remember something like that as well, his position with the band. The bottom line was it was great to meet him, and I have a very nice recollection of us talking backstage. I remember thinking I didn't know how far along or where he was at with the treatment, but I thought if he was open to any kind of "holistic assistance" along the way, it was something that I ... having just become vegetarian in the last year from that point there, I had been doing a lot of juicing, and I heard about the holistic connection between certain juices and how that could assist the body and healing. Probably within a month or so, I arranged to have a juicer shipped over to Eric's place. I sent him a juicer and got word back that he was trying some out. We might have talked by phone one other time since he got the juicer.

CARRIE STEVENS: When he was at Sloan-Kettering getting chemotherapy, we used to go to the arts and crafts room. We'd learn how to make silly things like jewelry, and he made me this heart-shaped key chain and melted a red stone in it. It's silver with a red stone. I just found that in my jewelry drawer the other day. We used to say to each other when we were at Sloan-Kettering, "We feel like we got off on the wrong floor." We were taking the elevator up to the arts and crafts room, and we'd just look at each other and go, "We got off on the wrong floor," but we meant the wrong floor in life. Like, we're not supposed to be here. I'm like this budding starlet, and you're this rock star. We're not supposed to be in the arts and crafts room in the cancer ward. It was very surreal that whole time.

He was very upbeat. I don't think he ever really thought he was going to die. We never really discussed that he would die, even though he knew the doctors gave him two to five years. He's the one that told me that. But like me, he never believed that. The only time we ever briefly ever had a remote conversation about death is when he said that his only two regrets was that he never had a child and that he didn't do anything with the *Rockheads*. So that's the only conversation we ever had about death. He was always pretty upbeat, even when he was puffy and pale and tired and nauseous. I used to be so scared. This is in Manhattan, when I was staying there with him through the chemo. I gave up my apartment—I just gave everything to my roommate. I'm like, "Here, take everything. I'm going to be with Eric." I left to be with him.

I remember he would take a lot of naps, and I was such a nervous wreck. I was getting up to see if he was still breathing. It was very scary. But he never seemed like he was being defeated, and we did so many things during that time. We went to every museum, every zoo, and took trips to see my grandparents and his, and where I grew up in Massachusetts. It was a wonderful time, even though he was sick. It was such a great, bonding time. People don't take time to do those kind of things in life. Everybody's like, "Go, go, go." It sounds strange, but it was a really special time. It wasn't like he was laying around going, "Oh, I'm going to die." It was like, "Let's go to the zoo today, we don't have chemo today." We went horseback riding. We did things that you don't do.

EDDIE TRUNK: Unfortunately, I never visited him in the hospital, but there was a reason for that. And, yes, I was in contact with him, very much so. But what happened was around the time ... it was very hard to get information about what was really going on. The one guy that I had befriended through Eric was Gary Corbett. Gary would give me some information from time to time. Ace was long out of the band, I knew Bruce a little bit. But Gene and Paul, for as long as I've known them, we had an up-and-down relationship, because I've been outspoken about how I feel about the band as a fan, and I've never had a relationship with those guys where it's "pick up the phone and let me give you a call." So Eric was always "my guy." And it was really hard to get a handle on what was going on. Gary would tell me some things.

CARRIE STEVENS: I do remember when people were sending him cards—when he was sick—seeing a return address from Peter Criss. And I remember thinking, "That's really cool. 'To Eric Carr, from Peter Criss,'" like a nice card.

EDDIE TRUNK: The one thing that I will never, ever forget is, I don't remember what month, but Eric called me, and he said, "You're not going to believe this. I've got some great news." He had had an open-heart operation, and he had done my radio show after that—he came in and was talking about the operation. He had gone back to get a check up, to make sure nothing had grown back or there were no complications. And he called me up and said, "You're not going to believe this ... I just got a clean bill of health from the doctor. It's gone. I'm good. Everything's great." I said, "This is amazing, thank God! This is great, I'm so happy for you." It was a great moment. I said, "What are you doing calling me? Did you call everybody else? Did you call your parents?" He said, "No, I'm just making calls now." I said, "Call everybody and tell them. This is great—this is the best news in the world. I'm so happy for you." And that was the last time I ever talked to him.

MARK SLAUGHTER: The last time I saw him was at the *Bill & Ted's Bogus Journey* premiere, which Kiss had "God Gave Rock n' Roll to You," and we had "Shout It Out." He looked great and seemed real happy.

BLAS ELIAS: I ran into him, I think it was the movie premiere for *Bill and Ted's Bogus Journey*. I saw him there. He had that bout with cancer, and it had gone into remission. So he was really happy and looking forward to getting back into the groove of things. He seemed in great spirits. He was positive about music and life and everything.

CARRIE STEVENS: I remember meeting [Bill Aucoin] at the premiere of *Bill and Ted's Excellent Adventure*. Bruce, Eric, Christina, and I ... if you go on WireImage, there's pictures of us from that event together. That's what I remember Bill Aucoin from, because he said something to Eric, like, "Wow, your girlfriend is so pretty." I remember seeing Shannon and Gene there, and Tracy Tweed was Paul's date. He always took Tracy, Shannon's sister, when he couldn't get a date. When he *didn't* have a date, rather, because I'm sure he could have got one.

MARK SLAUGHTER: He was like, "I'm feeling really great. I feel really good. I'm stronger than I've ever been." The typical Eric. He was getting his ass kicked, and the guy was still fighting.

GARY CORBETT: He went through—if I remember correctly—four sessions of chemotherapy, and was told that he was cancer-free, was totally fine, and was basically done with it.

CARRIE STEVENS: After he got sick, I told you I gave up my apartment and everything to go be with him, and that same week that he was here, we got me an apartment at Studio Colony. We went to IKEA, and we bought all [the] furniture for it, down to the plants and silverware. Everything, because I had nothing anymore. And we stuffed my car with it. I just remember that moment when we were sitting outside IKEA, with my car stuffed with stuff he bought me. I just looked at him, and I don't know where it came from, from the depths of the bottom of me, I said, "I'm sorry, and I'm sorry for every fight we've ever been in, and I'm sorry for any hurt that was ever between us." It was better than a thank you, you know what I mean? He just looked at me back and said, "I know, me too." We put my apartment together, and he paid the first six months' rent for me. And all my bills were in his name, by the way—my phone bill, my electric bill, and everything. I said, "You don't have to do this for me," and he said, "I want to. I want to give back to you what you've given to me, because you've given my life back." Because he thought—as I thought—that he was better, and that me standing by him all those months and then every day in the hospital and those doctors' appointments, that being there for him, he wanted to be there for me. The same way that I was there for him. So getting me on my feet again, that was his way of doing that.

ROD MORGENSTEIN: I also remember speaking to Eric some months after that when he was on cloud nine, because he said that he got a clean bill of health. His cancer was in remission, and he was on top of the world.

CARRIE STEVENS: We thought that he was cancer-free, and I was in all these appointments with him, every doctor appointment. There were x-rays where you could see the "cloudy" cancer in the lungs. And then after the chemo, we went back, and they were clear. I saw them with my own eyes—we thought he was cancer-free. So we came back to L.A., and I threw him a surprise party. Gene and Paul came. [White Lion drummer] Greg D'Angelo was a friend of his, he was there. I'm sure Bruce and Christina were there [and] Gerri Miller from *Metal Edge*. There were pictures of the event in *Metal Edge*. So I threw him this surprise party, and we all celebrated Eric being cancer-free. It was at this club called Black and Blue, and he was so shocked. I made up this story that we were going out to dinner with somebody. He walked in the room, and everyone yelled, "Surprise!"

GARY CORBETT: Did Carrie talk to you at all about the party? Did she tell you that Gene and Paul did not go to the party, and also, told Bruce that he couldn't go to the party? So she's throwing this party for him, and how it was put to me was they were already planning on letting him go from the band, because they weren't comfortable with the fact that they were afraid of a relapse in the middle of a tour, that he would not be able to actually withstand how grueling a tour can be. They were planning on letting him go, so they weren't going to the party, and also, told Bruce that he could not go to the party. Gene and Paul ruled ... see, the one thing about that band, once it was no longer the four original guys, Gene and Paul were very deliberate in hiring guys and keeping a very tight rein on those two guys. They called the shots, and for Bruce, they told him he couldn't go to the party. So basically, if he went to the party, he probably would have lost his job. That's the way those guys were.

CARRIE STEVENS: No, that's not true at all. [Gene, Paul, and Bruce] were there. I remember thinking they wouldn't come and being surprised that they did come. I have it somewhere. It was written someplace in *Metal Edge* magazine, and there were some photos. I don't know if Gene and Paul were in them. There's a photo of Eric and I, I don't remember who else. I have a distinct memory that everyone was "anti-Gene and Paul" then, and I remember saying, "They probably won't go." And they did come—I'm fairly 99% sure. I think I would have remembered if they didn't.

MARK SLAUGHTER: He was positive. Eric always had a very upbeat, positive attitude [of] "I'm going to beat this." We'd start talking a lot about the *Rockheads* projects, making some music, and just hanging out and being creative.

CARRIE STEVENS: Yes, we did [talk about marriage], a couple of times. The saddest part of it was that was the last thing he was ever able to say to me. He called me, I said, "Hello," and he said, "Will you marry me?" And I started laughing. He said, "Why are you laughing at me?" And I said, "Because you're not serious." And he said, "How do you know I'm not serious?" And I said, "You know us. We'd get to the end of the aisle, look at each other, and go, 'Nah.'" Then we both laughed. The other time we talked about it was on my twenty-first birthday. We had dinner at Spago [in 1990], and I said next year I wanted a ring for my birthday, and he said, "If things are going as good in a year as they are now, you will be getting a ring on your birthday."

JACK SAWYERS: Eric and I made plans that night to meet up before he went back to New York. But he was juicing a lot—he was doing the carrot juice and all the stuff, just trying to keep his body healthy. He got on this trip about, "I want to do a drum instructional video—'The Eric Carr Drum Instructional Video.'" So we made an appointment to meet, and I guess about ten days later, we met up at Jerry's Deli at Studio City for breakfast. We sat there for two hours, just talking about everything in life, plus the video. It's funny, because I just remember him asking me a couple of times, "Does this wig look fake?" He used two different ones. The one he used in the video was real long and "rock n' roll," and the one that he used not on stage was shorter but long. They both looked fine. I said, "You look fine. Stop worrying about it."

So we were planning on doing this drum instructional video in October of '91. I had it all set up to shoot it at Universal at Florida. He was like, "Cool, because I've never been to Disney World before." And I was like, "Me neither ... let's go! There's a studio there that we can shoot." He was going to bring Carrie, maybe his niece, and maybe a couple other people. We were planning it out, and I was doing the logistics on it. We were going to use lipstick cameras on the drumsticks, just stuff that hadn't been done yet. We wanted to make it really cool. So we had that phone conversation. I had gone back to New Jersey, and I was hanging out at my mom's house for a few weeks and waiting to get everything going. I talked to him a couple times, and then I didn't hear from him. I was just like, "Whatever. He'll call."

GARY CORBETT: At the time, I was playing with Cinderella, and I was over in Japan. I got a phone [call] from my wife, that Eric had a stroke, a brain hemorrhage.

CARRIE STEVENS: This is so sad ... the next day [after the party for Eric in L.A.], he flew back to New York, and the phone call I told you about took place, where he called and said, "Will you marry me?" And a couple of hours later, I got a call from Bruce. And he said, "Did you hear about Eric?" And I said, "No, what? I just talked to him." And you could hear the panic in Bruce's voice. Apparently, he had a very, very bad headache, took some aspirin, called an ambulance. He went into a seizure, which turned into a coma. I got on the next plane to New York. The cancer was obviously not gone—you just couldn't detect it. It was a rare kind of cancer that you can't see. So we thought it was gone, but it was in fact spreading like wildfire. It had gone to his brain, his lungs, and his kidneys. So he had brain surgery.

When I got to the hospital, there were bandages on his head. And he was paralyzed on his left side, and he was left-handed. He could never speak again. He tried to write but couldn't really do it. He would kick. It's really painful for me to remember this, but he was so frustrated, that he would ... even if they sat him up or laid him down, he took that one leg and just kicked and kicked. I could tell he was trying to mouth the words, *"Fuck!"* Can you imagine? Trapped inside of his body, not being able to communicate. I would be there like 21 hours a day, until I was forced to go home. I'd read to him, put his earphones on his head, brush his teeth for him, massage his feet. I mean, we found a way to communicate. I swear, I found a way to argue as we always did! There was just such love between us. It's like I figure it that he kind of helped me into the world and shaped who I am, and I was there to help him out. I never imagined—even back then, as bad as things were—that he would die. I pictured for the rest of my life having to dress him and button his shirts for him. I knew he would probably never be normal again, but I never imagined that I wouldn't be with him.

LARRY MAZER: I lived in Philadelphia, [the other Kiss members] were based in L.A., and Eric was in the hospital in New York. I know Gary Corbett was there all the time, and I think he has his own personal feeling that Eric was abandoned by them. But they lived in California, what were they going to do? They weren't going to sit in a hospital in a vigil.

CARRIE STEVENS: [Gene and Paul] went there for the heart surgery, but they never came during the chemo or when he was in a coma. I don't know what they were doing, but they were on the west coast, and he was in New York.

CHRISTINA HARRISON: To this day, it's my lowest point ever, because we didn't go visit him at the hospital. We were going to visit him in the hospital—we weren't doing anything—and then Carrie told us, "No, he doesn't want you to come. He looks really bad. I'm telling you, don't come." And we didn't go. In hindsight, even though the girlfriend says not to come and Eric's telling us he doesn't want us there, we should have went anyway. That was just the right thing to do. We should have went. I'm sure Bruce regretted that. But if I was sick, I know there are people I wouldn't have wanted to see who are really good friends. I would have done the same thing. I wouldn't want people there crying at my bed.

GARY CORBETT: Gene and Paul at that point, Eric's family—his parents— were not really thrilled with them, let's put it way. I basically felt the same way. They allowed me to come to the hospital. They allowed a friend of his that he grew up with to come to the hospital and one other person that wasn't a family member to come to the hospital. Everybody else was not allowed near the hospital. And I was told by his parents that I was not allowed to talk to Gene and Paul about how he was doing. The reason why they put that on me was because he was paralyzed on one side of his body. And his family was afraid—because they knew that Gene and Paul were planning on firing him—that now that he was physically unable to play, that that was going to happen. If it did, he was also going to lose his health insurance. So I was forbidden to talk about how he was doing, and if Gene and Paul called me, I was not allowed to give them a report of any kind, of what was actually going on. And I would come home from the hospital every night, and [on

Gary's answering machine], "Hi Gary, it's Paul." "Hi Gary, it's Gene." I just wouldn't return the calls.

CARRIE STEVENS: [The last time Carrie saw Eric alive] he was kicking, and he had bandages all over him. He fought. He fought a good fight, but it wasn't anything that he would have wanted anybody to see. It was no doubt that his mind was still OK. He was all there—he could understand you. But he couldn't speak, and he couldn't move on one side, and he was constantly getting poked at and prodded at, tested, and more surgeries. Basically, I was made to go back to L.A. because, literally, 21 hours a day, I was in that room with him. Until the doctors, the family, his friends—everyone—basically said, "Carrie, you're young. You've got your whole life ahead of you. You can't be doing this." So I agreed.

CHRISTINA HARRISON: Carrie was the one that was there for him, wiping up his throw-up. She was amazing.

CARRIE STEVENS: Even when he was in a coma, it never occurred to me that he was going to die. It was just too much to handle. In my world at that time, there was nothing bad. There was no pain. I just wanted to grow up to marry a rock star. And life was going to be easy. I was going to be a star, and that's the way it was. That was a real tough awakening, to find out about the real world that way.

SCOTT DAGGETT: Gene and Paul were great to me. But I heard some stories, and I don't know, maybe you'll be able to confirm them—Eric was fired while he was on his deathbed, in the hospital. I heard that it was Paul that did it, after he had lost his hair. They couldn't wait until after he passed away. They fired him while he was still alive, and literally, dying. I think that's despicable, and it hurt me. I'm sure knowing Eric, he laughed. But I was kind of freaked out when I heard that.

CARRIE STEVENS: I was there through all of this, and he was not fired. He died doing exactly what he wanted to do—to be the drummer for Kiss.

They did want him to quit. I was in the hospital room, I overheard many an argument. I can't remember who the guy was, it was the guy who worked in the Kiss office and was also Paul's psychiatrist or something. Some weird shit like that. There's some detail about how he used to be Paul's psychiatrist, and then he was running Kiss or something. It was someone that Eric was not very fond of, I can tell you that, and he did the dirty work. They were arguing, and they were trying to make him sign a resignment letter. They were trying to get him to resign, and he wouldn't do it. He thought they wanted to replace him with Eric Singer, and obviously, he was right. He didn't particularly have anything against Eric Singer ... he just knew. They took him in to record when Eric was sick or couldn't do it, and he was like, "They're going to replace me with Eric Singer." And look, Eric Singer is *still* in the band. He was right.

EDDIE TRUNK: I don't know what's true and what's not. Some of the things that I've heard are hard for me to believe that anybody could be that insensitive to that situation. I can't really comment, because I don't have any knowledge first-hand of what really went on. But I do know the stories that are out there are so hard to believe, that if they were true, that anyone could possibly be that insensitive—to be viewed as an "employee"—of the situation. If you look at it as that, even the biggest companies, I think it would be hard to do something like that, if indeed that did happen. But I don't know. All I do know is that there was definitely a wall put up at the time between much of the Kiss organization and Eric when he was sick. And I also do know that Eric was completely convinced that his days in Kiss were done, if he had regained his health. What that was based on, I don't know. He was completely convinced that no matter what had happened with him and his health, that he was going to be on the back-burner, and [the] machine was moving ahead without him. He was very much trying to be proactive and asking me and other people that he confided in at the time about keeping their eyes open for gigs, because he was confident he was going to get healthy, and he wanted to play.

CHRISTINA HARRISON: I am sure they have regrets, but I also know they don't dwell on stuff like that at all. They don't have enough "Jewish guilt," I suppose. I'm sure to Eric, it was the ultimate proof to how he was always feeling, that it never was *a band* in the true sense of the word— band/teammate/partner. It was a business ... pure and simple. You work for a corporation, you get sick, the wheels must continue to turn, and we need a replacement to keep the car moving. It is not about love or sense of brotherhood, which is a real band, or supposed to be. It was business, and after all those years, that was a heavy blow. Yet a blow that should have not been all that surprising ... yet in the face of death, it really was. I'm sure Eric felt, "A-ha! I was right all along!" He probably felt justified when sitting in bars, privately bitching to fans.

Though when you are told you have cancer, you secretly pray your bandmates become true bandmates and friendship kicks in, and bygones should be bygones. What's a little moaning about money after all those years, really? You want to hear that they will be by your side, through thick and thin, that they will love you and support you, and heck, what's another tour? The fans will wait. But, alas, no—business first and foremost. Hey, they are successful for a reason, Gene and Paul are true die-hard businessmen! A lot of people don't get that rock n' roll is a business, eh? I saw so many bands come and go, one-hit wonders. Young guys that made some quick money and then overspent. Hey, that is America, is it not? Young musicians that didn't listen to the seasoned pros or didn't listen to the older, wiser managers, thinking that money would keep flowing in, and that if you have one hit, then of course, the next single will be a hit, too. Gene and Paul were smart, just seriously needed to be a tad more human when it came to life and friendship, and what makes the world really tick.

LORETTA CARAVELLO: There's really not much to say, than it was a time of our lives that you wouldn't want anybody to go through. It was fast, it was sudden, and there were so many more things that had to be done. That's it. It's a total emptiness.

November 1991

CARRIE STEVENS: I was back in L.A., I remember I was at the Mondrian Hotel. I was on a pay phone, and Gary's wife had called me and said to please call her, no matter what time. I called her, and she said it [that Eric had passed away on November 24, 1991]. I just remember dropping the phone—I was on my knees, completely hysterical, sobbing. They took me into a manager's office or something. I called Bruce and Christina, and they came and got me. I stayed at their place. I packed up and went to New York and stayed with Gary Corbett and his wife, Lenora.

CHRISTINA HARRISON: I remember Carrie called. She worked at a hotel, and she called Bruce and I. I'm 99% sure we were sleeping, because it was really late at night. She was crying, and she said, "Something terrible has happened. You have to come over here right away." Bruce and I got dressed really fast. We were in the car, and I remember exactly, we were on Cynthia Street where we lived, and we got to the first stop sign, and we're thinking, "OK, what could have happened? Maybe she got attacked. Maybe she got raped? Oh my God." And then right at the first stop sign outside our apartment, I went, "Oh my God ... *Eric died.*" It hit us right at that stop sign, and we knew of course that's it. We went to pick her up, and that's what it was.

BRUCE KULICK: Believe me, when we got the news, as much as it was something that I was expecting, when it happens, it hits you like a ton of bricks. The next thing you know, you're making plans to fly to New York to be at this funeral. It was unbelievable. I mean, it affected my marriage, where I remember Christina was a basketcase. It's not like she needed to go to therapy, but she was acting out in very weird ways. We all did, because how do you lose someone that young and that close to everybody? Especially someone that talented and wonderful. As much as he might bitch about some things, that's not a reason to get cancer at that age and die.

BOB KULICK: I do remember my brother's wife at the time calling when he passed. She was just totally in tears, as we all were. Nobody could understand. First he was better, and then all of a sudden, "What?" Like with Ronnie Dio recently. It's just heartbreaking. Just totally heartbreaking when somebody like that who you know and something like that happens, it really is devastating.

CAROL KAYE: I had to issue the death statement to the media. It's not something that I enjoy doing. Unfortunately, I've had to do a few of them.

JACK SAWYERS: Literally, I was asleep on the couch, MTV was on, and the MTV News came on [and] said that, "Kiss drummer Eric Carr died today." It was just like, *"Whoa."* That was exactly how I heard the news. In denial obviously, I immediately called his apartment number, and it was the answering machine. Obviously, nobody picked up. It was just one of those surreal things.

MARK SLAUGHTER: I didn't expect it, because the last time I spoke with Eric, he said, "I'm doing great. I'm healthy." We were working on our next record at that time, so my nose was in the studio 24/7. I remember hearing it, and it was just like losing a friend. When it's somebody like that, it's like, "Why couldn't it be the son of a bitch like somebody else I know, instead of this really wonderful, great human being who really gave his all as a musician and as a person." If anything, that's what I felt. I felt, "God, of all people."

TY TABOR: It was devastating. I knew it was coming, but when something is suddenly final, it's final. It always hits you differently when that moment comes.

MIKE PORTNOY: I remember the day he died ... didn't he die the same day as Freddie Mercury? What a surreal day, between Freddie and Eric dying at the same time. Dream Theater was in the studio recording *Images and Words* at that time, and I remember hearing about both of them that day. It kind of made me angry how Eric's death was so overshadowed by Freddie's— not that Freddie didn't deserve the coverage, because he was a huge rock icon.

But it was kind of like Eric's life and passing got overshadowed by Freddie's tragedy. It's kind of strange and similar to Farrah Fawcett and Michael Jackson, y'know?

BOB GRAW: I'll never forget it. I was sitting in McDonald's up on Jericho Turnpike on my way to college, and I was flipping through my newspaper, eating my Egg McMuffin, and it said, "Drummer of Kiss, Eric Carr, dies." I started crying. I remember sitting there crying, and I couldn't believe it. I was astonished. In fact, my initial thoughts were, *"It's over."* I thought Kiss was over. I really didn't think they were going to go on after that.

EDDIE TRUNK: I believe it was Gary who called me and said that he had passed away. I couldn't believe it. I said, "Gary, how could this be? He just called me and said everything was fine." Apparently, I never really got to the bottom of what happened, but cancer and the type that he had is such an unbelievably brutal thing that ... I mean, look, I was extremely close with Dio, and I had the same exact experience happen with Ronnie. I had seen Ronnie and had a conversation with Ronnie. He was feeling great, and everything looked great, and then the next call I got a week later, he was gone. That time frame of '91, obviously, communication isn't what it's like now with texting and emails, that everyone knows every move. But it just floored me.

GARY CORBETT: I was at the hospital the day he passed. It was really a rough thing. What happened was because his parents knew how close we were ... of course, they were distraught. They just lost their son. And they also didn't know the music business people, so they said to me, "You know all the people he knew. As far as letting people know and the word out ... " We even went straight from the hospital to his apartment, so I could help his mom pick out what he should be buried in. Because again, they knew that we spent a lot of time together, and I knew what his favorite outfits were. So we basically went in his closet. I remember being in his bedroom closet with his mom and picking the clothes. And his dad was inside in the living room. He had the TV on MTV, and while we were sitting there going through his clothes, they announced that Freddie Mercury had passed away. He died the same day.

His family wasn't sure about how to do the service, as far as doing something that was open to the public or being very private. They didn't really know what they wanted to do. We talked about it a bunch. Basically, I told his parents, "Eric was the nicest guy in the world to the fans. He was probably the fans' favorite guy, because he was the only one that would ... " not that Gene and Paul wouldn't stop and sign an autograph, but once they were in their rooms, they were in their rooms. Eric and I would come back after a show, change our clothes, go down to the bar and socialize. And like I said, he would sit and talk with anybody. As long as they wanted to sit and talk, he would sit and talk with them. So I said to them, "That stuff really meant a lot to him. I think he would want to have it be ... if not the wake, if not the funeral, something for the fans to be allowed to come to." And they actually did do that at the wake, and it was amazing. The funeral procession went for *miles*. I mean, there were state troopers escorting and blocking intersections. It was a really, really large group that ended up being at the funeral.

CARRIE STEVENS: Eric's best friend was Gary. That's who he palled around with on the road. That's who he trusted. They were both of the same mold, really down-to-earth, good people. It really killed Gary. The night Eric died, I went to stay with Christina and Bruce, and then I flied to New York, and I stayed with Lenora and Gary. We were all very close. When we were in New York, we hung out with them all the time. And Gary and Eric—on the road—palled around together all the time. I mean, Bruce was close to Eric, but he's a little more square and a little more ... I can't explain it really. But Eric and Gary were closer. They were goofy. They'd goof around together a lot and had the same senses of humor. And a trust, a real trust. Gary was just completely heartbroken when all this went down.

GARY CORBETT: He passed away on a Sunday, and if I remember correctly, it was the Sunday before Thanksgiving. Eric and I—one of our routines—we were very early risers. We would get up in the morning, call each other while we had our coffee, and just bullshit. And while we were bullshitting, we'd both have *The Howard Stern Show* on. We were huge Howard Stern fans. I had been on Howard's show before and participated in some things on the show, so I knew his producer, Gary [Dell'Abate]. Once his parents decided that they were going to allow one of the days of the wake to be open to the public, once again, I was the person that was the one that called MTV to let them know that he passed away. I was the one that dealt with the fan magazines. Anybody that needed to know, I was the one that made the call.

So the next morning—that Monday morning—I call up *The Howard Stern Show*, and I get Gary on the phone, and at the end of the show, [Howard] does the news. So I called up and said to Gary, "Eric passed away yesterday. I know Howard's probably going to talk about it during the news. I don't want to be on the air, I don't want to be part of it, but I would really appreciate it if he would give out the details for the service that was going to open for the public." And he said, "Sure, no problem." It was the last day before they were going on vacation for the Thanksgiving weekend. They get to the news, and they start to talk about it, and ... Howard's Howard.

I get a phone call after the show from Gary, and he said, "Did you listen to the show today?" "Yeah, I did." "Well, did you listen to what Howard said about Eric?" "Yeah, I did." "Did you think it was bad?" "No, it was kind of funny, actually." And he said, "Well, I just got off the phone with a very angry Gene Simmons, who demands a copy of the show, because he heard that Howard was making fun of Eric and all that stuff! And he demands a public apology from Howard, or otherwise, he's going to publicly punch Howard out." So he tells me this, and I say, "He heard everything third-hand from people calling him up. He didn't hear the show." And the way I felt about those guys at that moment, I said to Gary, "They weren't treating him good at the end. And now that it's a public thing, they're trying to make themselves look good, like they gave a shit. So fuck 'em. Don't send them anything. That's what I would say." And he said, "OK, fine," and he didn't send him a copy of the show.

Well, now we go to the funeral, and Gene and Paul show up at the funeral, which was a little awkward, to say the least. His family was not thrilled that they were there. At a typical Italian funeral, when the funeral is done, everybody goes out for dinner. So we went to this restaurant that they booked, and they had a buffet set up. I got my food, and my wife and I sat down at a table. And all of a sudden, Gene and Paul sat down at the table with us, because they weren't really welcomed at any other table. They weren't really welcomed at that one either, but I guess it was the one they were "least unwelcomed" at.

So we're sitting there, and Gene has no idea that I was the one who called Howard's show to start with. We're in the middle of eating, and he's sitting there. He's got his elbow on the table, and his hand kind of in front of his mouth. He asks me if I listen to *The Howard Stern Show*, and I said I did. He asked me if I listened the day that he spoke about Eric, and I said, "Yeah, actually I did." And he says, "Well, what exactly did he say, because I didn't hear it." And what he had said was that Eric had passed away. And he said how long Eric had been in the band and how long the band had been around. He goes, "Man, these guys have been around for so long ... I can't even name one Kiss song." So Fred [Norris] goes inside and comes out with Kiss *Alive II* I think it was. But that was still Peter. I guess it was a live version of "Beth" they put on. I guess it was actually vinyl—he puts the needle down on the turntable and starts to play "Beth." He plays two seconds of it and goes, "Oh God, that's crap! No wonder the guy got cancer. He had to play that crap every night?" Then he puts the needle down again, listens to a little more of the song, and goes, "Oh my God, *what a dirge*. They ought to play this song at his funeral. People will be jumping in the box with him."

I'm telling this to Gene, and I can tell he's trying to hold back laughing. He found it funny. I said, "He didn't trash Eric. If anything, he was trashing the band." And I said, "Gene, look, when Sammy Davis Jr. died and he had throat cancer, Howard was talking about that thing he used. He called it the 'cancer kazoo.'" And I went through three or four other people that were in similar situations, and I said, "It's funny when he does it and it's somebody you don't know. But you can't take it so personally because it's somebody that you know. That's Howard's way of paying tribute to somebody. If he didn't like him, he would have said nothing. So you really can't get mad at Howard for that." And that basically took the wind out of his sails. He was OK with it at that point.

Well, a few days later, they come back from their break, and Gary calls me up and goes, "Would you come on the air with Howard?" It was the first point in time since their break for Thanksgiving that they were going to have a chance to talk about what went down between Gene and Howard. So I went on the air and told them what I just told you about what happened about it. It was just a really funny situation. As a matter of fact, over the Christmas vacation, I got a bunch of texts from people saying, "Howard's on vacation. They do *The Best of Stern*, and that week, they played that morning show." I was on three of four times that week, and they had replayed all of that stuff.

CARRIE STEVENS: The hardest thing I ever did was walk up to that casket. I fell to my knees and started sobbing.

BRUCE KULICK: I remember the funeral was very moving, the outpouring of the people and the whole heaviness of the whole thing. It was a big sob-fest, I've got to say. And I'll never forget Paul seeing … y'know, Italians, they want the open casket, and him saying, *"That's not Eric."* And I know exactly what he meant. You're looking at a body. And we knew Eric was—as much as he might have been upset and depressed at times about things—the funniest guy and the most generous guy of the band. The most crazy, entertaining guy of the band. He was more the "Keith Moon" of the band. So that wasn't Eric, Paul was right. And I know it was a way for Paul to grieve, to say that to me.

I remember Carrie walking over to the casket and saying to Christina, "Touch him. Touch his hand." For me, it was just surreal. It was just freakin' crazy, the whole thing. And I remember some of the old girlfriends showing up, which was crazy, too. But look, we were there for him. I know the mausoleum that the family chose for him was really beautiful. And the fans, their outpouring and everything was incredible. There was a lot of other aggravation later on—his will and all that stuff. Again, Italians, y'know? I know when Eric wrote up the will, he knew something could happen, but I think if he could have revisited it, he probably would have wrote it a little better, if you know what I mean. And, oh boy, I had to handle the *Rockheads* with his family and everything … thank you! [Laughs] But I took that as a challenge, and I did the right thing. I got his music out there. I did my best for what he left behind.

CHRISTINA HARRISON: Did you ever see the episode of *The Mary Tyler Moore Show*, where she started laughing at a funeral? On the show, she worked for a TV station. Chuckles the Clown dies, and they go to his wake. And during the speech, Mary Tyler Moore starts laughing hysterically. Well, during the wake, I started laughing hysterically about something. I was at the back of the room. It was just really nerves and me not being able to handle it. And I remember Gary is like, *"Get her out of here!"* They knew what was happening. They knew that I'm not a total moron who would start laughing at a wake. Bruce was mortified. I remember they took me outside.

JOHN WALSH: It was Gary who arranged for me to be one of the pallbearers. I still have pictures here somewhere. There are pictures of me as a pallbearer, with Paul and Gene in the background at the church in upstate New York. It was Eric's wish that I would be there for him at the very end.

CAROL KAYE: We all went to the funeral upstate. I remember there were a lot of fans there that weren't especially nice to Gene and Paul. I'm not really sure why. Somebody starts a rumor, and then it spreads, and for whatever reasons, some fans thought that Gene and Paul were mistreating Eric or weren't fair to Eric. There's so much that goes on behind the scenes and on the business end that people are not aware of. It's very unfair to just assume. It was a very sad day. Gene and Paul were devastated—we all were.

LARRY MAZER: It was sad, it was a rainy day. I guess it was in Middletown, New York. It was an interesting thing for me, because I had managed prior to that, the Dixie Dregs, and the drummer was Rod Morgenstein, who was then in Winger, who supported Cinderella on their very first tour. And he and his wife—who has since died from cancer, also—came to the funeral. So in a way, it was very nice to see them, because I hadn't seen them in a long time on a social level. But it was a sad day. It was a church ceremony in Middletown, and I know that Gene and Paul came in the night before and came to the viewing, but I just came up with my wife for the funeral itself. A bunch of fans showed up—it wasn't just industry people. It was short and sweet, and that was that.

ROD MORGENSTEIN: My wife and I went to the funeral, which was a beautiful service. The church was just overflowing with people. There must have been 1,500 people inside, with people outside not able to get in. So it was obvious that he had a lot of fans. He was loved by a lot of people.

ADAM MITCHELL: No, I didn't [go the funeral]. We were in the Caribbean, and we made plans to be down there with family. And also, Eric wouldn't have cared, as I wouldn't. I mean, I don't care if anybody comes to my funeral. Eric and I had a great relationship in life—that's really what mattered.

GERRI MILLER: I did go to the funeral. It was really sad. Anytime you lose a friend, especially someone so young and talented, with so much to look forward to and do and accomplish ... and it's not there. It was a sad day for everyone, but it was very well-attended. I'm sure he would have liked that.

CHRISTINA HARRISON: The day of the funeral, it was like a president had died. They had police escorts, and people were lined on the street. I was really impressed with the fans. That was really emotional.

MARK ADELMAN: The amount of people that came was pretty intense. You never realize the magnitude of an artist until you see people flying in from different countries to attend the funeral of an artist that somehow touched their lives. Very, very touching to see his parents, his sister, and Gene and Paul.

JOHN WALSH: Gene and Paul came, and so did Bruce. I'm a humorous person as well, I try to look now at the humorous side—to see all those Jewish guys in a church. I kind of got a kick out of that! But a really emotional moment for me on top of the whole thing was being in the car with Gary Corbett and his wife, when we were going from the funeral to the cemetery, was on the New York State Thruway. The funeral procession went on for as far as you could see. The lights of all the cars, we looked back, and this is a New York state mountain country road. Gary and his wife said, "Wow. Eric would have been so proud." I turned around and saw all the cars with all the lights on, and it was as far as you could see—long, long. That was a very heavy moment for me. I'm glad that he had pointed that out. A lot of pride. We felt very proud to be part of this and to see what a valuable person he was. He deserved it. That's why we thought he would be very happy to know all these people came out to see him in a little town in upstate New York. It was very solemn, it was very sad, but we were also very proud to be part and to have known him.

EDDIE TRUNK: I do remember that his services were on the same day that my radio show was on. And I was faced with the decision of not doing my radio show and going to the services or doing my radio show, which I was going to completely dedicate to him and play nothing but music that he was on. And I was struggling with that. I had spoken to a few different people and said, "I don't know what to do." They said, "You know what? The funeral thing and all that is going to be a zoo." And there was a lot of controversy over who was going to get in, who wasn't. There was controversy quite honestly—it's well-documented—with the members of Kiss. That's a deeper, darker part of this whole story. A number of people had said to me, "Eric loved you, he loved doing your radio show, and he loved what you did on the radio. For his fans and everybody, I think people would love to hear you do that show, and he would, too. So you should go do your show." And that's what I did. I went on the air that night and did three or four hours of nothing but stories, interviews, and Eric's music. We did a whole tribute to him.

GARY CORBETT: After the *Revenge* album was done, the *Revenge* tour started in Europe. Before we did that, they did a bunch of dates, unannounced club shows [in April and May of 1992]. When we started doing these shows, all of the Kiss fans that I knew through the years, that I always saw with Eric, they would all come up to me, because they knew that I was the one that was closest to the situation that was happening. They would ask me about it. And what I found out really quickly is those diehard Kiss fans, they don't want to hear anything negative about Gene and Paul. If you say anything bad about those guys, you become "the scumbag." I was being honest about stuff, at least at the beginning I was. There are some of those diehard fans that are like *Star Trek* kind of fans. And then there were some, like Ed Trunk. I know Ed because he was a Kiss fan, and at the time, he was a DJ. He had a Saturday

night heavy metal show on some small station in New Jersey. And every once
in a while, Eric would go and guest-DJ with him. And I would go with him
occasionally and mess around on the radio. Ed was a diehard Kiss fan, but
you could tell, he wasn't weird or anything. He was just *a Kiss fan.* He was a
huge music fan all the way around, and we still keep in touch. But most of
the "diehards," when they asked me what happened, I thought they wanted
to hear the truth. But it turns out they didn't.

LARRY MAZER: I love Gary. Gary and Eric were very close, and at the end,
when the whole thing went down with Eric being sick and what transpired
with that, Gary I think got really upset with how Gene and Paul dealt with
things. I remember he was very angry at that point in time with things.

GARY CORBETT: I have no plans of ever working with them ever again.
It's been 20 years, and Paul still won't even say hello to me, because of what
went down between us. I let them know—let's put it that way—that I was not
thrilled with them and the way things went down. And I had conversations
with each one of them individually on the phone, because they all heard that
I was mad at them. My conversation with Paul, I wasn't nice, and I didn't
really care if I hurt his feelings. As a matter of fact, I was actually *wanting* to.
And I did it in a way where I did it very tactfully. Basically what I said to him
was ... he told me his side of the situation, which was that they were never
intending to fire him, that as soon as they heard that he was sick, they called
the best doctors that they knew, and they were trying to help him.
   And this one doctor told Paul that the type of cancer that Eric had was a
very aggressive and fast [type], and it wasn't a good prognosis. And he knew
that Eric was going to pass away, but they were never going to fire him.
And basically what I said to him was, "I'm really glad to hear that, because
I didn't think you guys could be that big of scumbags to take away the one
thing in the world that meant the most to him." It wasn't that long after
Rick Allen lost his arm. And I said, "You look at a band like Def Leppard,
and if anything was going to ruin a drummer's career, [it] was losing an arm.
But those guys stood by him like a band should. So it makes me feel a lot
better that you guys weren't going to fire him, because that would have been
a real scumbag move." And because he knew what the truth was, I guess he

basically took that as me calling him a scumbag. [Laughs] Which I was. And that was the last time he ever spoke to me.

WAYNE SHARP: I just want to say [that] it was so obvious to me [that] Gene really loved Eric. He had a real affection for him. And Paul is one of my best friends to this day. Business, I don't know, but on a personal level, I know they really did love the guy.

SCOTT DAGGETT: Gene loved him. Eric was Gene's little brother that he never had. Gene thought that he was just funnier than shit. I don't know how seriously he took Eric, but he loved him. Paul was, on the other hand, always in the background there. Paul comes off as a great guy, but Eric was certainly suspicious of Paul. He didn't trust him. It was just a feeling that he got. Paul, as I said, was great to me, [and] he was great to Eric. But Eric would tell me in his confidence he didn't trust Paul. And Paul, he said, was looking to bust his chops, when and if he could. But again, that's coming from two guys that were drinking a lot and everything else.

CARRIE STEVENS: I was angry at Gene and Paul then, and I even said it. Gene put me in *Tongue* magazine, and I said it right to Gene's face—"I used to hate you." And Gene loved it that I said that to him! Gene is like, "Tell me why. Talk about it." I mean, I'll probably be killed by Kiss fans who don't like Gene anymore for saying this too, but that's a real man. [Gene saying] "Tell me what you were thinking. Give it to me straight. Let me hear the controversy. Let me tell my side." You're not some pussy Kiss fan that's like, "Oh, now I see you photographed with Gene and Paul. You're such a backstabber to Eric." And it's like, it's not the case at all.

GARY CORBETT: I did the European leg [of the *Revenge* tour in May of 1992], and I just couldn't be around them anymore. Being on a tour bus with them ... the tour bus wasn't big enough for me to be far away. I couldn't even look them in the eye anymore. It got to that point. [The aforementioned phone conversation with Paul] was after that. I don't think he would have let me work with them again at that point, if I had done that before.

CARRIE STEVENS: Everyone can say what they want, but Gene was always nice to me. I think Gene's just Gene. Maybe he's not nice *to guys*. [Laughs] I judge everyone how they are to me. And he did adore Eric. He did. All that stuff in the end is fuzzy about the insurance, but he did love him. He did adore him. It was like his little buddy. He thought Eric was a sweet little guy.

LARRY MAZER: I left after [1993's] *Alive III*, during the making of the tribute record they did for themselves, [1994's] *Kiss My Ass*.

BILL AUCOIN: [Bill and Kiss] always talked. I tried to convince them to get back together again. Of course, they didn't want to, but eventually, it happened anyway. I told them it was the only way I thought they could really recapture the fame and glory of Kiss. But for many years, they didn't want to hear about it.

CAROL KAYE: It was years later when I was working with Ace and Peter, and they were doing their *Bad Boys Tour* [in 1995], that I engineered the first dinner that Gene and Paul had with Ace ... I think that was the first time they sat down and had a meal together in I think it was twelve years or something. Because Kiss were the keynote speakers at the CMJ Convention that year, so I knew they were going to be in New York. Paul would call me, Gene would call me, and I just felt, "You guys need to sit down and have dinner." And I remember they had dinner at Fujiyama Mama's, on the Upper West Side. Ace called me after their dinner and said it was really great. He was nervous, a little bit apprehensive about meeting with them. But I knew that if there was ever the right time to even think about a reunion, it was during that period. And then, it was *MTV Unplugged* [at which the original Kiss line-up played together].

BILL AUCOIN: They kind of lost the fans. It dwindled until they couldn't actually play on tour. The promoters wouldn't put up the money for them to play on tour. So that's when they decided that these Kiss Conventions, that looked like they were successful—they would do it themselves. And ironically, the Kiss Conventions is what brought them back together again, because they got to meet the fans first-hand in a close environment, which they realized how important the fans were. And also, that the fans wanted the make-up back. They wanted the real Kiss back [Gene, Paul, Ace, and Peter would reunite for the *Alive/Worldwide Tour* in 1996].

Eric Remembered

BRUCE KULICK: Clearly, I think he was a huge part of a certain period of Kiss that means a lot to a lot of fans. And I think the fans know that he really did care about them. He was more talented than they probably knew, but they certainly got enough of an idea of how great he was on the drums, how good a voice he had, and how much energy he had to play the role in the band. I think he was always the "cute guy" in the band as well, and many of the girls really loved him. I take pleasure in knowing that I had the opportunity to work with a great, talented guy, and he is of course sorely missed by all.

CARRIE STEVENS: From what I've been hearing from people, Eric did a really good job of setting his own legacy. I've been hanging around the rock scene a little bit again recently, and everyone knows who I am, because of him and *Playboy*. There's not a night that somebody doesn't come up to me, another guy in a band or a crew member, and tells me that Eric was one of the nicest people that they ever met, what a great drummer he was, and just what a down-to-earth, nicest person they ever met. I feel like people are extra nice to me and extra respectful of me because of him. So he's still supporting me. He's done a good job for himself, and I think he's being remembered exactly for what he earned. And he earned that reputation—no one can say an unkind word about the guy. I had to say, "Only the good die young," but believe me, I often thought, "Why him?" But I guess God probably needed him for something more important than what he was doing here. Maybe he's Gandhi somewhere else now, I don't know.

BILL AUCOIN: From my point of view, just as an incredible human being. I think of Eric as an incredible person, and a drummer second. Obviously, he was a great drummer, but I remember him as just an incredible human being. He was a sweetheart, willing to do anything for anyone. He was fantastic with fans. Fans would talk to him, and he would spend hours talking to them. He just wouldn't let it go. He couldn't have been a better person to have been with them during that time, when they were so disruptive and didn't know where they were going and weren't sure if Kiss would survive. If anything, he helped them through it because of that personality he had, and that "giving" emotion that he had. Not only to them, but to fans. I'm sure anyone who met him will never forget him.

BRUCE KULICK: He got a lot of fan mail, and back then, of course there was no emails or anything. This was all hand-written. He'd be reading them and writing back [to] people. I had fans show me hand-written responses from Eric, which was always very impressive to me. And I did it for a little while—I did the same, and I learned it from him. I was really, really impressed with that. There were times when we were on tour in Scandinavia and places like that, where the band is just *so* huge, and you really can't leave the hotel. And he'd go down to the lobby, and it would be freezing by the outer-door. Because they didn't want all these kids inside, he'd stand there and sign the autographs. There was no one in the band better to the fans than Eric. Period.

CAROL KAYE: Any time I spent with him, we always had a really nice time. He was funny, he was self-deprecating, [and] he was just a very happy person. He had a great vibe and a great energy about him. I always looked forward to seeing Eric. He was just a very special person. He really was. He became like your family.

JACK SAWYERS: I just remember him being really down-to-earth. And he was a practical joker. I remember one night on the "God Gave Rock n' Roll to You" video shoot, I just opened this Calistoga Water and had taken a big drink of it because I was so thirsty. And Eric comes running over to me and goes, "Jack! They just recalled all those Calistoga Waters because they were tainted!" Stuff like that. I'm sure there are many other stories. He was a funny guy. But through the most part of it, Eric Carr was who Eric Carr was. I really think that his legacy was always on his mind. I think that's what made him very aware of what he was doing, how he was treating people, and why he would stay the longest signing autographs.

There are stories of people, from what I've heard, that after concerts were waiting for buses and freezing outside, and Eric would see them and bring them back into the venue to wait for the bus where it was warm. There's all kinds of stories that you hear when you meet people who knew him. And I fortunately got to meet him when I was a teenager, and he was very nice to me. The fact that he remembered me every year. That turned into when I got out on my own, living life, meeting him again and actually becoming a friend, like with Bruce Kulick. I think that's what happens, man, [to] the nice guys in this business. It just seems like the stuff happens to them, and then everybody else who just trudges forward and doesn't give a shit, those are the people that succeed. Overall, knowing Eric Carr was definitely a good thing.

BOB EZRIN: I remember him as a very talented musician, but more importantly, a very warm, generous, gentle, and happy person who was a joy to be around.

MICHAEL JAMES JACKSON: As somebody as a musician was defined as much by the passion that he had for being a player, and the pride that he had in being a member of Kiss.

RON NEVISON: Just as a sweet guy. He was just a quiet, sweet guy. Paul Caravello. I don't know how he got "Eric" out of that. [Laughs] And where was he from, Brooklyn? So he was a nice Italian kid from Brooklyn, and a great drummer. That's how I would remember him.

CARMINE APPICE: I think he should be remembered as the guy who replaced Peter, and he did it really well. He added to the band, and he was a kick-ass rock drummer. He showed it every night that he played with them. I thought Eric's style definitely fit in. Eric Singer plays more like Eric Carr than he does Peter Criss.

MARKY RAMONE: He was a very nice guy. But I liked Peter Criss' style better, because to me, Peter had a style. Eric Carr was more of a technician. It's like the guitar player that plays for Kiss now—he's a technician. Ace has a style. What do I like better? Style than a guy that is technically advanced. He was a solid drummer—he seemed to be a very nice, gracious guy. And he was a short guy, but he knew how to play hard, so I said, "More power to you." He was able to do a really good job.

CHARLIE BENANTE: Genuine and one of rock's best drummers.

MARK ADELMAN: He really could have been one of the great drummers of our time had he lived.

ROD MORGENSTEIN: I would like him to be remembered as one of the good ones. This is an industry where musician or label or booking agency and all the people involved—it's a rarity to meet someone who you just get a beautiful vibe about from the instant you meet them. He's one of the few people in my thirty-some-odd years of being a professional musician that I did get that feeling about. And it wasn't a growing feeling. It was something that I felt from the moment I met him. It's just a rare treat when you meet human beings like that. I think he should just be remembered as that special kind of all-around nice guy. He had no "airs" about him. In being in one of the biggest bands in the world, [he had] no pretension. He was just a sweet, nice guy. It might sound boring, but I think it's like the highest compliment you can pay somebody.

AJ PERO: He was one of the best people that I've met, being in this fucked up business. Eric was one of the best fucking people that I've met. As big as he was, I just never met anybody like him. God took him too soon. I wish he was alive today, I really do. Me and him became friends, but it was too short. My father died when I was 25 years old. It was too short—I didn't have the time that I had with my father. That's how I felt about Eric. Right now, me and him should be hanging out. I feel cheated. I don't feel that I had enough time with the man to really become one of his best friends. The short time that I knew him was probably one of the best times that I've known anybody in my life, and I mean that from my heart. I miss him dearly, I really do. I never forget the times and the laughs.

FRANKIE BANALI: Eric deserves to be remembered not just by what a wonderful and powerhouse drummer he was—and how his skill and percussive technique drove Kiss on record, tours, and countless hits—but also by what a kind soul he was and will always be. God bless him, and may his family always find comfort in what a wonderful man he was. Rest in peace, Eric.

BLAS ELIAS: A great guy who never let rock stardom go to his head. Made everybody feel comfortable. You'd meet him, and in five minutes after talking to him, you feel like you've known him all your life.

BOBBY ROCK: To me, I think how you treat people is always going to be more important ultimately than what you achieved or accomplished. He was in one of the biggest bands in the world for many years, and so his career accomplishments are obviously undisputed. But my impression of meeting him and what I heard about him was he treated people well. And that to me is what I think will be the legacy, the focal point, even above and beyond of what great of a player he was.

BOBBY BLOTZER: I'd like him to never be forgotten, that's how I'd like him to be remembered.

LYDIA CRISS: People should remember Eric the way he was. Eric was a sweetheart. I didn't know him that well, but the little bit that I did know of Eric ... and anybody that did know Eric, always said that he was a really nice guy. The way he carried himself and the way he made himself known was that he was a nice guy. I don't know if anybody could deny that.

TY TABOR: As one of the most cool, positive, just really good people that I ever had the pleasure of getting to know.

JAIME ST. JAMES: More importantly than anything, what people mostly know [of] him is a great drummer, which he really was. But more than that, he was just a sweet, nice guy. I've never met anybody that I could instantly like more than him. He was just a good person.

BOB KULICK: One of the sweetest, nicest, most talented guys, and the worst thing that could happen, happened. To me, it's a sad story, because the ending was so bad. It's funny, the other day I was cleaning something up in the studio, and [Bob came across] one of the big tour books from back in the day. The thing's like three feet long! And Eric's in there. I'm looking at the pictures, and I'm just like, "Fuck ... look at his guy, man. *A total star.*" See, my brother was better at accepting his "station." That's what it is sometimes. I work with big artists, I produce big artists, but sometimes, they've said things to me that hurt my feelings. I had to accept that. "OK, I'll accept that." You know why? Because I'm a big boy. I can dish it out, but I can take it. Unfortunately, he had a hard time taking it. That was the problem. Other than that, the guy was just an incredible human being.

MARK SLAUGHTER: I'd like Eric to be remembered as the drummer who lived for drumming. The guy who had a great attitude, and furthermore, he was a part of Kiss for a lot longer than people perceive him to be. I think he, in a lot of ways, didn't really get the credit for what he had done. I mean, Peter Criss is an incredible drummer. Eric Singer is a great drummer. Understandably, any one of these guys that Gene and Paul have picked have always been stellar musicians. The reasons why they've been in Kiss is because they deserve to be in Kiss. And Eric—of all—deserved to be in Kiss, to be "that person." I'm very blessed to be a part of all that and see that, from behind the stage and behind his kit.

CHRISTINA HARRISON: I think he would have loved it if he was considered one of the best drummers in the world. He was super great, just a great guy, which he was in spades. I remembered the other night that when Bruce and I got married, Eric was so excited he had a suit made, and he kept going for the fittings. Then he went to one of the department stores we had registered at and got everything on the list! The presents starting pouring in. UPS kept delivering gift after gift. Just another example of how generous he was.

WAYNE SHARP: I'm sure everyone is telling you [that] he was one of the nicest people ever. When I got married, for my wedding gift—and I think I still have it—he made me a card. He was just starting to work on his *Rockheads* cartoon idea. But he sent me this great handmade card that had cartoon characters of me and my wife, and sent me a nice check. That was really touching. He loved his big hair. It would have never been big enough for him. I remember him sending me a card one time—when he was working on the *Rockheads* thing - he had like 15 strands of hair that he put into this card! He would count the number of hairs that would fall out of his head. He would brush his hair and keep track of how many strands of hair he found in his hairbrush. He was *obsessed* with his hair. That was the other thing, too—when I saw him last and I saw he was wearing a wig, I just thought that was heartbreaking.

SCOTT DAGGETT: He was always there for money if I wanted it. He gave me plenty of Christmas presents, and what I was doing at the time was Eric would send me a bonus in the mail, and I would usually just spend that check ... he was writing music at home with one of Paul's old throwaway guitars—one of the "breakaway" guitars. For the show, one-third of one truck was filled with nothing but brand new guitars from probably BC Rich. [Paul's] tech would saw through half of the neck and just about all of the truss-rod that runs through the neck. Every night at the end of the show, Paul would break his guitar. So Eric had one of those old guitars that he was writing music on. I got him a very nice acoustic guitar for Christmas that year. But the thing was he would spend money on me, and I would usually spend everything he spent on me. I'd take that check and go to a music store or a jewelry store or whatever and buy something for him. He was not stingy. He was good with his money.

CHRISTINA HARRISON: He didn't die with much money, because he was always giving it away. I know he helped his family a lot, he helped Carrie. That guy was not cheap. He was really a generous person.

LORETTA CARAVELLO: He was on a basic contract. I have some copies of his contract, and I think it's been out there a while. Don't ask me how the fans got it, but they did. It was pretty standard. From anything that I see as the years go by in his paperwork, I did not see any kind of royalty from merchandise. I did see some royalties from a few of the songs he co-wrote. But other than that, he was just a contract player, and his contract was pretty standard. He was just happy to be in Kiss.

CARRIE STEVENS: We had a ton of fun together. I mean, obviously, or we wouldn't have stayed together. I remember us being so goofy, being in Manhattan, and it would start to rain, and we'd be jumping in puddles and singing, and then ducking in restaurants, having Mexican coffee, and going out in the rain and jumping around again. I think he loved that young kind of spirit that I had, because he was very immature, too. [Laughs] He was really into watching movies. I know he said he wanted to grow up to be Paul McCartney when he was a kid. I used to call him and play Elvis songs on his answering machine ... and Winger songs. [Laughs] He liked old classics [movies]. I remember I'd be like, "You like these *old* movies." And he's like, "Well, you're an actress. You should be watching movies." But I wasn't as into it as him. We used to love the animated *Little Mermaid*. He loved that.

EDDIE TRUNK: I loved Eric to death. He was one of my most favorite people ever. I miss him to this day. He was not only immensely important to giving Kiss a kick in the pants when they really needed it, but he was a guy that for a replacement member of a band was extremely well-loved by the fans. And that's something that people don't really connect with as much, maybe who are younger or didn't live through that period. A great, fun-loving, prankster of a person. And a *monster* drummer. I just don't think he got enough credit for the drummer he was and the "kick" he gave to Kiss. And vocally, he was such a huge part of Kiss. He even sang lead vocals on a couple songs—not only recorded, but you talk about the *Lick It Up* album, during that period, they would do that song, "Young and Wasted." Even though Gene sang that on the record, [when it was done] live, Eric always sang the whole song. So he was such a big part of the harmony and the vocal sound.

Just such a driving force in that band. I think they couldn't have found a better guy. His persona, his character, his warmth and love for the fans, and his talent I think were key. I question if Kiss didn't hit a home run with bringing him in as the first replacement member, I don't know if Kiss would have survived it. Because that's a sensitive, delicate thing, at a time when they were falling apart in every way. Then you go and endure a line-up change. If you don't bring the right guy in, and you brought in some schmuck or someone who didn't connect or didn't work, and a year later, you're bringing in another guy to take that spot and the revolving door starts, that really could have been the death blow for that band to totally not recover. But because of what he did persona-wise, musically, how relatable he was for fans, how much the fans pulled behind him, I really think that it gave the band a boost in a lot of different ways.

BOB GRAW: He's always going to be remembered as probably the member of the band that I would say was the easiest to talk to and the nicest guy. When *Creatures of the Night* came out, he changed the sound of that band and brought them back to prominence. He's always going to be remembered as probably Kiss' best drummer. I love Eric Singer, and I love Peter Criss, but Eric Carr was Kiss' best drummer. Absolutely, 100%, their best drummer.

ADAM MITCHELL: Eric had a warmth about him and a warmth about his drumming. Eric's drumming in a way was "analog sounding," as opposed to "digital sounding." Now, Eric Singer and Tommy Thayer ... the last time I saw Kiss in Nashville four or five years ago, technically, they're the best band that Kiss ever had, in some respects at least. They're a tremendous band. But Eric Carr was so warm, so big, so handsome-like. To me, he was the best drummer in that respect that Kiss ever had. I'd have to say he was a great drummer, of course, which he undeniably was. But truly, as a great and warm person. I couldn't even imagine anyone who didn't like Eric. And there's not that many people you could say that about. Everybody liked Eric—the fans liked him. The fans took to him, which is no mean feat. He was just an all-around warm, funny human being. The thing I miss the most about Eric, it's not just that I miss seeing him play, I miss that he's not around to talk with and laugh with. But life is like that sometimes.

SCOTT DAGGETT: In the rock n' roll industry, I would like him to be remembered as one of the most creative minds, and probably, the best drummer for Kiss and with Kiss that they ever had—technically, look, and everything. But I'd like people to remember him for what a kind person he was and what a helpful person he was. He was child-like—not childish, but very child-like. And he cared for a lot of people.

NEIL ZLOZOWER: As a great drummer, as a warm human being. Nice guy. As a member of one of the greatest rock n' roll bands of all time—Kiss.

MARK WEISS: I'd like Eric to be remembered as someone who was happy at doing what he did, and he lived the dream. It sounds cliché, but [he was] probably one of the nicest guys in the business. He was kind of ahead of his [time], making a niche for heavy metal drumming. He seemed really natural. It just seemed like Kiss was the perfect band for him. I couldn't imagine him in any other band than Kiss at that point. I think he did better without the make-up with them than with the make-up. He was more of himself.

GERRI MILLER: As a really important contributor to the era. He was definitely well-liked, fun, and good to be around. I think he brought a lot to the party.

NINA BLACKWOOD: As for Eric Carr, his drumming was superb. I never had the opportunity to interview him, but knowing what I did of the man, he was the sweetness and sensitivity within the group. He could've been "the hawk" as originally intended. Then of course he became "the fox" ... but he most easily could've been "the pussycat." A pussycat who could strip the skin right off a set of drums. His death was a tragedy for the millions of members of the Kiss Army, and all others who were inspired by the unstoppable force known as Kiss.

WAYNE SHARP: He was one of the nicest human beings I've ever met in my life. I never saw him yell or scream at anybody. If he was pissed off about something, he kept it to himself. I just wish more people would have gotten

252 The Eric Carr Story

to know him off stage, because he was one of the nicest and sweetest human beings I've ever met. I'd be shocked if you could find anybody for this book that had anything bad to say about the guy. The other thing that I remember about him—if there was something bothering him, and I don't know if it was something with a girl, the band, his family, or whatever—he would just go into this depression for like days at a time. He just wouldn't talk to anybody and keep to himself. He wasn't interested in trying to irritate people or take whatever was bothering him out on anybody. That's the kind of guy he was. If something was bothering him, he wasn't going to push it off and make you feel bad about it, too.

JOHN WALSH: I don't believe in clichés, but he gave 100% all the time. He really left it all out there on the drum riser every night. Everything that he did, he really gave of himself completely. He loved the fans. He was so happy to be in the position that he was. Always ready to sign an autograph. He would take pictures with everybody. He just enjoyed it so much. And I think because of that, he was such a happy guy. He got to do what he always wanted to do. He wanted to play drums, and he wanted to be in a band. And he found a band that he could really give his all for. Everyone else will tell you [that] he was a terrific man and a great guy. He really gave it all.

LARRY MAZER: He was a great drummer in a great band. People should remember him just like they remember other great rock stars who they're fans of. I'm sure a lot of people right now are going through the same thing with Bret Michaels, who just had a cerebral hemorrhage. It's a sad thing. You want to see rock stars live forever. When you realize Jimi Hendrix, Janis Joplin, Jim Morrison, and Kurt Cobain were dead at 27, and you see Bret Michaels who is in his early 40s, and who knows what's going to happen, it's sad. I mean, he was a very important member in one of the greatest bands in the history of rock n' roll. People should remember that.

CAROL KAYE: As an amazing drummer and as a very integral part of Kiss. And as a really kind, warm, loving person. When people talk about Kiss, they kind of gloss over that period, and I know had Eric still been alive, that he would be right there beside them today.

MARK SLAUGHTER: We dedicated "Days Gone By" to Eric Carr on the second record, *The Wild Life*, as well as we dedicated that to Freddie Mercury. Two rock n' roll legends right there.

BRUCE KULICK: [1999's *Rockology*, which featured unreleased Eric demos] was a labor of love. It was a little hard to get it all together. I wanted to really do it right, both musically and lyrically. Musically, I had it covered. I only had certain materials. It was pre-Pro Tools, but I made sure I got it done the best I could. And I was really pleased with the results. But there was a while when it was a little hard to figure out the business angle of it, between the family and Adam Mitchell and myself. You know when you're doing something that's a legacy product because the person is passed away, you have to be careful about the legal issues with it.

I remember for a little while, it was really frustrating. There was some confusion about the direction and would these issues be worked out. Would everybody be happy? And I had a very vivid, very clear dream about Eric. He was talking to me in the dream—I mean, full color. And he's telling me everything is going to be OK. I can't really sit here and say I know for a fact when you have those dreams you're really experiencing their essence or their being. But it was as real as day, and shortly after that dream, everything did work out. So I kind of did always feel that Eric would talk to me.

CARRIE STEVENS: I think *Rockheads* was ahead of its time. I think right now it would be really great. Someone told me the other day that Slash has this animated project, and I go, "Oh, what is it?" They described it, and I go, "That sounds like a rip-off of *Rockheads*." I think Gene and Paul ended up with that. I wonder who has it now? But they didn't do anything with it—it was never developed. He did the drawings, but they're not walking and talking.

BRUCE KULICK: The next time I "heard" him or "saw" him was when I was doing "Dear Friend" for Union's *The Blue Room* album [released in 2000], which was a song written for him. I remember I was kind of struggling with some of the lyrics or just getting a little stressed—"I'm going to sing the song." I guess whether or not it's my own subconscious figuring it out or you really are capable of being visited, I once again felt that he reached out and kind of comforted me in my mind. It's happened a few times. Those are the ones I remember the clearest. So I clearly felt that he was grateful of me getting it out there. And *Tale of the Fox* was fun, too, even though I didn't really spearhead that. It was Jack Sawyers and Loretta. But I was very honored to be a part of that. The materials released on Eric are great, considering you never have an idea that someone could pass away so young.

JACK SAWYERS: I always had that on my mind, this whole unfinished business of Eric Carr. I wanted to do something. [2000's DVD, *Inside the Tale of the Fox: The Eric Carr Story*] we did for zero budget. We just sort of had video cameras and flew around interviewing. That's why the production on that is basically like a video magazine kind of a thing. But I felt that it was necessary, because I wanted to do *something.*

EDDIE TRUNK: I'm happy to talk about the man, because he was a friend. Again, it's hard to believe that it's 20 years coming up. Every year on my radio show around his passing, I always play a set of music for him—a set of songs that he was on.

GARY CORBETT: One of the nicest guys in the world. One of the best rock drummers. Great showman, and a great person, a really great, generous friend and loving person. I miss him dearly. I really do.

CHRISTINA HARRISON: Seriously, he would give you the shirt off his back. That's the type of guy that you wish you had as a friend. You know how they say, "If you can count five friends in your life, then you're fortunate." He'd be a good one.

MIKE PORTNOY: He was a genuine, kind soul. It's kind of sad that a lot of people, it takes them to pass away before people realize how sweet, gentle, and kind some people are. I saw the same thing recently when the Rev died, or Dimebag died, or Ronnie James Dio. It's sad. It takes somebody to pass away for people to appreciate how great they were. And Eric was one of those type of people. It wasn't until after he was gone that everybody came out of the closet saying, "What a sweet guy he was." It's just an example of you've [got] to appreciate people when they're here. And when you have a nice and genuine person like he was, you've got to appreciate people like that while they're still here on Earth with us.

CARRIE STEVENS: It's almost his birthday, and I'm finally 41. I'm finally the age that Eric died. And when I turned 41 this year, it really hit. And it is depressing to me—I'm still in love with a dead guy, and I'm still single. I would have jumped off a bridge if you told me back then, "Carrie, you're still going to be crying over him 19 years later. You're never going to find a guy that was as good as he was to you." It's so weird. I just went to the Rainbow ... which Eric, Bruce, Christina, and I went to on his 41st birthday, which turned out to be his last. I was there with my friend last Friday night, and when we were there, I told her that. And then as we were leaving, I was still talking about him. We turned on the radio, and his version of "Beth" was playing. My jaw dropped. This stuff happens to me all the time. It's like he's there. He's like, "Hey, *I'm watching you.*"

LORETTA CARAVELLO: As far as fans go and as far as the Kiss world, I would want him to be remembered as a great drummer. And as a person, a good human being who would go way out of his way to help people. And never asked for anything other than friendship. He was just a kind person, a funny person. I wish he was here. Even if he wasn't in Kiss, it probably would have been a better trade-off to have him here and fixing stoves rather than playing on stage. If this is the way it was meant to be, I'm sure the trade-off would have been better as far as I'm concerned.

AJ PERO: He was a class act. Billy Joel said it correctly—"Only the Good Die Young."

www.ericcarr.com

Visit www.ericcarr.com, the only official website of Kiss drummer Eric Carr. Besides finding the latest news, archives, rare photos, fan-submitted stories, and official merchandise, there are also links to view rare pieces of memorabilia which were personally owned by Eric.

Official merchandise for sale on the site includes custom signature drumsticks, pins, bobbleheads, lithographs, posters, DVDs, guitar picks, shot glasses, patches, and for the true hardcore Eric/Kiss collector, rare one-of-a-kind personal items owned, worn, or handwritten by or from Eric himself.

The Official Eric Carr Website also features links to our own Facebook and Twitter sites, so all of Kiss' and Eric's fans can share their thoughts and cool stories with each other. Visit www.ericcarr.com today!

[The Official Eric Carr Website is in no way affiliated with the author or publisher of this book. It is solely owned and operated by Eric Carr's family.]